Springer Series on Life Styles and Issues in Aging

Series Editor

Bernard D. Starr, PhD
Marymount Manhattan College
New York, NY

Advisory Board

Robert C. Atchley, PhD
M. Powell Lawton, PhD
Marjorie Cantor, PhD (Hon)
Harvey L. Sterns, PhD

Colleen L. Johnson is Professor of Medical Anthropology at the University of California, San Francisco. She has conducted research on ethnic families during processes of assimilation, the family in later life, and grandparenting during the divorce process. Since 1988, she has had a MERIT Award from the National Institute on Aging to study adaptation of the oldest old. In addition to numerous scholarly articles, her books include: *Growing Up and Growing Old in Italian American Families; The Nursing Home in American Society;* and *Ex-Familia: Grandparents, Parents, and Grandchildren Adjust to Divorce.*

Barbara M. Barer is a Senior Research Associate in the Division of Medical Anthropology at the University of California, San Francisco, where she has been affiliated since 1978. She has collaborated with Colleen Johnson on major studies of caregiving, inner-city elderly, grandparents and divorce, and the oldest old. Her particular interest is in the application of research findings to policy and practice. Her publications include, "A Critique of the Caregiving Literature," and "Men and Women Aging Differently," as well as numerous articles co-authored with Dr. Johnson.

Life Beyond 85 Years

The Aura of Survivorship

Colleen L. Johnson, PhD

Barbara M. Barer, MSW

SPRINGER PUBLISHING COMPANY

Springer Publishing Company, Inc.
536 Broadway
New York, NY 10012-3955

Cover design by Margaret Dunin
Production Editor: Kathleen Kelly

99 00 01 02 / 5 4 3 2

Library of Congress Cataloging-in-Publication Data
Johnson, Colleen Leahy, 1932–
   Life Beyond 85 years : the aura of survivorship / Colleen L.
Johnson. Barbara M. Barer.
     p. cm. — (Springer series on life styles & issues in aging)
   Includes bibliographical references and index.
   ISBN 0-8261-9540-7
   1. Aged. 2. Aged—Social conditions. 3. Aged—Family
relationships. 4. Gerontology. I. Barer. Barbara M. II. Title.
III. Series. Springer series on life styles and issues in aging.
HQ1061.J549 1996
305.26—dc20
                                                96-35185
                                                CIP

Printed in the United States of America

Contents

Foreword

A wonderful title! An aura of survivorship is what I have often experienced when interviewing an individual beyond 85 years of age. But why the aura? What emanations are given off so that I experience an aura? Is it because I too would like to survive to my late 80s or my 90s and, if possible, beyond 100? I, of course want to, and not very differently than the apparent one-half or so of persons of advanced old age who are able to carry out their activities of daily living. Recall Ben Franklin who said, "All would be long lived but none would grow old."

It is, however, more than a wish to survive intact to a ripe very old age that evokes the experience of an aura of survivorship. One part of the experience is how ordinary people, who have often lived what only can be considered rather mundane lives, have a sense of well-being in spite of the many losses associated with advanced aging. Also a part is how well they are coping in the here-and-now. Another part is how I forget the age of the octogenarian as she or he tells a life story. I have been visualizing the person as a younger person living a life, but then as I get up to go, I suddenly come back to reality. I have been talking to a very, very old woman or man and not to a coquette in her courting years or to a vigorous tradesman in his most productive years. Then too, on reflection later, that is the acceptance of death.

An understanding of why I have invariably admired, but not always liked, very old individuals has been helped by this stimulating report from the 85+ Study. As I sit talking to the wizened old lady of 87, I realize that she is doing okay although barely mobile because of crippling arthritis and bereft of spouse or friends. She is managing, so Johnson and Barer tell me, by behavioral and cognitive coping. Of course, I say. Behaviorally she has contracted her daily environment, her apartment, to make it manageable, and cognitively has redefined what she can do to be in control. Feeling in control, the world is controllable. Then too, she has narrowed her time frame to the manageable here-and-now and disengaged from formerly significant others who are now departed, to accept a quiescent, withdrawn equanimity.

Would I manage as well if I were to experience her kind of losses? Not at my age of 64. The losses would be premature, too early in life. They would be "off-time," to use the words of my mentor, Bernice Neugarten. On the other hand, the 85+ are "outliving time." They know it. How else can we explain the Johnson and Barer finding that at follow-up an improvement in physical functioning is reported by them? Yes indeed! They know they are outliving time and we feel it. The aura becomes demystified.

Also, and surely, if death was approaching, I would not find it acceptable. It too would be premature and I would feel that my life has been foreshortened. There is a business yet to be done, of nonbeing, as the concern shifts to fear of the process of dying, of dying immobile, in pain, intractably confused and alone.

When I began my studies of aging, I did not believe it was possible at any age to accept non-being with equanimity. But now I know that when there is no unfinished business at the end of the life course, that accepting death is inherent to the aura of the oldest of the old. Facilitory to accepting death in my Chicago and Northeast data, has been the belief in a hereafter that contains reunions with departed loved ones. This religious belief, also quite evident among centenarians in Georgia, was apparently absent among the secularized white respondents in San Francisco, the site of the 85+ Study. Yes, California is indeed a different kind of place! To add complexity, however, Johnson has recently told me that African Americans in the San Francisco area are very likely to introduce religiosity in their interviews.

Puzzling on how manifestations of early socialization and later life experiences may affect the psychology of the 85+, I keep returning to my metapsychology beliefs: There is something like basic personality or identity that never changes. Family members or close friends of my parents that I have known for more than half a century are still themselves, and even more so. Yet, are they not also different? They, like the wizened old lady, when asked how they have changed, may take out a picture of themselves from their young adult years. Chuckling, this decrepit, admirable woman shows me an ancient picture taken of her when she was in her early 20s and then says, "This is me but I have changed just a little." How can we best conceptualize the dramatic, and drastic, changes with the experience of never having changing?

Although Johnson and Barer emphasize transformations of the self to maintain adaptation, every vignette (and indeed there are many illuminating vignettes) reveals the uniqueness of the individual. When somewhat similar catastrophes have occurred to two octogenarians, one may be found to react with despair whereas the other with transcendence. The likely explanation for this kind of difference is that some stable inner core from earliest socialization is retained that makes some people sturdier than others. Still, I must recognize that within this stability, there are profound changes. I am forced to ask myself: Is my sense, or even conviction, of being the same person I have always been only an illusion of sameness and continuity as I continually adapt to new forces? Is not there a core in me that will persist? If not, in turn, there is something strange, potentially frightening, about being a different person, a "not me," when adapting to the oldest old years? Of course I will still be me but, strangely to say, also a different me.

Independent of my ruminations on myself are both the insights and challenges in the reading of *Life Beyond 85 Years: The Aura of Survivorship*. The insights capture the reality of the inner lives of very old people and why they emanate an aura. The challenges reside in integrating these insights with other extant knowledge and in, moreover, absorbing into one's psyche, especially mine, an appreciation for normative transformations that are yet to be encountered.

SHELDON TOBIN

Acknowledgments

This research was funded by a MERIT Award from the National Institute on Aging (R37-AG06559). We wish to thank Katrina Johnson, the Project Officer over most of the eight years, for her continual support and enthusiasm for the project. Over these years, we have benefited from the contributions of numerous people. Initially Leonard Pearlin was a consultant who advised us on critical aspects of the conceptual framework and the research design. Throughout the research activities, Lillian Troll participated at all levels of the research process, and we are indebted to her for her many contributions. While both authors conducted as many interviews as time permitted, we were most fortunate to find very talented and sensitive psychologists who were superb interviewers. Susan Boxer contributed to the first few years, followed by Nan Harvey, who worked on several waves of interviewing. Beth Krackov then worked in the last stage of the project. Without their contributions, the insights into the lives of many respondents would have been far scantier. Finally, in the past year, Nicolas Sheon has organized our materials and made himself indispensable in processing the data and assisting us in preparing the manuscript.

We also wish to thank others who assisted in the final preparation of this work. Frank Johnson made valuable suggestions for the chapter on emotions and, in fact, enlightened us on a new perspective. Sheldon Tobin made most productive suggestions in the final revision. Christian Simon assisted in identifying how the oldest old define their health. Others who worked on the project for a time include Norah Schwartz, Julie Parisian, and Kathleen

Coll. Brian deVries read an earlier version of this manuscript and was most helpful in pointing out much-needed improvements in our conceptions and our style. Needless to say, we alone are responsible for the outcomes.

PART I

The Study

Chapter 1

Introduction

In recent years, profound changes have occurred in the age distribution of our population. Not only are the numbers of older people increasing, but also members of the oldest age category are now the fastest growing group in the United States. In fact, researchers have now come forth with a new age label, "the oldest old," designating those 85 years and older. This, last in a succession of convenient but arbitrary labels, refers to those who are two decades beyond 65, the age when social security begins for a predominantly healthy and active group. Even by age 75, many do not qualify for the usual stereotype of inevitable decrepitude in the senium. By another decade, however, most survivors have some disabilities and have experienced social losses as well. As a consequence, this unprecedented prolongation of life has far-reaching implications, not only for the aged themselves but also for their families and society in general (Taeuber & Rosenwaike, 1992).

In response to these concerns, we began our study eight years ago with the conviction that there is much to be learned about the aging process by focusing upon the oldest old. In the study of their adaptation, we began by posing a simple, straightforward question about adaptation aimed at Maslow's lowest level of needs (Maslow, 1954). What competencies are needed to survive and continue community-living with a modicum of strain? Then we went on to explore the objective and subjective experiences of daily life, and those capacities needed to manage both the physical and social environments and sustain a sense of well-being.

Those of us who are investigating the oldest old population have moved into previously uncharted personal worlds, where exceptional demands are placed upon survivors. These respondents must deal with persistent pain, problems with mobility, loss of vision and hearing, the recurrent deaths of contemporaries, and even the onset of old age among their children. Understandably, it is not unusual to encounter those who feel a sense of aloneness as a result of outliving all or most of their significant relationships. Nevertheless, it is puzzling but reassuring to learn from our research that the onset of disability does not necessarily lead to demoralization or despair. In fact, most of our respondents have retained a sense of well-being and pride in their special status as long-term survivors.

Early in the interviews with the very old, we were impressed by how these respondents dealt with their losses. When they should be having difficulty coping with pain, disability, and deaths of loved ones, most were handling their lives competently and with good spirits. Moreover, respondents discussed their lives and their experiences with a profound grasp of the practical and philosophical aspects of long-term survivorship. In other words, they were adapting well to seemingly impossible odds and, on the basis of the current research literature, we could not explain it. Thus our task has been to find out why. As findings accumulated from repeated interviews, we began to speak of an "aura of survivorship," a subjective impression that something emanates from them that hints at their special status. This book then stems from our conclusion that, in many respects, the oldest old are quite different from younger old people, as they have the unique status of having outlived the predictable life span.

We set out to examine not only how very old individuals adapt to daily challenges, but also how they maintain a positive outlook as they face the risk of losing their linkages to the outside world (Tobin, 1991). These linkages refer not only to social network connections, but also to their physical, sensory, and cognitive connections to their environment. We will demonstrate in the following how, over time, most of the very old continue to view their health as good and to express contentment about their lives. The question thus is posed: By what means are they able to sustain well-being despite seemingly insurmountable odds?

Rethinking Conceptions of the Aging Process

Our findings also point to the need to reconceptualize both popular and scholarly conceptions of the aging process that are commonly taken for granted in gerontology. Most ideas stem from the Panglossian view of aging that denies, minimizes, or overlooks the predictable problems of advanced old age. Perhaps this view results from the fact that few researchers have methodically made age distinctions after age 65 or 75. Consequently, they miss those age-specific events and situations occurring during the final stage of life among long-term survivors.

First, gerontologists are particularly prone to counter well-known conceptions in the field by labeling them as myths. Subsequently, these are then replaced by generalizations that become countermyths that eventually are subject to the same scrutiny and revision. The changing conceptions of the family in later life is a particularly good example. Ideas about the family were revised over a decade ago, when Ethel Shanas (1979b) shot down as a myth the idea of family abandonment, aptly illustrating from survey data that the old are not necessarily bereft and neglected. Instead, she found that older people were in frequent contact with children or, in their absence, other relatives. Thus the principle of substitution came to dominate our thinking about the late-life family—a proposition inferring that all elderly have at least one family member available to help them. Until recently, however, no one paused to inquire whether this conclusion also holds true for the oldest old? As our research reports here, as many as 24 percent of the very old respondents no longer maintain face-to-face family relationships. Since those living into advanced old age may face the risk of outliving their family members, we need to revise our conceptions of the late-life family to take into account the families of the very old.

A second widespread conception in social gerontology stems from theories on the efficacy of activity and a sense of control. According to these views, self-direction, activity, and social involvement are reported as positive forces, while passivity and disengagement are considered signs of unsuccessful aging (Maddox, 1965). These ideas also need rethinking when examining the situation of the oldest old, since their high level of disability can prevent them from exerting effective control over their physical environment. Similarly, their disabilities often lead to difficulties in socializing, so they become less active as their social environment shrinks. These changes, as noted above, do not generally undermine their well-being. When social involvement becomes too complicated to sustain, and physical problems make the social environment too difficult to manage, the oldest old usually welcome increased detachment and aloofness from potentially bothersome, demanding, or stressful roles and relationships.

A third assumption we are questioning here concerns how the current conceptions of the life course may be incongruent with the subjective and objective situation of the oldest old. The predominant emphasis assumes that successful adaptation during the aging process entails continuities in the self concept. To be successful, according to this view, older people should progress through life making transitions preferably on time and with a minimum of disruption (Neugarten, Moore, & Lowe, 1968). While such assumptions on continuity may pertain to some young-old cohorts, they tend to be less applicable to most of the oldest old in our study.

In agreement with recent views that are now rejecting any unitary conception of the self (Baltes, 1993; Ryff, 1993), we suggest that, within a temporal context, individuals are continuously reconstituting their self-representation in response to new situations faced in late life. Such a process, we will demonstrate, constitutes an effective adaptive technique.

Consistent with these formulations, we propose that long-term survivorship tends to stimulate changes in both cognitive and emotional processes, wherein conceptions of social relationships, the self concept, one's orientation toward time, and even the meanings of life and death tend to be reconstituted. Sometimes these changes occur following a brush with death, the loss of a final contemporary, or simply with the realization that one has become an "accident of time" or "beyond time."

We conclude that it is time to go beyond the bipolar conceptions of the process of aging as either successful or unsuccessful, that one experiences either integrity versus despair, or that one's life should be characterized by activity rather than disengagement. More appropriate in the study of the oldest old is the recognition that usual aging during the last stage of life entails widespread disability (Siegel, 1994). Then we can go on to study individual variability in adapting to the formidable but typical challenges in late late life.

The Conceptual Framework of Adaptation

In defining adaptation as simply the capacity to survive and to continue community living with a relatively low level of strain, we went on to collect information about three types of competencies the oldest old require to sustain themselves in the community.

First, the very old need to devise the means by which they can manage their physical environment and carry on daily routines, so that basic physical needs are met. Second, if they are too disabled, they must mobilize help from others and determine the level of social integration appropriate to meet their needs for sociability and support. Third, psychological adaptation rests on the capacity to sustain motivations and a sense of well-being.

Very old individuals are continually confronting the challenges that result from having to cope with numerous physical and social losses (Lawton, Greenbaum, & Liebowitz, 1980). Consequently, their status day-to-day is rarely characterized by equilibrium and homeostasis (Riegel, 1975; Thomae, 1980). In confronting these dynamic and problematic situations constructively, we assume that the individual is an active agent in responding to the typical problems of late late life by two means: 1) behavioral attempts to manage the physical and social environment, those coping strategies directed to specific situations; and 2) cognitive and emotional processes that monitor and define the meanings of these adaptive challenges so as to have a sense of control over one's life. Data collected in these domains include objective indicators of physical status, and the numbers of social contacts and supports. Also included in our data are subjective indicators, namely, the individuals' discussions of their perceptions, explanations, and interpretations about their adaptation to long-term survival.

In recognition of the great variability among the oldest old in both objective and subjective indicators, the outcomes are also variable, because they can be personally defined or be "in the eyes of the beholder." For example, they can define their adaptation as successful when they are housebound or even bedfast, just as others are successful when they are active participants in the outside world. With these propositions in mind, we conclude that adaptation is basically a process of "fine tuning," that is, the ability to arrive at a balance or congruence between the individuals' capacities, objective and subjective resources, and the demands posed by their survival into late late life.

A Variety of Adaptive Strategies

Throughout this book, case studies illustrate a range of life experiences of the oldest old. Here it is appropriate to describe four individuals in our study who provide a study of contrasts in their adaptive styles. We begin by comparing two women who share a prior social position and currently a very disabled physical status, yet their lives have taken very different pathways. Then we describe one of the few participants in the study who had no impairments after six years in the study, and who remained a robust survivor actively in control of his life. He can be compared with one of the few centenarians in the study at the outset. This woman, at 103 years, lives out her life by devising a system of personal meanings that helps her to transcend her very disabled body mentally.

Contrasting Developmental Pathways

Mrs. Allen and Mrs. Bascom differ widely in their responses to similar adaptive challenges in late life. Both are functionally impaired, in continual pain, and mostly housebound, but their capacities to sustain their motivations and sense of well-being vary greatly, with Mrs. Allen being cheery and resourceful, and Mrs. Bascom, anxious, unhappy, and intermittently hostile to the interviewer as well as to her full-time help.

Both Mrs. Bascom and Mrs. Allen were born into a prosperous upper middle-class family, but Mrs. Bascom experienced unsettling events throughout her long life that may have affected her today. She is an unhappy and probably clinically depressed woman, who makes incessant demands on everyone. Over five years in the study, she was mostly housebound and needed full-time help. At the last contact at 97, she rarely left her bed. Like Mrs. Allen, she had painful arthritis but, unlike her, she constantly complained about her pains and her life in general.

Mrs. Bascom's father had died shortly after her birth, and her mother left home almost immediately thereafter to seek a career in the arts. Thus, she was left to be raised by her grandparents whom she remembers as warm and loving. When she was eight years old, a woman appeared at the door, who proved to be the mother she never knew she had. Her mother had meanwhile married a wealthy industrialist and wanted her daughter back. Mrs. Bascom remembers living with a loving stepfather, but a cold, aloof mother.

She concludes, however, that she had a happy childhood, taking numerous trips to Europe, having her own horse, and attending private schools here and abroad—all accoutrements of upper-class life. That ended at 18 when she fell in love with an Irish Catholic man. When they subsequently married, she was disinherited by her stepfather, a 33rd degree Mason, who left her one dollar. She noted, "I was born with a silver spoon in my mouth, but now I'm left with only a wooden spoon." After World War I, her husband's career progressed successfully, but her fortunes changed when he died prematurely of cancer at age 35. Having spent their savings on his terminal illness, she was forced to work for the first time in her life in order to support her two young children.

Only in her 60s was she reunited with her mother. She feels that her mother re-established the relationship mainly because she needed a caregiver. After taking care of her mother for five years, her mother died, leaving Mrs. Bascom $10,000 and a house where she still lives. She remarried after her mother's death, but her new husband died suddenly after one year. The final tragedy of her life, from which she says she has never recovered, came 12 years before she entered the study, when her two daughters died of cancer within six months of each other. These daughters, both in their 60s at the time, had been important social anchorages for Mrs. Bascom. Since their deaths, she has only intermittent phone calls from her biological grandson who recently had moved to England. She has lost contact with two adopted granddaughters and her great-grandchildren. Because of her long period of disability, she was unable to maintain a friendship network, so her only contacts were with her round-the-clock hired helpers. Even then she complained constantly about not having help that she can talk to in "regular English."

Over the course of the study, her sparse social environment contracted even more. By the last contact, visual problems prevented her from watching TV, and listening to her radio made her nervous. The direct call buttons on her telephone had become accidentally switched, so she no longer had any contact with the outside world. Instead, she reported she spent her days thinking about her past life and worrying about the future. With her control over her environment minimal, she was completely dependent upon her full-time help, and upon her lawyer, who managed her dwindling financial resources. In her attempts to keep up her home and maintain full-time help, her economic problems became severe. She claimed she had only enough money for the next two months. At the end of the last interview, she said, "All of this makes me so confused. My mind is not working so good. Why has God let me live so long?"

Mrs. Allen's adaptation was markedly different. By our criteria of adaptation, she had impressive competencies to adapt to major disabilities.

From her wheelchair in senior housing where she lived alone, she competently managed her physical environment, maintained adequate social integration, and sustained a positive outlook about her life. She is a lively, animated, and opinionated woman, with her arms waving vigorously in order to emphasize her convictions. Small and frail looking, she maintains her links to others with the help of two hearing aids and very thick glasses. Her favorite hobby is reading, even though she must hold her droopy eyelids open in order to see. To ease her pains, she keeps a water bottle under her right arm and a heating pad on her left knee.

She frequently referred to her happy childhood. Of Dutch background, she was born in Philadelphia, the youngest of eight children in a prosperous mercantile family. Her early years were happy ones, "We were into everything—I had a very lively family. It was always fun. My brothers played the mandolin and we'd move the furniture out and dance." After a short marriage to a Jewish man whose family never accepted her, she remarried at the age of 32. At age 45, she had her first and only child, a daughter. A few years later she was widowed, and she is still proud of the fact that she supported her daughter alone. "I was a businesswoman my whole life— I had a man's job in sales of heavy equipment."

Her senior housing is suited to her needs. It offers some supervision and weekly transportation to stores and a senior center. She uses a walker and a cane in addition to her wheel chair. Even with her difficulty in mobility, she lives alone in her apartment and has hired help only two mornings a week. Her daughter stocks her kitchen, and Mrs. Allen microwaves her own meals. When asked about her health, she replied, "It is lousy—I have real bad arthritis." Despite this, she was highly motivated to maintain her social ties. She ordinarily took Tylenol for her pain, but on her day at the senior center, she added codeine to be assured of having a good time. She felt fortunate that she still had her mental skills—unlike some of her friends who had strokes. Four friends in the building visited her daily and her daughter stopped by frequently. She clearly enjoyed all these contacts. Although her income was only $800 a month, her housing was subsidized and she felt her economic resources were sufficient.

As to sustaining her morale, she explained, "I don't think anything upsets me any more. I don't let things bother me. I flush away my worries.

I am pleased with everything." As to her impending death, she said, "You have to meet death. It's part of life. It doesn't upset me." Six months later, she died after having two strokes. According to her daughter, she maintained her contentment right up to the end.

To illustrate the importance of developmental factors, we have contrasted two women who began life with similar social advantages but from almost the beginning, the events impinging upon them took a very different form. By their late 80s, they were dealing with similar disabilities and dependencies, yet the emotional aspects of their lives varied greatly. Mrs. Bascom tragically lost both of her children and, for all intents and purposes, had witnessed the demise of her family and friends. Except for her daughter, however, Mrs. Allen too was without family contacts, but she compensated by making friends easily. A life course perspective thus is useful in examining these survivors.

A Self-Reliant Survivor

Only a small minority could be termed successful adapters if the conventional definition was used—namely, that they remained healthy and actively in control of their lives.

Mr. Friedrich is one of those exceptions. From age 86 to 92, he retained his health, his functioning, and his active lifestyle, concentrating upon action-oriented strategies to cope with specific problems. He is a youthful-looking, wiry older man, always immaculately groomed, and at each interview dressed in a brightly colored shirt that he himself had sewn. His cheerful spotless apartment bespoke his excellent housekeeping skills.

When he joined the study, Mr. Friedrich still seemed to mourn the death of his wife four years previously. At each contact, he described the six years of caregiving throughout her protracted bout with cancer. His grief, however, was moderated by the formation of a close relationship with a woman he met at a senior center.

Perhaps reflecting his German background and his career as a machinist, Mr. Friedrich approached life with a meticulous, methodical daily plan. "I get up at seven, make breakfast, clean up, make my bed, and never leave this place untouched. A good day is when I wake up alive and hungry and ready to begin my activities—housework, sewing, seeing my companion, and even just riding street cars around the city." He spends half of his time in the country where he is restoring a vacation home and building a new deck and a garage—strenuous work he continues to do unaided, even though he's in his 90s.

When in the city, his life centers around his companion, whom he meets each day at the senior center, and then goes to her home for dinner. They travel together and share the same interests and activities. He insists that their compatibility is strengthened, because they never interfere with each other's lives. He is cautious about the relationship—"I do not want to wear out my welcome. Fancies can change to distance and arguments." He has no children and has no contact with his few surviving relatives. Instead, his companion's children and grandchildren have become his family.

He attributes his contentment with life to his "positive thinking" and to the fact that the many years of caregiving for his wife taught him to withhold his feelings and complaints. His philosophy of life is, "Don't look back. Look forward. Life is what you make it." He insists that he is always happy and contented, that he is never angry, and that he is always level-headed. Although taking personal responsibility for his life, he also acknowledges some divinity. "I am not religious, but I know there is a God and an afterlife. God has been good to me to let me live so long. My way of life is perfect. My whole life has been good. My parents were perfect. I was never out of work, and I always made good money."

His capacity to exert effective mastery over his life was evident when the rent on his airy, spacious apartment was raised. He immediately moved into a one-room efficiency apartment with no complaints. In fact, he views the present as the best time in his life. When asked about his thoughts on his death, he replied, "I've already committed myself to obligations until the year 2001, so I intend to be here to meet them." Since his mother and father survived into their late 80s, he had always anticipated a long life. He concluded, "I don't think about dying. I bought my burial plot 25 years ago, so that's all taken care of."

This remarkable self-reliant man with a good physical status and a positive sense of his own competence continues to be in control and the master of his environment and his own fate. Fortunately his exceptional physical status is compatible with such an orientation. His adaptive strategies, however, illustrate only one form of adjusting to long-term survivorship.

A Centenarian

In contrast to the very practical Mr. Friedrich, Mrs. Bloom, at 103, draws upon her intellectual and artistic competencies to arrive at personal meanings to sustain her well-being in the face of her physical declines. She has 1 surviving daughter, 7 grandchildren, 16 or 17 great-grandchildren, and 1 great-great-grandchild. She has outlived another daughter and a great-grandchild. Many relatives, friends, and former students visit her frequently. Throughout her long life and, in fact, until shortly before her death at 106, she maintained an active interest in music and literature, and she was a published author. She lived in a small, comfortable house overflowing with books and family pictures. She had full-time help because she was unable to walk unassisted.

> She began the interview, "I don't know what's so wonderful about living to 103. Life just goes on and on and then you are alone. I have to have nurses. I can't stand alone. I can't cook. I need help with everything. I'm irked to have someone always at my elbow." Yet, despite her disabilities, she claims that, by living so long, she has new eyes to see the world. This new status, she says, has brought contentment to her life. As an onlooker, not a participant in life, she says she has developed more flexibility and openness about the world around her.
>
> She then laid down her guidelines for the interview—that she would answer no questions about time. As a result, there are gaps in the chronology of her life.

> *I have no truck with time. I've always been that way. I never dated anything I wrote. Oh, I keep a few dates in mind—my wedding anniversary, my daughter's birthday, but that's about it. I don't like to be asked when something happened. It's been both a good and a bad thing. Sometimes I would like to organize my life chronologically, so I could see how I arrived at this or that. But with my attitude about time, there is an advantage—I don't dwell on being so old.*

As to her health,

> *It is wonderful. I have only a little arthritis. Even my eyes are good, so I can read all the time. I can also write. For me writing is like breathing. I am most happy when I am writing. I am out of my own mind and just concerned with what I'm writing. If I believe in my unconscious, something comes to me. I also have periods of aloneness. I don't get lonely, but I go through periods when I feel unrelated to what is going on about me. When I get these periods of aloneness, I just make peace with them. These feelings come even though I am never alone—I have all this help around me. My daughter comes a lot and so do friends. But some days, I am lost on all calendars. A bad day is when no one comes."*

When her husband died 10 years earlier at the age of 98, Mrs. Bloom still drove and was relatively independent. "The person I valued most in the world was gone, the house was empty. We had to have full-time help to take care of him, then they all left. I felt so alone that I became disoriented for a time."

She refers to her grandchildren and great-grandchildren as her intimate relations and avoids being judgmental about their lives.

There is no generation gap. Our interests are the same. I know only what they choose to tell me. Of course, I hear rumors, but I try not to think about them. All but two have been divorced. Naturally, I would have liked it if they got on during their marriages, but I have no desire to push it. Their lives are their own. I am only an onlooker and should not comment. I never say what is right or wrong. I'm more tolerant than when I was younger.

She considers herself as in another stage of aging. For example, she mentioned her 86-year-old friend who was also in our study. "We are close even with large differences in our age. You know, she is the only one left who knew my parents." When asked about her own death, she replied,

At 103, you can't help but think about death. But I enjoy my way of life. I put time out of my mind. I push away death thoughts. I look forward, not back—I put a frame around what I want to see and ignore the rest. There is no way to die gracefully, except by not worrying others. But I should modify that; these ideas are all right for my days. My night dreams are different. My unconscious takes over and I have no control.

• • • •

The chapters are organized into three parts. This chapter and the next introduce the study, its rationale, and its research approach. The second part explores the context in which adaptation takes place: the age-related problems that challenge the oldest old and the physical and the social resources that facilitate their survivorship. The third part analyzes the cognitive and emotional processes indicating the psychological interior of the oldest old and then goes on to illustrate varied patterns of adaptation of the survivors and their preparations for death. As we map the lives of the oldest old, we let the respondents speak for themselves, so as to illustrate how they perceive and interpret their world, and thereby convey the aura of their survivorship.

Chapter 2

Studying the Oldest Old

When the request for proposals on the oldest old was first issued in 1984 by the National Institutes of Health, very little was known about members of this age group. Beyond scattered demographic and epidemiological findings, most studies of older people failed to make age distinctions after age 65 or 75. Since little information was available on whether the oldest old faced problems unique to advanced old age, exploratory inductive research seemed particularly timely. When we began preparing a proposal on the oldest old in 1987, we were surprised to find that, in the meantime, few had taken advantage of that incentive and secured funding to do exploratory studies with members of this age group. By now in the mid-1990s, plentiful findings are coming from large data sets, but still few reports are available that flesh out the context of life in late life.

Special Research Considerations

Some have commented that the lack of research on the life experiences of very old people indicates that most researchers find this age group too difficult to study. Of those difficulties we are now all too familiar. Potential respondents of advanced age are a very small proportion of our population and, hence, they are hard to locate with opportunity sampling or even costly random sampling procedures. As many as 22 percent live in institutions and, not surprisingly, once a community sample is located, many are too mentally or physically impaired to participate. Thus some screening by necessity prolongs the process of drawing a sample.

Likewise, interviewing is more difficult with the oldest old than when studying younger old people because of the high incidence of vision and hearing problems as well as memory loss. We did not use proxies, except in later stages when we were tracking respondents in the attrition group. Even then, a family member only gave an account of why that respondent could no longer participate. Finally, in studying the oldest old over time, attrition is high and, thus, those lost to the project also need to be studied to determine whether they differ from the sample of survivors.

The study of a vulnerable population requires some specific skills. One major consideration was the effects the research itself would have on them. Because of our repeated contacts, we understandably developed a special relationship with those respondents who remained in the study, but a relationship that posed a dilemma. If we cultivated that relationship in such a way that conferred a special status, halo effects might influence how they responded to later questioning. Consequently we decided to retain selected individuals as informants, those who had a special interest in the study and who helped us design the interview protocols. Other than these informants, we limited contacts with participants to scheduled interviews at 14- to 16-month intervals and declined invitations to stop by in between. We did send out certificates of appreciation acknowledging their participation, and we later spotted them usually framed and prominently displayed.

Respondents' continued participation in some cases became a source of humor. At the end of the first interview, when we said we would be back the next year, a common response was, "Don't count on it. I'll probably be dead by then." How to respond to such a remark was a source of lengthy staff discussions. Saying "I hope not," or "I'll be sad if that is so," seemed too serious a reply to their light-hearted comments about their imminent death. Instead, we commonly joked in return, "You have to be here. We need you in the study." At subsequent interviews, some predicted our closing remarks by saying, "I know, I know. I have to be here for you next year."

Interviews were often conducted under difficult circumstances. By standards of younger people, most residences were overheated and stuffy. Probably the most difficult problem, however, was the prevalence of hearing problems. On occasion, respondents did not come to the door, even though we had no difficulty in setting up the interview if their telephones had amplifiers. Thus the interviewer had to call from a public phone to request they come to the door and let us in. To adjust to their hearing problems, respondents often planned a seating arrangement ahead, so the interviewer sat by their good ear. In some cases, the standard instruments had to be abandoned because of hearing problems. Some items on mastery and mood were too abstract and brought either no responses or unusable ones. Such items most likely were too remote from their typical concerns as very old people. Because of problems with eyesight, we never considered using pen-and-paper tests to administer structured instruments.

Another difficulty arose in scheduling interviews because of their health problems and frequent visits to the doctor. If respondents said they were in pain or felt too lethargic, we conveyed our regrets and said we would call later. Usually after repeated efforts, we reached them on a day they felt well, and they often invited us to come right over. In other cases, the interview had to take place over two sittings because of their lack of stamina. Very few people refused to participate in subsequent contacts. The few that declined at later dates were usually those who gave brief responses initially, and they eventually told us they had already told us everything we needed to know. Only one respondent dropped out of the study, because she was upset about our questioning. Quite to the contrary, most respondents looked forward to each interview and welcomed the opportunity to discuss their lives with us. In fact, some said they were able to discuss issues with us that they avoided telling their own children. Some respondents prepared for the interview by making lists of topics they wanted to discuss.

More serious decisions had to be made when we observed minor neglect or rude treatment by home-care workers. Since help is difficult to find, we did not want to jeopardize what was often a carefully arranged formal service plan. Never did we encounter a situation that we felt demanded interference. On occasion we anonymously lobbied for the immediate need to implement delivery of meals on wheels. In a few cases, we observed that drug regimens carefully set out by a visiting nurse were not being taken regularly. Far less serious were dilemmas on accepting refreshments when it was an eight-ounce glass of prune juice, or whether or not we should tell a respondent with hearing problems that her telephone was ringing or the tea kettle was whistling.

Impact of the 1989 San Francisco Earthquake

A natural disaster can have serious effects on an already vulnerable population. Since the 1989 San Francisco earthquake occurred during the second round of interviewing, we had an opportunity to assess the effects of this event. Two respondents suffered injuries. One woman hit her head against a table as she attempted to save her Tiffany lamp. Miss Taub, who is described in Chapter 4, felt her health was permanently affected by being knocked down by the tremor and left alone unconscious for almost two hours.

Others experienced considerable dislocation in their lives. In fact, at that time our attrition rate was higher than at any other time over eight years. When the earthquake damaged their apartment or home, those who were having difficulty managing alone often decided it was time to move to more protective housing. Some finally responded to a child's insistence that they move to the city where they were living. Others were inconvenienced by damage but stayed where they were. Many respondents lived in high-rise apartments or senior housing where elevators did not work, and electricity, water, and telephones were unavailable in some cases for several days. Without telephones, some who were living alone went through an anxious period until their families or friends reached them. One of the frailest women in the study had to leave her apartment that was flooded by a broken pipe. She refused all assistance except a borrowed chair where she sat for several hours in front of her building until her children arrived on the scene.

Others reported more anxiety and sleep problems after the earthquake, particularly if they had gone through the experience alone. Predictably the earthquake for some evoked memories of the 1906 earthquake. Some reported they felt less secure and jumped nervously at the slightest noise. Some bemoaned the loss of fine china or mementos of their past, because their china cabinet had been knocked over.

Given these imposing obstacles to research on the oldest old, our rationale and research design at every stage of planning had to take many factors into account. This chapter will describe these hurdles and how they were surmounted.

Rationale and Conceptual Framework

While anthropological research on this little-studied population seems warranted, such studies are rarely cited in model-driven studies or reports from epidemiologists and demographers. Consequently, uncertainty existed at the outset as to how to design a research project that could generate hypotheses from qualitative material on the subjective and objective dimensions of long-term survivorship. The findings to be reported here come from one of the few or perhaps the only intensive qualitative study to date of the oldest old. Some statistical findings are presented here only to document significant differences and associations between variables. These tests also demonstrate how representative our sample is to the national population of oldest old.

Five methodological decisions rested upon the premise that an intensive study was needed that could inform and contextualize the findings beginning to emerge from large data sets. First, our goal has been to use ordinary conversations in an open-ended interview format to secure the point of view of the respondents, what Sankar and Gubrium (1994) refer to as an approach that is empirically grounded in everyday experience. Consequently, the research design needed a sample size small enough so that an intensive open-ended interview technique was feasible, yet a sample large enough so that statistical tests could be used where appropriate. We also needed sufficient numbers to compensate for high attrition. The research project needed to draw a sample that represented an ordinary or typical group of individuals 85 years and older, who initially resided in the community and were mentally competent. We started with 150 respondents and, where possible, we went on to interview those respondents who entered institutions during the course of the research.

Second, given the size limitations, it was necessary initially to control for ethnicity and race, yet permit socioeconomic status to vary. If we were to study cultural differences, particularly in a city like San Francisco, we would need at least 50 respondents in each ethnic group. Because of the small numbers of oldest old surviving in each ethnic group, and because of the need for interpreters with Asians and Hispanics, accounting for ethnicity would turn this study into a much larger and cumbersome enterprise than seemed needed in exploratory research. Although we began adding black oldest old three years into the research, this book is confined to the white oldest.

The rationale for excluding blacks from this book is twofold: Since black oldest old are now being interviewed for the third time, it would be impossible to analyze adaptation over the same time span that we have for whites, and early comparisons of 122 black and 150 white oldest old revealed major differences on almost all indicators of adaptation. We concluded that a book that paused at each presentation of findings to account for racial differences would be invidious to both samples of respondents. Predictably, this cohort of blacks suffered from more limited opportunities, lower education level, and poorer economic resources. Few had had stable marriages, and many were currently experiencing some effects of the breakdown of the inner-city family. Nevertheless, their situation was superior to white oldest old in key aspects. While fewer blacks than whites had surviving children to see to their needs in late life, they were immersed in more active helping networks of their own devising (Johnson, 1996). Perhaps as a reflection of higher social integration, they had a significantly higher level of well-being than whites. For these reasons, a decision was made to study each group in its own right, so a report on the black oldest old will follow at a later date.

Third, the importance of repeated observations has been an important part of the research design (Siegel, 1994). This community-dwelling sample of 150 white oldest old has been assessed at five interviews at 14- to 16-month intervals. Thus it has been possible to generate hypotheses at one contact to be tested more systematically in later contacts with the respondents. For example, initially we found that friendships seemed different among very old people than reported in the literature on friendships of younger old people, so at Time 2, additional questions were added to explore that phenomenon.

Fourth, because the age range was narrow, it was difficult to single out the effects of chronological age as compared with functional age. Consequently we added a sample of 100 individuals 70 to 84 years of age, who where drawn from voting records, the same source as the oldest old.

Fifth, conceptually, this research design has drawn upon both the applied and theoretical literature in gerontology. At the empirical level, we have been interested in the chain of events taking place which determine the extent of fit between the needs of the individual and the personal and social resources they have available to address those needs. Understandably, physical resources can be evaluated in rather clearcut fashion as can the numbers and types of social supports and the level of social integration. In contrast to behavioral indicators, the cognitive and emotional dimensions of adaptation at this stage of life involved indicators that are more difficult to assess except by an open-ended interview format. Unfortunately most instruments tapping the psychological variables are inappropriate for very old people because they have difficulty with the abstract nature of some questions. Moreover, such instruments cannot be self-administered because of vision problems, while hearing problems interfere with understanding the syntax of many items in instruments.

Research Design

Finding the Oldest Old

It bears repeating that the study of the oldest old is particularly difficult at all levels of research activity. The first problem we faced was determining how to locate a representative sample. After ruling out random sampling as too expensive and time consuming, we turned to public voting records, because they gave the date of birth. Since we were confining the first sample to whites, we identified those city precincts that had high proportions of whites yet also had diverse socioeconomic status.

Since the intent was to study normal aging, it was necessary to draw a community sample that was representative of a white urban population who lived outside institutions. We concentrated our efforts in two neighborhoods in San Francisco that had a high proportion of individuals who met our selection criteria. This area had also been extensively studied in two research projects by Todd and Ruffini (1983). Since one project used a household survey technique, their demographic data were useful in augmenting the 1980 census data.

These neighborhoods had another advantage in having a high proportion of older people. We estimated that over 1,700 individuals in these districts were 85 years and older in 1988. Because these neighborhoods also had a low proportion of minorities at that time, sample selection was facilitated. Todd and Ruffini's survey of 434 households indicated an adequate distribution of older people with diverse socioeconomic indicators, and representative distributions of the major religious backgrounds. These researchers also found that the elderly population in these districts were not concentrated in high-density senior housing, but rather dispersed throughout the neighborhoods. Since 70 percent of the residences in these districts were one-family dwellings, we were able to reach the less visible portion of the older population. We viewed this housing pattern as an advantage, for it permitted us to study those individuals who were able to maintain their homes.

Initially all samples were drawn from voting records in San Francisco, and then snowball techniques were used with some respondents from voting records then referring us to their age peers. Approximately 20 percent came from the latter technique. Letters were sent to respondents that were followed by a phone call to determine eligibility and schedule an interview.

Sample Characteristics

Table 2.1 presents the characteristics of the sample at each wave of interviewing over six years, when the mean age rose from 88.9 to 92.9, and the mean education level was 12.0 years. Throughout the study, approximately one quarter of the sample were men. The proportion married declined from 20 to 13 percent, yet the numbers living alone ranged from 52 to 58 percent. The proportion with at least one surviving child also was similar at each contact, 68 to 74 percent, while the numbers with children in proximity increased, most likely with the increased needs of the survivors at Time 5. Over half had no complaints about their economic resources.

In their physical status, a majority, 64 to 73 percent reported that their health was good or excellent throughout. While the sample at each contact remained much the same on most variables, they did become progressively and significantly more disabled on both the Activities of Daily Living for personal care and the Instrumental Activities of Daily Living. In fact, at Time 4, only 8 percent were

TABLE 2.1
Characteristics of Survivors at Five Contacts over Six Years (by percentage)

	Time 1 (n = 150)	Time 2 (n = 111)	Time 3 (n = 93)	Time 4 (n = 63)	Time 5 (n = 48)
Mean age	88.9	90.1	91.2	91.9	92.9
Mean years education	12.0	12.1	12.1	12.1	12.1
Gender					
Male	26	23	24	25	23
Female	74	77	76	75	77
Married					
Yes	20	18	16	16	13
No	80	82	84	84	87
Household					
Alone	58	56	52	52	56
With others	42	44	48	48	44
Parental status					
Child present	68	69	69	74	73
Child nearby	55	58	59	63	65
No children	32	31	31	26	27
Economic status					
Good	61	56	49	50	52
Fair/Poor	39	44	51	50	48
Perceived health status					
Excellent/Good	73	69	70	71	64
Fair/Poor	27	31	30	29	36
ADL impaired					
None	83	78	70	68	60**
1 or more	17	22	30	32	40
IADL impaired					
None	25	21	15	8	13***
1–3	39	37	32	31	15
4 or more	36	42	53	61	72
Informal social supports					
None	53	36	34	37	31*
For 1 or more ADL/ IADL	47	67	66	63	69
Formal social supports					
None	44	40	11	17	27
One or more service	56	60	89	83	73
Mood (means on scale of 8–32 with 8 = good)	16.7	16.8	16.3	16.2	15.2

*$p < .05$; **$p < .01$; ***$p < .001$.

free of disability on the latter scale, and by Time 5, 13 percent were so. These differences between Time 1 and Time 5 were significant. Consistent with rising disabilities, informal supports increased significantly, although the use of formal supports did not. Interestingly enough, the mood of the survivors at Time 5 was not significantly better or worse than the sample as a whole at Time 1.

Information available on the oldest old indicates that our sample is more or less representative of the white population in a national survey (Kovar, 1986), a London study of the oldest old (Bowling & Browne, 1991), and the National Institute on Aging epidemiological study of New Haven (Cornoni-Huntley et al., 1986). In family characteristics, the same proportion of oldest old are married as reported by Kovar (1986), but somewhat fewer live with others. Approximately the same number of San Franciscan oldest old have no surviving children as found in New Haven and London, and those who have children have approximately the same level of contact with them, a factor indicating the same level of geographic stability. In physical status, the San Francisco oldest old are more disabled, yet they are more likely to report that their health is good as found in the national survey (Kovar, 1986).

Sample Attrition

Figure 2.1 presents a survival curve over six years indicating the proportion participating at each contact and those lost because of death, incompetence, or other factors such as moving away. As to be expected, attrition is high. With interviews at an average of fifteen month intervals, 74 percent of the original sample participated at Time 2. By Time 3, 62 percent participated, 42 percent at Time 4, and 33 percent by Time 5. Most of those who were lost to the study had died, ranging from 16 percent at Time 2, 21 percent at Time 3, 31 percent at Time 4, and 38 percent by Time 5. From 6 percent at Time 1 to 19 percent by Time 5 were lost to the study because of mental or physical incapacity, while 4 to 10 percent moved away, refused, or could not be located.

The large attrition group was a unit of study in itself. The question was addressed as to whether those who became incapacitated or died differed significantly from the survivors. Using variables at Time 1 as possible predictors of later outcomes, Table 2.2 makes *t*-

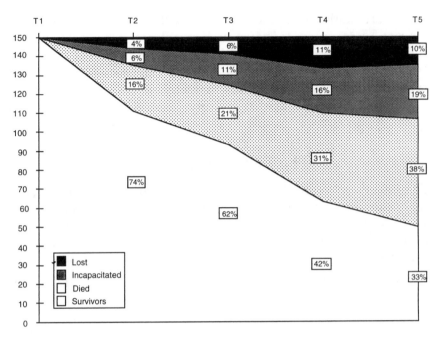

FIGURE 2.1 Reasons for attrition from oldest old sample over six years

test comparisons between survivors and those lost to the research at both Time 3 and Time 5. There are far more differences at the earlier time. At Time 3, those who survived for 30 months had been significantly less disabled at Time 1 on their activities of daily living. They also were more active with family and friends and in community associations, and they had better ratings on their mental status. By Time 5, however, few predictors of attrition were found, except that those who were ultimately lost to the study were more impaired at the outset on the Instrumental Activities of Daily Living. Consequently the predictors of attrition appear only earlier in the study. Over time, the survivors, like those lost to the study, become more disabled, less socially involved, and perhaps more forgetful, so after six years, they come to more resemble those who became incapacitated or died.

While those who developed prominent dementia no longer participated in the study, interviewers' assessments of mental status indicated increased problems with memory and, in some cases, reality orientation over the six years. At the first contact, only 13 percent were noted to have such problems, a proportion that steadily increased to 42 percent by the fifth interview (Figure 2.2). Most often these problems centered upon the recall of dates and events of the past. Also common were increased difficulties in responding to questions that required them to deal with abstractions.

The Focused Interview

The interviews were conducted at 14- to 16-month intervals and, with a few exceptions, they were held in the respondent's home. They generally lasted two or three hours. The focused interview format was used, one that combined both structured and open-ended questions. Pilot interviews with our informants assisted in designing the interview protocol. Interviews focused upon both

TABLE 2.2

T-test Comparisons of Survivors with the Decedents and Incapacitated at Time 3 and Time 5

	Time 3				Time 5			
	Survivors ($n = 90$)		Decedents and Incapacitated ($n = 47$)		Survivors ($n = 48$)		Decedents and Incapacitated ($n = 85$)	
	M	SD	M	SD	M	SD	M	SD
Physical status								
Perceived health	2.2	.80	2.1	.80	2.3	.08	2.1	.73
ADL	6.5	1.10	7.0	1.80*	6.5	.68	6.8	1.70
IADL	10.5	2.90	11.3	4.00**	10.5	2.90	12.8	3.90*
Social integration								
Family	2.5	1.3	3.0	1.35*	2.7	1.40	2.8	1.30
Friends	2.8	1.30	3.2	1.30*	2.8	1.30	3.1	1.20
Associations	2.6	1.40	3.2	1.50*	2.6	1.40	3.1	1.50
Mood	16.8	4.40	16.7	5.30	15.2	4.50	15.5	4.70
Cognition	1.2	.50	1.5	.70***	1.6	1.90	9.4	2.80

*$p < .05$; **$p < .01$; ***$p < .001$.

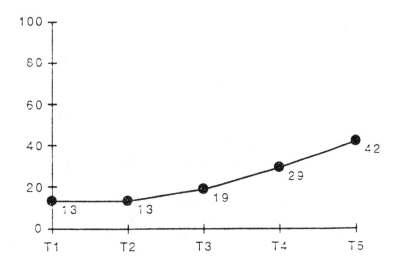

**Percentage of Respondents
with Cognitive Losses over
Five Contacts (Six Years)**

Comparison of Cognitive Losses.

FIGURE 2.2   Cognitive losses over six years

reported behaviors or factual material and the respondents' subjective experiences. Such a technique under skilled interviewers can result in an in-depth understanding of an individual's interpretations, reactions, and emotional responses, as well as knowledge of the cultural, social, and personal contexts in which they occur.

Trained interviewers assisted us in conducting these interviews. They were instructed to follow the conventions of ordinary social interactions so respondents, if they so chose, could determine the course of the discussion. For example, if a respondent, in answering questions on health, began discussing her daughter's caregiving activities, the interviewer turned to the questions on family relationships, so the flow of conversation was not interrupted. If the respondent digressed too lengthily, he or she was redirected back to the interview questions. This interview technique is not as open-ended by ethnographic standards or by those that elicit reminiscences, for our interviewers play a more active role in guiding the discussion. Verbatim notes were taken throughout the interview and transcribed by the interviewer soon afterwards.

The Interview Protocol. A basic interview protocol was designed to elicit information on demographic characteristics, health, economic status, typical daily activities, social network resources, responses to changes, and stressors and problems. Standard instruments measured functioning on activities of daily living, mood, and mastery. Most questions were used as guides to the discussion, but those questions that became variables to be measured were specified and asked at each contact regardless of what else was covered (see Appendix A). At each wave of interviewing, other questions varied. Respondents also were encouraged to discuss subjective or existential issues. For example, they were encouraged to reflect on their childhood, and some gave extensive life histories. They discussed their concept of self and how it might have changed with advancing age. They also described their attitudes about their longevity and death.

Data Analysis

Coding. Approximately halfway through each wave of interviewing, a code book was designed that coded open-ended responses and transferred the structured responses to a code sheet. In addition to fairly direct topics such as self-reports on health variables, we also coded global five-point measures on the key elements of adaptation, namely, control over environment, social integration, mood, and motivation. Interviews were coded by two members of the research staff, and differences were resolved. Their agreement each time was above 80 percent.

A productive although time-consuming process was used to analyze qualitative data. The respondents' constructions of meanings included their explanations and rationalizations about their situation. To identify patterns, these data were decontextualized by disassembling the interviews and filing together all discussions on the meanings of life, coping with problems, and attitudes about death. We then read the comments in each file and condensed the responses into categories. As categories were combined conceptually, consistent patterns were discerned.

When patterns were identified, we recontextualized the finding by referring back to the entire interview in order to examine the context in which this pattern occurred. For example, we wondered whether detachment was occurring because of depleted networks or because of personal preferences, so we needed to examine the interviews. This analytic strategy was used to address those research questions that were not amenable to direct questioning or use of standard instruments. For instance, the questions posed as to whether a sense of invulnerability was associated with survivorship could only be addressed at this point by analyzing the respondents' comments regarding how they dealt with stressors, illness, or impending death. Likewise, to attempt to account for the higher morale we found over time, it was necessary to examine the entire interviews and do a content analysis of the discussions.

Case Study Analysis. Respondents on the extreme ends of the curve were also singled out for a special analysis. For example, interviews with those in complex active families were analyzed and compared with those with few ongoing family relations. It was also very useful to examine their life histories so as to identify the course of events that contributed to these outcomes. Case study analyses were also useful in analyzing adaptation. For example, using such variables as living alone, being disabled, and poor, we could identify the most vulnerable respondents. Then by comparing them to the less vulnerable, it was possible to understand how socioeconomic forces influence adaptation. Productive insights likewise came from exploring the commonalities found among the effective adapters.

Statistical Analysis. In cross-sectional analyses, exploratory descriptive statistics were run with each wave of interviewing. A profile of each sample at each point in time was then constructed. These analyses also examined whether coded variables of qualitative data were sufficiently valid and reliable to be used in the further statistical analysis. For example, we found, our five-point coded measure of family integration was more powerful for some analyses than social contacts with family members, because it tapped aspects of the relationship that operated without face-to-face contacts. If coded measures were not adequate discriminators of variation in the sample, they were used solely for exploratory purposes or as a means to identify examples of adaptive strategies.

To determine whether significant changes had occurred over time, nonparametric statistics were used for most longitudinal analysis where tests of differences were run on variables between each contact. In some cases, multiple regressions were warranted, such as in indicating how the predictors of friendship changed over time. Where multivariate statistical techniques were used, coded measures were not used. Given the inductive nature of the research design and the wealth of qualitative data, complicated modeling did not seem warranted.

Conclusions

The techniques used here are neither entirely anthropological nor social psychological, but are intentionally chosen to satisfy some of the requirements of both qualitative and quantitative researchers. In the current scholarly community, as, for example, on the program at the annual meeting of gerontologists, qualitative or quantitative research seems to be an "either/or" methodology presented in separate sessions. Although most researchers recognize the need for thematic material or descriptions of the context in which questions are posed, the use of qualitative techniques is usually an adjunct as in pilot research to design surveys and test protocols. If themes are needed, they are usually compartmentalized from the "real" data coming from forced-choice instruments.

Qualitative researchers have developed their own networks, journals, and even an organization within the professional field. Rather than interaction between the two approaches, where one type of data informs and augments the other type, each approach usually stands alone. Certainly a melding of these two research philosophies would be productive intellectually in developing theories about the aging process. At the present time, unfortunately, there seems to be distinct bipolar views of the optimal approach to conduct research on older people. Even worse, members on one side do not quite believe the findings of the other. Such polarity is indeed unfortunate, since gerontology is interdisciplinary.

What we have attempted in the research findings on the oldest old presented here is a combined approach that demonstrates how both qualitative and quantitative data can be used. Our aim here is to convey the experiential side of long-term survivorship, that of real people adapting to difficult situations. At the same time, our statistical findings can place the research within the framework of the burgeoning literature on aging.

PART II

The Context of Survivorship

Chapter 3

Are Very Old People Different?

T his chapter presents findings on age differences after age 70 and addresses the question, does age make a difference in dealing with the typical problems of old age and in adjusting to late-life transitions? We will focus particularly on age-related problems individuals are likely to face. Additionally, a cross-sectional analysis identifies the timing of the major transitions occurring in later life and how the age at which changes take place influences adjustment. What happens when one loses a spouse, relocates or changes from living with others to living alone, or undergoes that transition from being independent to being dependent upon others for help? Are gender and age important determinants of adaptation?

When we recruited the initial sample of subjects age 85 and older, we followed what was then the official designation for the "oldest old" stipulated in the 1984 National Institute on Aging Request for Proposals. Even a short decade after this designation, however, there is no clear agreement about just when one becomes "oldest old." Is it 80 or 85 or even 95 years? One of the few books specifically on the oldest old has some authors who make the cut-off at age 80, while others use 85 years (Suzman, Manton, & Willis, 1992). Now when the oldest old, and particularly centenarians, are receiving widespread attention, others seem to suggest that the onset of being oldest old is as old as 95 (Perls, 1995). Undoubtedly the use of chronological age in studies of change in later life is pervaded by some confusion about the parameters of one of the most commonly used variables in aging research.

After analyzing data from our first round of interviewing, we realized that the narrow age range of 85 and older made it difficult to single out the effects of chronological age. Therefore, in order to make comparisons by age we broadened the age range in our research to include a sample aged 70 to 84 years. After making these age distinctions, the choice of an identifying term for the younger group became a problem. However much we disliked having to pigeonhole our respondents, an age referent was needed to differentiate two age groups. The terms "old" and the "elderly" had seemed adequate in earlier gerontological research, until Neugarten and her colleagues (1968) pointed out that those in their 60s and early 70s were more like the middle-aged population than the older one. They suggested two categories, the young old, ages 55 to 75, and the old old, or those 75 years and older. With an emphasis on very old people today, we wondered what we should call our younger sample, those who are "old" but not as old as "the oldest old?" Given this variation, we too have to make an arbitrary distinction and, for utilitarian purposes here, we refer to the "oldest old" as those 85 years and older and to the "younger old," our age comparison group, as those ages 70 to 84.

Does Age Make a Difference?

Comparisons of these two age groups indicate important but predictable differences between them. At the outset, the oldest old had a mean age of 88.9, and the younger old, 76.8 years. Table 3.1 indicates that the oldest old are significantly less likely to be married, they are more likely to have witnessed the death of a child, and they have a lower mean education level. In their physical status, they have significantly worse perceived health, and they are much more disabled on both measures of activities of daily living. While they do not vary in their family integration, they are less involved with friends. Finally, scores on the Bradburn Affect Balance Scale indicate that the oldest old have comparatively lower morale.

Thus the oldest old are more disadvantaged than their younger counterparts in key aspects of adaptation. They also differ from the

TABLE   3.1
Comparisons of Oldest Old and Younger Old at
Time 1 (by percentage)

	Oldest Old ($n = 150$)	Younger Old ($n = 100$)
Mean age	88.9	76.8
Mean years education	12	14***
Gender		
Male	26	34
Female	74	66
Married		
Yes	20	36**
No	80	64
Household		
Alone	58	47
With others	42	53
Parental status		
Child present	68	72
No children	32	28
Child deceased	32	9**
Economic status		
Good	61	53
Fair/Poor	39	47
Perceived health status		
Excellent	18	45
Good	55	34
Fair/Poor	27	21***
ADL impaired		
None	75	97***
1 or more	25	3
IADL impaired		
None	30	78***
1–3	39	16
4 or more	36	6
High family integration	47	47
High friendship involvement	38	50*
Mood (means on scale of 8–32 with 8 = good)	16.8	14.1***

*$p < .05$; **$p < .01$; ***$p < .001$.

younger old both in the types of problems reported and their coping responses. We asked all respondents, at the first interview, "What is the hardest thing you have to face these days?" This question was followed by, "What are your major worries?" From these discussions, we were able to construct an age-specific problem list (Table 3.2) that was used in coding spontaneous responses in subsequent interviews.

The mean number of total problems listed in Table 3.2 did not vary significantly by age, but significant differences were found in specific problems. As many as 69 percent of the oldest old complained about limited mobility in comparison to 42 percent of the

TABLE 3.2
Self-Reported Problems: Oldest Old and Younger Old

	T2 Oldest Old ($n = 111$)	T1 Younger Old ($n = 100$)
Physical problems		
Limited mobility	69%	42%***
Illness	42	31
Sensory loss	28	17***
Physical environment		
Housing	15	24
Neighborhood	15	10
Economic	19	30*
Social relationships		
Loss of friends	53	45
Child problems	27	40**
Spouse's problems	7	20
Conflict with others	26	42**
Isolated	11	7
Insufficient supports	12	5
Psychological problems		
Emotional state	13	31**
Lonely	29	21
Fear of dependency	15	11
Feeling useless	10	6
Memory loss	14	7**
Mean total problems	4.4	4.0

*$p < .05$; **$p < .01$; ***$p < .001$.

TABLE 3.3
Feelings of Mastery among Oldest Old (Time 3) and Younger Old (T2)

Instrument adapted from Pearlin & Schooler Mastery Scale	Oldest Old ($n = 78$)	Younger Old ($n = 76$)
1. I have little control over things that happen to me.	3.03	3.37
2. There is no way I can solve some of the problems I have.	2.91	3.38*
3. What happens to me in the future mostly depends on me.	3.14	3.84**
4. There is little I can do to change many important things in my life.	2.42	3.35***
5. I often feel helpless in dealing with the problems of life.	3.35	3.92*
6. Sometimes I feel that I'm being pushed around in life.	5.12	4.12
7. I can do just about anything I really set my mind to.	3.35	3.37
8. I feel personally responsible for the well-being of others.	2.71	3.28*
Mean Total Scores	25.40	28.37

Note: 1 = strongly agree; 5 = strongly disagree. Items 3, 7, 8 reversed.
*$p < .05$; **$p < .01$; ***$p < .001$.

younger respondents. The oldest old also complained significantly more about sensory loss. Other differences indicate that the oldest old had withdrawn or detached themselves from many of the worries typically reported by the younger old (Table 3.2). They were significantly less likely than the younger group to complain about their economic situation. Moreover, since significantly fewer of the very old reported worries about a child or conflict with others, they may have detached themselves from typical social irritants. The fact that they had fewer emotional problems is consistent with the conclusion that they are coping well.

The Mastery Scale offers further evidence that the oldest old have detached themselves from some concerns affecting the younger old (Table 3.3). Very old people were somewhat less likely than younger participants to exercise overall mastery ($p < .07$). They were significantly more likely to agree that there was no way they could solve their problems, that there was no way that they could change important things in their life, and that they felt helpless in dealing with their problems. They were less likely to agree that they were personally responsible for another. They also agreed that their future depends mostly upon their own actions. These seemingly inconsistent responses most likely reflect the recognition that, while adhering to self-reliant values, the oldest old also recognized that they can no longer realistically exercise mastery over many areas of their lives. We propose that they accept the fact that they have less control over their lives, a response that is adaptive, because it is congruent with their declining functional capacity.

Such findings suggest too that many oldest old come to terms with their limitations by reassessing their capabilities and by modifying those responses requiring control or mastery. We have been impressed by the presence of subjective transitions into late late life, where the oldest respondents move beyond worry and responsibility and accept their new situation as long-term survivors, some with relief, others with resignation, and still others with detachment (Johnson & Barer, 1992; 1993). In fact, some oldest old respondents commented that such a change was one of the positive aspects of living so long.

A Closer Look at Age and the Context of Reported Problems

A review of the comments on their problems illuminates age differences in coping. In their social affairs, only a few of the oldest old respondents reported they worried about their children, mainly because they concluded there was little they could do to help. "My son has angina. I am concerned, of course, but what can I do at my age?" Their responses also reflected the fact that fewer oldest old were still able to carry on reciprocal social relationships. A typical reply was, "How can I help others, when I can barely take care of myself?" Additionally, the oldest old were less emotional in their discussions. They usually commented upon their physical and mental inactivity with little affect. "My biggest problem is the length of the days. With nothing to do, I go to bed at 5:30."

While 42 percent of the younger old reported having physical problems, these difficulties did not usually dominate their interviews. They tended to worry more about their social and psychological problems rather than their health. In contrast to the oldest old, who are remote psychologically from many of their problems, the younger respondents were far more bothered by family problems. Complaints about their children were common, particularly about their not meeting parental expectations. Some respondents in the younger old group were themselves sometimes adjusting to a new marriage and dealing with stepchildren. Still others were involved as caregivers for their spouse, or they were adjusting to widowhood after a spouse's recent death. Also quite noticeable, as we will see in the following, some were making decisions about selling their home and moving to more convenient housing. In contrast, the oldest old had fewer housing worries, because many had relocated to more easily maintained housing some years earlier.

Instead of the resignation observed among the oldest old, the discussions of the younger old usually were permeated with emotion. They were particularly distressed when they realized they were getting old. Rather than the acceptance of aging so noticeable among the oldest old, they mentioned "aches and pains" or "nervous problems." Even a few complained about how they were perceived as old by others. They also expressed discontent with their aging because of the recent deaths of spouses, friends, and other age peers.

Unlike the younger old, who, as noted above, complained more about their advancing age, the oldest old more often mentioned their age as a positive factor in influencing how they felt about their lives. "Everything is smooth, but why shouldn't it be? At my age, it is natural to have lost so many family and friends." Others report that their pleasant memories sustain them. One widow commented, "My memories protect me from worry. I think of all the beautiful sunsets I watched with my late husband."

A review of direct responses to questions about their worries or problems suggests several patterns. Problems with their disabilities dominated the discussions of the oldest old; most of their problems focus upon the ripple effects changes in their physical status had to other areas of their lives. Yet a strong survivor effect permeated their discussions: they were proud they had lived so long. Fewer of the very old faced the usual difficulties confronting younger adults—problems with money, housing, and family responsibilities. They seemed to conclude that they had already experienced the typical problems of later life and had long ago adjusted to them. Only a few of the oldest old were continual worriers, like Mrs. Raymond, "I am a hostage of fortune. The longer I live, the more I accumulate to worry about." However worse off they may be physically, most oldest old would agree with Mr. Keller, who said, "I have outlived my worries."

Transitions in Late Life

Developmentalists are particularly interested in the timing of normative transitions, especially those that require some adjustments to changes in status and roles (Hagestad, 1990). If changes occur "on time," they are normative, predictable, anticipated, and even rehearsed, so adjustment to a transition is easier (Neugarten et al., 1968). We propose that chronological age may affect adjustment to key transitions in old age.

By the time individuals reach their mid-80s, they have usually been affected by one or more of three major transitions that entail alterations in their physical status, their family life, and their social networks. First, older people, particularly older women, experience the end of their marriage and a transition to a single status (Lopata, 1973). Second, usually as a direct effect of the loss of a spouse, older people are likely to undergo a change from living with others to living alone (Aldous, 1990). Also at a later age, relocation is likely to entail a move from a home to more protected housing. Third, with the predictable increases in disability with advancing age (Manton & Suzman, 1992; Verbrugge, 1984), the status of older people is likely to change from independence to being in need of some help from others, a situation that potentially places more responsibility on younger family members. Consequently the age at which these transitions occurs is of importance (Johnson & Troll, 1996).

Loss of a Spouse

The ease of transition following the loss of a spouse differs between men and women, and it is influenced not only by the age at which this occurs (Bass & Bowman, 1990; Brock & O'Sullivan, 1985), but also depends upon the recency of the event (Lowenthal & Haven,

1968; Moen, Dempster-McClain, & Williams, 1992; Pihlblad & Adams, 1972). Since marriage in later life is more commonly terminated by the death of a husband than a wife, there are more studies of widows than widowers. Most stress the importance of the timing of this transition and focus on bereavement (Bennett & Morgan, 1992; Blau, 1973; Brock & O'Sullivan, 1985; Gallagher, Thompson, & Peterson, 1981; Herth, 1990; O'Bryant & Straw, 1991).

Only a small minority of our sample ended their most recent marriage by divorce or separation. Much more common in later life is the risk of losing the companionship of a spouse because of dementia. In such cases, a spouse no longer has the mental capacity to sustain an intimate relationship, so he or she "is no longer the person I knew." Again, much of the research on caregiving to a demented spouse focuses on a younger age group and addresses the burdens and stress on the family (Fitting, Rabins, Lucas, & Eastham, 1986; Pruchno & Resch, 1989; Zarit, Todd, & Zarit, 1986). In contrast, older caregivers, who had a long, meaningful, enduring relationship with their spouse may actually benefit from their caregiving role (Clipp & George, 1993).

Widowhood. Table 3.4 presents the timing of three transitions from ages 70 to 103, and then describes the consequences in terms of caregiving and social supports. In the transition from marriage to widowhood, we find that over one half in their early 70s are married. That proportion drops sharply to 29 percent among those in the 75 to 79 age group and further declines at 90 years of age, when only 14 percent are married. Consequently, for these respondents, the transition to widowhood is most likely to occur in the mid-70s.

We found that one half the widows under age 85 had lost their husbands within the previous five years, whereas one half of those over the age of 85 had been widows for over 20 years. As would be expected, many of those in the younger age group were still adjusting to the loss when we interviewed them. For many, two problems had not been resolved: the economic effects of losing a spouse and the practical problems of maintaining a home alone. Nevertheless, being younger and healthier, most were able to continue their social involvements.

In contrast, most of the oldest women in our study had adjusted to the loss of a spouse a decade or more before, so they generally

TABLE 3.4
Late-life Transitions and Family Resources (by percentage)

	Age 70–74 (n = 39)	Age 75–79 (n = 34)	Age 80–84 (n = 27)	Age 85–89 (n = 93)	Age 90+ (n = 57)
Transitions					
Marital status					
Married	52	29*	22	20	14
Not married	48	71	78	80	86
Household status					
Alone	38	53	52	61	53
With family	58	41	41	37	28
With others	4	6	7	2	19
Onset of disability					
No disability	82	97	52***	38	18*
One or more	18	3	48	62	82
Family resources					
Family caregiving					
Family caregiver	8	3	19*	30	46
Potential family caregiver	76	85	52	42	29
No family caregiver	16	12	29	28	35
ADL/IADL help					
Help from family	5	3	26*	36	44
Help from formal support	21	26	48	71*	81

$*p < .05; **p < .01; ***p < .001.$

had some years to adapt to the change. Even recently widowed women in advanced old age expressed their sense of loss differently from younger widows. For the older women, such a loss is predictable, and may even be overshadowed by concerns with their own poor health or mounting disabilities. With increasing age, they have inevitably survived other deaths of family and friends, so that they have had experience in coping with loss.

The loss of a spouse is most often a female experience. Fewer than one fifth of the men in the 70- to 84-year-old age group had been widowed at Time 1, compared with one half of the women. Of these, only two men lost their wives within the past five years. Most widowed men soon remarry (Longino, 1988), while few prospective husbands remain for the older women. Among the younger old men, consequently, the role transition from being married to being widowed is often short-lived. They are much more likely to remarry, and they tend to marry younger women.

Unlike younger widowers, those widowed in their 80s and 90s usually do not anticipate remarriage. Having been unexpectedly left on their own, these men have difficulty adapting. At the practical level, they are unfamiliar with managing the home and arranging social involvements. An 85-year-old summed up a typical situation. "When my wife was alive, we had a social life. Now I don't visit anyone and nobody visits me. This is the worst kind of life!" Another commented on the loss of a confidant, "When I had a wife, I shared my thoughts with her. Now I have no one."

Some retained evidence of their late wife's presence. When we interviewed oldest old widowers, we commonly noted her belongings as if awaiting her entrance—a cane propped up in the corner, her knitting bag by her chair, or even her glasses by an open book. One 91-year-old man explained, "I haven't touched any of Effie's things. I consider myself still married. To remarry would be abandoning her."

Widows in their late 80s and 90s present a very different picture, because most have long been widows. In fact, for some, the length of time as a widow equalled or even exceeded the number of years of marriage. One woman talked about her marriage as being "so long ago I feel like I'm dreaming when I think about it—as if it were another life." Others engaged in what Lopata (1979) has described as the sanctification of the late husband. For example, "I was blessed. He was a sterling type of man—all for his home, his wife, his son." The comments of another woman who had been married for 48 years and widowed for 26 years are characteristic of her cohort, one in which marriage was a woman's central adult role. "I had a perfect husband. He took care of me—I never had to work a day in my life." Some very old women widowed late in life found the loss of their spouse after 60 or more years of marriage less problematic than having to deal with their own disabilities. "I just stopped driving—that's more of an issue than the loss of my husband. He had been ill for 20 years."

Marital Loss with Dementia. When dementia develops, it is not unusual to experience the same sense of bereavement as after a death. In both age groups, husbands and wives alike pointed out that not only have they experienced the same loss of companionship as a widow or widower, but they also must take on a burdensome caregiving role. Some case examples illustrate the problematic transition from the companionship of marriage to a constricted and stressful life caring for a demented spouse. For example, one woman said, "My husband is lost to me. It's so tiring. Last night I wanted to cry—I'm with him all the time, but it's like he isn't here. I am really on my own."

A recently widowed woman after several years of caregiving captured the essence of loss that dementia imposes upon a marriage. "The most difficult time was before, not after, his death. When the deterioration came, there was little communication, so those few years were tough. I felt he was gone long before he died." An 87-year-old woman, who had already lost her first husband and had outlived two sons, was caring for her second husband, a 97-year-old cognitively impaired man. She said, "After 56 years of marriage, I am waiting for him to die, so I can follow him. At this point, I feel like he'd be better off dead. I can't go before him and abandon him." Men caring for their mentally impaired wives raised similar issues. As one man said, "I'm waiting for my wife to die. Running my business was easier than this. I'm nursemaid, housekeeper, and everything else." The death of a demented spouse can come as a relief.

> *My wife began to become senile. She had this problem with her memory, but I didn't understand that something was happening. Sometimes she'd swear—such awful language. You'd have to know my wife, that she never said an unkind word. Then there were times when she thought I was her father. I was very upset. Half the time she didn't know me. That puts a chill in you. I was devastated. The doctor wanted me to put her in an institution, but I said, "I'd never put her away. As long as I'm alive I'll take care of her." I had to cook, clean, bathe her, and watch over everything.*

Although anxiety and demoralization were readily observed among these caregivers, over time most eventually came to terms with their loss. An 84-year-old woman who visited her institutionalized husband daily was already making plans. "I've been thinking of moving to a retirement home, because I'm alone now." Similarly, another said, "I'm in the process of getting on with my life." In anticipation of his death, she was exploring travel possibilities for a safari to Africa or a cruise to the Azores. Another caregiver redirected her affection to her dog. "Everyone knows I'm nuts about Skippy. That's what keeps me going."

Transitions in Living Arrangements

Housing is a source of vulnerability for older people (Tobin & Lieberman, 1976), largely because increasing functional problems with age create greater environmental pressures (Lawton, 1982). When the environment becomes too difficult to control, individuals begin to think about relocation. Three types of transitions in living arrangements occurred during the course of the study. First, with the loss of a spouse, individuals undergo a transition from living with others to living alone. At every age, older women are far more likely to live alone than are men. Second, others move from a longstanding residence to a more convenient living situation. This, "the second move," is intermediate between a long-time home and institutional care, and it most often occurs among those in their early 70s (Longino et al., 1991). Third, after age 85, individuals are more likely to enter an institution. Twenty-two percent of the population over the age of 85, most of whom are women, reside in nursing homes (Hing, 1987).

Among our oldest old respondents, 46 moved during the study, of which 28 or 61 percent moved to a nursing home or board-and-care home, 28 percent moved to senior housing, and only 11 percent made a lateral move to similar housing. In household composition by age, a majority in their early 70s, 58 percent, still live with a family member, usually a spouse, and only 38 percent live alone (Table 3.4). But among those 90 years or older, the situation is reversed: 53 percent live alone, and only 28 percent live with a family member. Those who continue to live alone are likely to be unmarried women who are functionally more independent and less impaired than those living with others. Men who comprise only 26 percent of our sample are significantly more likely to be married and thus to live with their wife (Johnson & Troll, 1992).

Aging in Place. Over two-thirds of our respondents remained residentially stable throughout the study. In fact, most had lived in the same home or apartment for some years; the mean length of residence for the oldest old is 26.8 years and for the younger old, 22.1 years. As many as 21 percent of the oldest old have remained in their own home for over 50 years. As people reach their eighth and ninth decades of life and their mobility becomes increasingly limited, the home environment can become more important, because much more time is spent there (Rubinstein, 1990). Homeowners particularly have strong attachment to their homes. "Staying in my own home is the most important thing to me. All my memories are here." A widow who had lived in her own home for 54 years agreed, "I really love this place. I feel so surrounded by my past here and supported by it." Even with increased crime and fears about safety, individuals are reluctant to move. Mrs. Morgan, in her 90s, did not consider leaving her deteriorating neighborhood even though her home was repeatedly vandalized. She refused to change the home in any way even by adding to her security by putting bars on her windows. "I won't be caged in. I'd rather live in jail."

Age-Segregated Environments. When forced to give up their home, many turn to senior housing as a means to remain in the community. Twenty-six percent of the original sample of oldest old were living in senior housing at the outset of the study, and another 13 percent relocated to senior housing or a retirement residence in the course of the study. Among the younger old, many were anticipating such a move in the future. A typical dilemma for them is deciding when to make the move. "The hardest thing is deciding when to go into a retirement home. You have to give up so much but it's important to do it before it's too late." In the younger sample, ages 70 to 84, those who changed their living arrangement rarely did so because of physical disability. For example, a few individuals moved to a new area to provide caregiving to an older relative or to assist a child. Others simply made a lateral move to similar housing in a different neighborhood. Over three years, only 3 percent of our younger old respondents experienced declines in mental or physical capacity that warranted a move to a nursing home.

Adjusting to Congregate Housing. Age-segregated congregate housing generally consists of a small room with a bathroom and an efficiency kitchen, and the provision of two or three meals a day. Adjustments must be made to a reduced living space and a loss of some privacy. Voluntary moves rather than those forced on one because of disability are usually less problematic (Schulz & Brenner, 1977). "Some time ago I looked to the future and knew I'd have to make this move. Now I don't feel as stressed as I did before. I'm thankful I can still get around the way I do, as old as I am." Others concluded that relinquishing some measure of independent living was timely, and making an adjustment was a matter of pride. For example, Mrs. Lewis, at 93, reported,

> *I know I'm not as strong as I was. I have a good feeling about being here, it makes me feel secure. I look at it this way. I get three meals a day. If I need something, I ask at the desk. I know a lot who can't get around like I do. It's a mental attitude that I have. I always had a positive attitude—I consider myself well off for being my age.*

Like Mrs. Lewis, others were resigned to the move and were satisfied. "I've adapted pretty good. I just made up my mind, that's the only way." A recently relocated 94-year-old man asserted, "I'm a very optimistic person. I think I'll be all right if I just let things take their course. I am so glad to live so long—how could I complain?" Others point out the advantage of having fewer worries in senior housing. "If I stayed in my home, I would have had insurance bills, painting, and repairs to deal with. Here everything is taken care of, and I have more time to read." Many welcome the opportunity to remain active. "There is lots of entertainment—tai chi, discussions on world affairs, social hours on Friday afternoon, and even some dancing." The opportunity to socialize is also welcome. "We've made many friends already. We're all in the same boat and have lots to talk about. It makes time go quickly." Finally, with so many services available to them, they feel more secure.

Complaints were also common, most often because physical impediments hampered adjustment to a new setting. For example, a recent newcomer to senior housing acknowledged problems with her failing eyesight. "My trouble is meeting all these new people. I can't see their faces, so I don't recognize them the next time I see them. I hope they don't take it for a snub." Several complained about their fatigue or hearing loss that prevented socializing with other residents. "At meal times I don't talk too much. My hearing aid makes too much noise, and I can't distinguish what they say."

Others experience the depersonalization typical of institutions. Ironically, a retired physician, who had been a prison doctor most of his career, equated his retirement residence to a jail. "If you took away the keys and put up bars, it would be the same." A 91-year-old woman concurred, "In this living situation, you lose your sense of self-worth. You're fed and cared for, but you lose your freedom." A retired navy man was equally displeased with his move. "Before I came here, I was busy all the time. Now here I have nothing really to live for, because there is nothing to do."

Mealtimes in congregate living are an important focal point in structuring the day and a source of sociability. Some find it an advantage, but for others, it is the bane of their existence. On one hand, respondents point to the positive effects, particularly as an opportunity to make friends and socialize with others. Some welcome the regulated meal times as providing a source of meaning to the day. "I have a busy schedule here, three times a day, for breakfast, lunch, and dinner." On the other hand, negative effects were traced to the regimentation of the day and, in some views, enforced socialization. Residents almost universally disliked the precise timing of meals and the inconvenience of being properly dressed three times a day.

Sociability in the dining room is governed either by the policy of the administrators or the informal norms of residents. In some settings, residents are encouraged to rotate table mates, an enforced sociability that was often criticized or ignored. "They make it so you have breakfast with different people every morning. I won't do it. It's strange when you don't know the people you're sitting with." Some residents take control of the seating arrangements. "We reserve a table for lunch. We're supposed to move around, but I like to sit with people I know." Having to eat with people of "a different sort" also brought complaints. "I don't like the women that sit at the table with me. They have no personality. They all smoke, and they cough all through the meal."

Nevertheless, most social interaction takes place in the public areas of the facility, and particularly around mealtimes. These contacts generally substitute for hosting visitors in one's apartment, a situation most choose to avoid.

> A group of us have formed a breakfast club, one man and three women. It's so much fun. We sit together at breakfast every morning. We live for that hour. It's wonderful. It makes the day begin very happy even though we go our own way afterwards.

Another explained,

> *I'm not interested in all the planned activities here. I've done all that. We prefer to get together in the dining room at lunch. I sit with my new friends, Millie, Lily, and Harriet. We converse, we understand each other, and we share our problems.*

Involuntary Relocations. While few of the younger old needed protective housing, adult children of parents in both age groups were particularly prone to alleviate their own filial anxieties by encouraging their parents to move to more secure housing.

> *My daughter wanted me to go into a retirement home near her. She found a place a few minutes from where she works, so she could come over for lunch. She thinks it's getting unsafe here, but I like this neighborhood—it has all the advantages, I see nice quiet people here, and I can get to the laundromat and church by myself. Just to shut up my daughter though, I will look at the place.*

Another woman was less amenable but responded with humor at the affront of her children's pressure. "My daughter-in-law was checking out rest homes for me. I started laughing that they would even think I would go to a rest home. First they thought I should use a cane, and now it's a rest home!"

Some adult children essentially force an involuntary move, whether it is insisting a parent move nearer to them or urging senior housing upon them. One 88-year-old woman regretted moving from her native Chicago to live with her unmarried son in San Francisco. "It was hard to leave my old friends. I see almost no one here, because I can't navigate these hills." Another complained about having to learn new bus routes just to get to a drugstore. "When I was living back home I could just hop on a bus and get downtown. Here I'm much more confined." An 86-year-old mother of seven acquiesced to her family's insistence that she move from her apartment in the heart of the city into a basement apartment in a daughter's home in the suburbs. Shortly after the move, she grumbled,

> *The family wanted me closer, but I get kinda down in the dumps here. I don't have visitors since I moved here. My daughter's gone all day, and I'm more lonesome. Where I lived before, I knew people in the building, and every day I'd see someone. Delivery men would leave packages with me, and I'd see my neighbors when they picked them up.*

The children in another family formed an alliance in order to force their mother to move to more protective housing. They even made a down payment without consulting her. Such actions were reported indignantly, "I didn't decide to move! My daughters decided. I didn't have a choice!" Similarly a 98-year-old woman described the pressure as an act of aggression, "It was an assault from my son and daughter-in-law. I didn't know when they brought me here a year-and-a-half ago that it was a permanent arrangement. When they brought in my plants, that's when I knew they didn't intend for me to go back home." Another who was reinterviewed in her new senior residence was somewhat more conciliatory. "A few months ago my daughters brought me here, and they gave me no chance to say no. I guess I'm satisfied. I'll soon be 90, so I can't stay alone forever. It's more or less a concession to my daughters, so they won't have to worry about me."

Institutionalization. When respondents entered an institution, we attempted to reinterview all who were mentally competent. This final relocation was generally precipitated by an acute change in health status, cognitive decline, or the death or incapacity of a care-giver. In most cases this move was considered as a last resort, when the family or the respondents themselves found no other options. Some individuals reacted with anger. One 88-year-old woman was emphatic, "I want to live in my own home. Although I'm old, I can still struggle. I told the children, throw me in the ocean, but don't put me in a home."

Usually a chain of events in combination led to relocation to an institution. As will be noted in Chapter 4, a fall or illness often led to a hospitalization and then discharge to an institution, because the former support network could not be re-established. One widow with three children had lived alone in a large dilapidated home. After her daughter died of cancer, most of her needs were left unmet. Her son lived several hours away and could only come once or twice a month. When he placed her in a board-and-care home, she became very depressed and angry and died soon afterward. In other cases, changes in mental status made it too difficult to retain help, as with a widow who entered an institution when her memory and eyesight worsened. Seldom is relocation to a nursing home voluntary and without some precipitating incidents. One rare exception was a woman who commented, "Nothing drastic happened. I just became a drain on my family as I got weaker and more dependent."

Cognitively intact respondents usually adjusted eventually to a nursing home, and a few went on to exert impressive mastery over their environment. Such a sense of control in managing their external world certainly enhanced their morale. Mr. Holman had moved to a board-and-care home following a slight stroke. Always a personable man, he had previously been an active participant in many senior programs. He boasted about his good memory and past athletic abilities.

> *Baseball, basketball, and rugby gave me a good foundation. I can't walk very good any more, but I can still sing and dance. Yesterday I got up and did the hula dance here, and they were all screaming with laughter. I've made friends with everyone. We have great times here, many parties, birthday celebrations, decorations for special occasions, and wine with dinner on Sundays. I'm living comfortably and I have everything I want. I don't even feel that old.*

In contrast, as Mrs. Donaldson's physical condition deteriorated, and her family could no longer provide sufficient care, they placed her in a nursing home. This fiercely independent and forceful woman had sufficient financial resources to simulate her former lifestyle. Within the institution she managed to not only recreate a home-like setting, but also insisted upon maintaining her previous daily rituals. Refusing to share a room, she chose a corner room with a garden view and had it converted from a double room with two hospital beds to an "apartment" for herself. One bed was removed, and an upholstered loveseat and a matching pink velvet easy chair were installed. "I had my favorite chair recovered in rose color. I want to enjoy my own things around me." The decor was completed with a coffee table, footstool, and a glass-doored bookcase filled with family mementos. Other homey touches included many house plants, brightly colored afghans, some stuffed animals, and fluffy pillows. Prominent on the wall was a large framed drawing of her home of 52 years. In maintaining her usual routines, she disassociated herself from the other residents by having meals brought to her in her room.

> *I don't want to go to the dining room where I see them feeding people. I have my own schedule and routine here, and I tell the help that when they are in my room, they must do as I ask. In here, I'm the boss. Out there, they are in*

*charge. At home I had apricot brandy and graham crackers at 4:20 and sipped
it 45 minutes before dinner. So here I have it every day at 4:20. I have to
maintain my own schedule; otherwise I'd be like everyone else here. I'm the
only one with an apartment. I'm paying the highest rent in the place.*

Transitions to Neediness

The transitions to widowhood and living alone usually occur some
years before individuals become disabled. Defining disability by
the activities of daily living, we find that a large majority of those
in their 70s, from 82 to 97 percent, are fully independent in their
functioning (Table 3.4). In contrast, among those aged 80 to 84, just
over one-half are independent on all activities, a significant decline
from those in their 70s. Of those in their late 80s, only 38 percent
are independent in handling daily tasks, and after 90, only 18
percent are. Thus, the transition from independence to being in
need of some help from others occurs for most older people when
they reach their 80s. Those who survive into their 90s usually
require outside help (Kovar & Stone, 1992), and as we have
noted above, increased numbers have a nonrelative living with
them. The effects of this timing are important; at an age when
help is really needed, very few are married and over one-half live
alone.

Conclusion

This chapter began by asking whether chronological age makes a
difference? What can we learn about the aging processes by looking
at 250 individuals whose age ranges from 70 years to 103 years of
age? To address these questions, we began by examining the types
of problems these respondents discussed and the age at which
specific problems were likely to occur. We find that age certainly
makes a difference in terms of the nature of stressors confronting
older people. For the oldest old, major problems were related
to physical status, particularly their limited mobility and sensory
and memory losses. There were no age differences in reports of
illnesses.

The younger old faced different types of challenges, really more
like those faced by people in middle age. They complained more

about their spouse and children's problems, about money, and about the general emotional tenor of their lives. Age differences were also significant in response to the mastery scale, where the oldest old willingly exercised less mastery, they had less sense of control over their future, and they felt more helpless in dealing with the problems of life. This combined evidence supports our impressions while doing the interviews: that the oldest old have moved to a stage of life when the usual stressors and demands have less effect on them.

The second half of this chapter examined the typical transitions in later life and asked whether the age at which they occur affects adjustment to change. Certainly the transition to widowhood has differential effects depending upon gender and age. The loss of a spouse is likely to occur for women at a much younger age than for men, and it involves quite different demands for a woman in her early 70s than for a man in his late 80s. By the time men reach late life they are unlikely to remarry. Having been married during a time before androgynous roles were adopted, they are left helpless after the loss of a wife. They no longer had someone to take care of them, arrange their social life, provide companionship, and most were unable to find substitutes. Women at most ages were usually more embedded in family and friendship networks that could step in to fill the gap when widowhood occurred, plus they have more age peers who share their status. Needless to say, the loss of a spouse because of dementia was a stressful, unhappy time, irrespective of age and gender.

The transitions in the living situation are also affected by age. The younger old are often in a decision-making process about when to sell their home and move to more easily maintained housing. In contrast, many oldest old had already made that transition some years in the past. For them, the major fear was being forced to move to an institution or to regimented congregate housing where they had to adjust to group living. In reading the many examples, we find that most had adjusted to relocation as a tradeoff, an exchange where more security was welcome even if it meant some loss of freedom. Children are prominent instigators of relocation, even against their parents' will, most likely because it alleviated their own filial anxiety about caring for a parent.

This chapter concludes by including findings on the transition to neediness, that age when individuals must turn to others for help. For those on the normative track, that transition usually occurs some years after they have lost a spouse and were left to live alone. Consequently, when help is most needed, it is not readily available. In the next chapter we will trace the trajectories of the oldest old's physical status and examine how individuals manage the predictable changes of late life.

Chapter 4

Stability and Change in Physical Status: A Naturalistic Account

T he research literature on the oldest old is dominated by reports on their physical status and the social and economic repercussions that their disabilities create. Some refer to this emphasis as a medicalization of social gerontology. Such an emphasis is relevant, nonetheless, for recent longitudinal surveys have repeatedly found higher levels of disability with increasing age, a rate that is particularly high among the oldest old. Given the high rates of disability, the very old are frequent users of health care services (Manton & Soldo, 1992; Soldo & Manton, 1985). Since each year of active life expectancy gained is accompanied by increased disability, the needs of the oldest old may differ substantially from younger old people (Brody & Miles, 1990). With the unanticipated declines in mortality after age 85, yet little change in the rates of morbidity, researchers and policy planners are attempting to estimate the future needs of this population (Manton & Soldo, 1992; Soldo & Manton, 1985; Suzman et al., 1992; Verbrugge, 1984).

Research findings also indicate that with the incremental deaths of family members and friends, informal networks also need to be bolstered (Antonucci & Akima, 1987; Cornoni-Huntley et al., 1986; Johnson & Troll, 1992; Rathbone-McCuan, Hooyman, & Fortune, 1985).

Some questions, however, remain unanswered. For example, how rapidly do health and functional characteristics change over time? On the practical side, the question arises as to whether anything can be done to slow the pace of decline in physical status. Also missing from some of these reports is information on multiple outcomes or trajectories, that plot not only declines in functioning, but also those cases where conditions are stable and declines are reversed.

Recent publications have pointed to needed changes in the direction of research on the oldest old. One serious gap concerns variations within this age group, an omission we are addressing here (Guralnik, 1991; Manton & Suzman, 1992). Only limited information is available on transition points when declining functioning becomes irreversible (Cornoni-Huntley et al., 1986). Also needed are distinctions between change at the population level and change at the individual level (Manton & Soldo, 1992). Longitudinal surveys have found, for instance, that rather than unilineal declines in functioning, some individuals actually improve over time, some remain stable, and some decline in functioning (Suzman et al., 1992). Thus, functional change among the oldest old does not always entail continuous decrements. In fact, a recent report on a small sample suggests that some people in their late 90s are healthier and more robust than younger old people (Perls, 1995).

Health researchers emphasize the importance of documenting changes in functional status, since a sudden decline in functional ability can cause permanent declines in performance and health (Svanborg, 1988). Furthermore, the onset of disability is likely to trigger detrimental changes in other aspects of an individual's life (Cornoni-Huntley et al., 1986). Studies of changing functioning can also indicate how declines in one area of functioning can precipitate declines in others (Palmore, Nowlin, & Wang, 1985). It seems that older people are particularly at risk following a hospitalization (Mayer-Oakes, Oye, & Leake, 1991; Wu, Rubin, & Rosen, 1990), or where mental status changes. Epidemiologic studies report the incidence of dementia at 15.8 percent after 85 years of age (Regier et al., 1988), but in areas such as East Boston it is reported to be as high as 47 percent (Evans et al., 1992).

While descriptive studies can by no means substitute for representative surveys, they do have the potential to address such discrepancies in the literature, for they can focus specifically on the subtle repercussions occurring with increased disability. In this chapter we will examine stability and changes in physical status in late late life by first describing the physical status of the survivors,

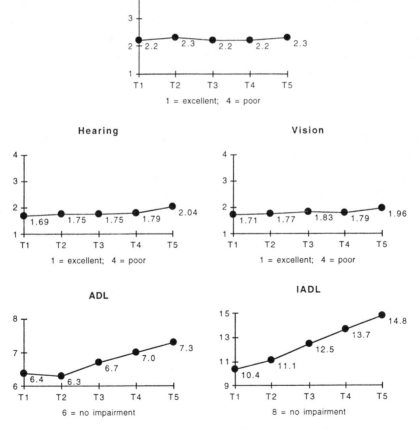

FIGURE 4.1   Changes in physical status over six years

defined here as those remaining in the study for six years. Then to explore intragroup variations, we have identified three trajectories occurring over time: those whose physical status remained stable at an adequate level of functioning; those who had a stable status but with high disability; and those whose functioning declined, in some cases, precipitously. Then we identify the outcomes in terms of morbidity and mortality for each trajectory.

Physical Changes in Survivors over Six Years

Figure 4.1 maps major indicators of physical status of the 48 survivors over six years. Perceived health remained at virtually the same level with most reporting their health as good or excellent. There were few changes in hearing or vision over that time. Functioning on the Activities of Daily Living (ADL) for personal care also changed significantly, but not like the larger and more significant changes that occurred in functioning on the Instrumental Activities of Daily Living (IADL). Figure 4.2 indicates the use of health care services remains the same over six years. Despite the increased disability, the frequency of physician visits and hospitalizations did not change significantly. These mixed findings raise intriguing questions that will be addressed here. To understand more about the pace of changes at an individual level and the subsequent repercussions, we will examine the three trajectories over time and the differential risk of morbidity and mortality.

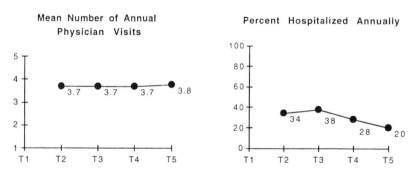

FIGURE 4.2   Changes in health care utilization over six years

Physical Trajectories and Later Outcomes

It is useful to distinguish between two types of effects with changes in physical status. First, a health problem can have ripple effects that create other problems. For instance, many report a "slowing down" or a feeling of being "dragged out." Such lethargy often creates problems walking which, in turn, create the need for help with transportation, shopping, and most activities outside the home. The synergistic effect can continue with limited mobility leading to constraints on social activities that in turn result in loneliness. Such effects are common among the oldest old, but in some cases, they can be reversed by assistive devises that permit individuals more mobility.

Second, a cascade effect is a concept sometimes used by geriatricians to refer to a process in which disease conditions and iatrogenic effects of their treatment combine to initiate a downward spiral in a patient's status (Johnson & Catalano, 1983). Such a process is more common among the very old by virtue of their higher disability and the effects of both acute and chronic diseases. Thus they can experience far more serious consequences from physical changes than observed among younger old people.

To trace a fairly common chain of events, for example, a problem with walking may lead to a fall and a broken bone, which then requires a hospitalization. Given the greater frailty of the oldest old, the hospitalization can have serious side effects. Some experience cognitive changes because of the iatrogenic effects of the hospitalization, for example, those caused by changes in medications. Even a hint of dementia can prevent older people from returning home. Some are institutionalized for "rehabilitation." In fact, those without a strong support system may lose what little help they received before admission, so they are particularly at risk (Johnson & Catalano, 1983). When no family member is present to mediate with discharge planners, the institutional setting is likely to become a permanent residence.

Time 4 has been singled out as a baseline for determining later outcomes, because four years in the study is sufficient time to identify trajectories, and sufficient numbers, 63, are still in the study. We categorized these surviving respondents into three empirically derived groups, whose outcomes we could determine at the next round of interviewing 15 months later. The first group, defined as the *functionally fit* include 24 of the 63 survivors, who were identified as being impaired on three or fewer activities of daily living (ADL/IADL) over almost four years. This cut-off point was determined by our analysis of the interviews that indicated those individuals could still maintain some independence at that level of disability. The second group, the *chronically disabled*, consists of 17 individuals, 27 percent, who also remained stable but at a high level of disability, being impaired on four or more activities of daily living. The third group, the *increasingly disabled*, includes 22 respondents or 35 percent, who had experienced a steep rise in their disabilities. This group is of particular interest because most of the morbidity and mortality took place among these participants.

The Functionally Fit Survivors

Among the 38 percent who had a stable physical status with an adequate level of functioning, none died and no one became incompetent or entered an institution in the subsequent 15 months. Throughout the four to five years, these individuals remained relatively independent. Few had arthritis or problems with their lower extremities. Despite being more functionally fit than others in the sample, however, members of this group were just as likely to be plagued by falls, sensory losses, and acute episodes, such pneumonia or heart problems. In fact, 25 percent were hospitalized for surgery or severe illnesses such as pneumonia from which they recovered or, at best, moderated the symptoms so as to avoid per-

TABLE 4.1

Trajectories

Time 1 (n = 150)	Time 2 (n = 111)	Time 3 (n = 93)	Time 4 (n = 63)	Time 5 (n = 48)	Outcomes	
					Mortality	Morbidity
The Functionally Fit (n = 24)					0	0
The Chronically Disabled (n = 17)					2	0
The Increasingly Disabled (n = 22)					3	7

manent declines in their functioning. Although some were depressed or demoralized, few experienced declining cognitive competence. The following two examples are fairly typical of these respondents.

The Fourth Life of Mr. Sarkosian

Mr. Sarkosian reported good health and adequate functioning even though he had serious health problems.

At age 88 at our first contact, he summarized his health status, "What can I say? I've had by-pass surgery twice. I now have shingles, I'm isolated, and lonely. I'm losing my confidence in myself, but glory be to God, my health is good." He was leading an orderly life, taking pride in cleaning his house every day before breakfast. "I cannot begin a day without the house being clean. I don't even eat breakfast until I have mopped the kitchen floor. I guess I am a prisoner of my compulsions." These rituals provided an effective means to demonstrate his independence and his ability to take care of himself without help.

The interviewer described Mr. Sarkosian as a distinguished looking man who spoke with a strong accent. He had had a long and tumultuous life, referring to himself as "the son of the revolution," and later as one who led three lives. Born in Russia of Armenian descent, he lost both parents in the Bolshevik revolution, but he managed to escape Russia at the age of 13. After some years as a displaced person, he began his second life, settling in the Balkans, receiving a college degree, and marrying. With the beginning of World War II, his third life began when he and his wife became refugees again and eventually came to the United States, leaving behind a daughter whom they never saw again. At the first interview, he had been widowed for 13 years. His only friend at the first interview was someone he had known in his work life.

At our next contact, he reported he was feeling better, and he was driving and getting out more. He had been hospitalized in intensive care for his heart, but he was relatively unconcerned. "My doctor says my body is strong or I wouldn't be able to resist these heart attacks. I take so many drugs, it's like I run a pharmacy." By the third contact, he described his health, "It's not good, but I wouldn't go so far as to say it is poor. I cannot care for my house as I used to, because I get very, very tired. I still have shingles, but they are not as painful as last year."

By the fourth contact, he was more active, greeting the interviewer as he returned from a lecture on displaced persons. He was dressed in what looked like a new suit with a color-coordinated shirt and tie. He described his health as fair, about the same as the previous year. His social life had improved considerably having been enriched by his efforts to help

Armenian refugees. He was particularly fond of a young couple he was assisting. "I have a feeling I make satisfaction for them. To do something for others is good—to help out or have words to say." His main problem was his anger at someone who ran into his car, but he continued to drive. At the fifth interview, his life remained much the same, and his functional status was stable. He did develop shortness of breath because of an enlarged heart, but medications controlled some of the effects. He continued to complain about his health, but with a sardonic sense of humor reflecting a strong sense of fate.

Reaching 100 and Doing Well

Mrs. Leach offers a clear contrast to Mr. Sarkosian, because, except for being legally blind, she had only minor chronic health conditions. In fact, she was the only one out of 150 who reached 100 years of age while in the study.

She was 96 at the outset and had been a widow for 50 years. She has witnessed the death of her daughter, the declining health of her son, and crippling arthritis of a grandson. At first, she was living with her late daughter's husband, a situation chosen for financial reasons, not because she had to live with others. A granddaughter, her major caregiver, assisted her by installing devices on her telephone and stove to compensate for her poor eyesight. She also handled Mrs. Leach's finances, shopped for her, and took her to the doctor.

Throughout the study, she had no other chronic conditions, and continued to do her own cooking and housework, even climbing the stairs frequently. She described her health, "It's fair. I manage to look after myself. The doctor takes my blood pressure and says I am in wonderful shape for my age. I'm not so good in the morning, but I feel better as the day goes on. But I am not very robust—I don't know why I have lived so long." By our next contact 15 months later, she had moved with some relief into an apartment of her own. She responded to questions on her health, "My eyesight has gotten worse, but I can't do anything about it. I put things down and then can't see them. It takes a long time for me to find them. As to my health, I'd rate it as good. I had the flu a few weeks ago, but I took care of myself."

By the third contact, she still rated her health as good. "I haven't spent a day in bed in years. I did have skin cancer that had to be removed this year—it was nothing. My major worries are not about me, but my son who has a bad heart but who won't tell me much about it. I don't have enough money, but somehow I manage." Her health was reported to be equally as good at the fourth contact, "I'm just tired—no illnesses. I feel older, but I never spend a day in bed. I'm too busy. It takes me all day just to keep up this apartment." A subsequent interview after she turned 100 found little change despite recent falls. "I just bruise, but I get up and go on about my life. I don't tell anyone about it. It's not so wonderful being 100 now, except I am very interested in my descendants—my five grandchildren and four great grandchildren." Although she complained of memory problems, she was still living independently with her health and functioning remaining unchanged.

The Chronically Disabled Survivors

In contrast to the functionally fit, who remained so even after episodes of acute illnesses, 17 individuals, 27 percent of the survivors at Time 4, had a poor level of functioning throughout almost four years in the study. Two had died by Time 5 and no one became too incompetent to be interviewed. Among this group, functional problems could usually be traced to chronic conditions rather than to life-threatening diseases. They were more likely to complain of arthritis, painful joints, and limited mobility. Falls accentuated their difficulties. Generalized complaints were also common and reflected the unremitting effects of most chronic conditions.

"I'm just tired."

"It's just a cold hanging on."

"It's the flu I can't shake."

As some reported, "The only thing wrong with me is old age." Reports of unhappiness and depression were typical. The following case studies illustrate how a ripple effect works, with health problems, even minor ones, affecting social and psychological status.

Sinking into Weakness

Mrs. Bronson was 85 years of age at the beginning of the study. A widow with two children in the area and live-in help, she was impaired on four or more activities of daily living throughout the study.

From all outward appearances of this attractive, petite woman, her hearing aid was the only sign of her impairments. Nevertheless, she had numerous chronic physical problems. She attributed her health declines to two serious bouts with pneumonia a few years ago.

I've always had respiratory problems, but until the pneumonia, I was able to fight them off. I have cataracts and hearing problems, but I can handle that. It's the pain in my neck and shoulders that keeps me from sleeping. Then I have to rest for three hours during the day. The rest of the day is filled with reading and writing letters to friends.

At the second interview, she reported her health had deteriorated.

I'm not as sharp as I used to be. I can't follow some of the things I read— my mind is too slow. I also had bronchitis from Thanksgiving to Christmas. It's harder to shake at my age. My hearing is much worse. I can't hear the notes when I listen to music. It's not that I am tired, but it's a gone feeling, like I'm sinking with weakness. I feel the drawstrings of my world pulling a little tighter—not all at once. It's a gradual thing. I always worry I will be a drain on my family.

By the third contact, she reported that she had broken her arm by just turning over in bed. "It was very painful. Then last week, I was dizzy and was always bumping into furniture. I tell myself I am getting older and probably won't live another 10 years. I'd like to have more energy—I get depressed when I can't do things." By the next contact, almost four years after the first interview, she reported,

I'm perfectly healthy except for one episode of tachycardia that went away in an hour. Even then, they put me in the hospital for three days. After a week back home, I felt fine, but then I twisted something in my back by just pulling a weed in the garden. That made me feel languid and weary. Now I don't go to my son's country place any more, because there is no emergency treatment there. I don't drive as much, so I've given up going to meetings. Once in a while, I'm a little anxious. I feel out of things. I don't understand cartoons in the New Yorker anymore and I don't know what's on at the opera or ballet. These things I've sorta blotted out.

In a subsequent interview, her functional status remained much the same, but she complained of increased weariness and fatigue as well as some cardiovascular problems. At the fifth round of interviewing, her functional status remained quite impaired.

Pain from Head to Foot

Mrs. Resnick, also 85 years old initially, lived with her unmarried daughter.

In the four years prior to the first interview, both a son and daughter had died. After reporting these losses, she added, "Having lost two children, I am not worried about dying." Most of her adult life was spent in New York City, but she came to her daughter's home a few years previously after breaking a leg and being unable to manage alone. "I've had two knee replacements but still have a hard time walking. I use a walker when out of the house and get around the house by hanging on to furniture." Like the majority in the study, her string of complaints were followed by the claim, "I'm in constant pain, but my health is excellent. I'm pleased when I look at others and realize how lucky I am to have all my faculties—I can think, and I can read even with cataracts." At the first interview, Mrs. Resnick went to a senior center three times a week and had made new friends there. "It's a lot of fun to go there, but otherwise my life is very boring."

By the second interview, few changes were noted, but Mrs. Resnick seemed depressed and had greater difficulty walking. This time she described her health, "It's poor because I can't stand up. I'm confined to my chair. I can't walk at all. It's painful climbing out of bed. Even taking a shower is hard. Now all my days are bad. It's frustrating, but at least I don't have heart trouble." Despite these complaints, she later talked about her television programs and her delight in her painting class at the senior center. "The people there mean nothing, but they hug me—that's nice. The people on the van that picks me up are nice too—it's a happy van. I have a lot to be thankful for. At this stage, my life couldn't be much better than it is now."

By the third contact, she had increased her attendance at the senior center to four times a week; it was the central source of contentment in her life. Second to that, she also was pleased with the births of great grandchildren. She described her daughter as an "angel" for all the help she was providing. As an example of her optimism, she had not given up hope that this 64-year-old daughter would eventually marry. Yet her disabilities persisted, "I have pain from head to foot and can barely move. I fall a lot, and sometimes it takes me an hour to get up."

At the fourth interview, she discussed her health, "I feel okay even though I can't taste food. I did have a terrible fall. I lost my balance, my knees buckled, and I went down, thump! Now every bone hurts. Dressing is hard. I get cramps in my fingers, so I can't knit and crochet. Sometimes I get so angry for no reason. I'm getting to be a cranky old lady. I try to control it. I want to say I'm content, but I'm not 100 percent content." Shortly after this interview, she had a slight stroke and developed some problems with her speech and memory. For example, one time when taking a cab home from the center, she couldn't remember her address. Nevertheless, she had not changed her lifestyle, continuing to go to the center and enjoying her life in general, despite her many disabilities.

The Increasingly Disabled Survivors

To visualize the trajectory of change, Figure 4.3 depicts a potential chain of events that can occur among the increasingly disabled. First, a precipitating incident such as an acute illness, an accident, or a surgical procedure entails a hospitalization. At that point, a

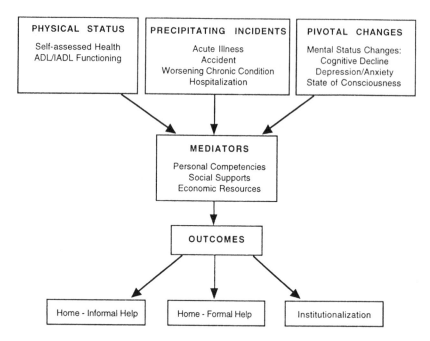

FIGURE 4.3   Model of functional changes occurring over time among
the increasingly disabled

cascade effect may occur, with pivotal changes in mental status
happening in conjunction with physical changes. The mediating
factors in this model refer to the individual's resources, such as adequate social resources, financial resources, and those personal competencies needed to cope with declining health. The outcomes for
this third trajectory include morbidity and mortality, institutionalization, or return home.

Of the surviving 63 individuals at Time 4, 22 experienced rapid
declines in functioning, as measured by increasing impairment on
four or more activities over the course of the four years. By Time
5, three of those with rapid declines in functioning had died, and
seven became too incapacitated to continue in the study. As many
as nine suffered from injuries from a fall and nine exhibited cognitive losses. Of the 22, 16 had been hospitalized at least once in the
course of 15 months.

This subgroup is of interest, because they are the most vulnerable and at risk of physical and psychological morbidity. The cases
described in the following indicate how rapidly physical status

can change, and how, in turn, these changes have ripple effects to other areas of life. Because over one-half were able to maintain community living, however, they offer information as to how institutionalization may be forestalled despite sharp drops in functioning. While the complex interactions among physical, social, and psychological effects cannot be fully accounted for here, hopefully the findings can address in part the questions posed by Manton and Suzman (1992). What can be done to improve outcomes, and how do individuals with impairments manage to remain independent? In some cases, mediating effects such as personal and social resources were important in easing the problems. For example, those returning home were more likely to have adequate social supports available and could draw upon various personal competencies to cope with their declining status (see Appendix B).

These processes are similar to Uhlenberg's (1995) reference to functional status changes as transitions, where thresholds act as markers of change. He suggests that once thresholds are established for cognitive and emotional changes, sensory or energy losses, and loss of mobility, then destinations or outcomes can be studied. These outcomes are influenced, as we will indicate, not only by physical factors, but also by the social and psychological resources of the individual.

Precipitating Incidents. An acute illness is one such threshold, where changes in functioning occurred among 11 individuals. In nine cases, the threshold resulted from injuries, such as from a fall. Thus only two individuals experienced a decline in functioning without noticeable acute episodes. The acute episodes were varied: strokes, mastectomy, viral infections, and bleeding ulcers. Accidents entailing broken bones or a concussion often led not only to a hospital stay, but in some cases also to institutionalization (Johansson, Zarit, & Berg, 1992). Thus, these already frail individuals who experienced a health crisis faced serious risks.

Lasting Impact of an Earthquake

Miss Taub declined in functioning over the years, but she attributed the onset of serious declines in her health to an injury incurred during the 1989 San Francisco earthquake.

She was 89 years of age at the first contact, a retired school teacher who had never married, a situation she deeply regretted in her last years. Her only relative, a brother, died a few years previously. Initially she looked far younger than her age and, as a reflection of her active life, she was to receive a community award the next evening for her work with disabled children. She described her health as fair. "I have borderline pernicious anemia that makes me weak, but I eat natural foods to help. The pain from arthritis comes and goes, but I'm the type that ignores that. I like to keep busy. I go to the opera and symphony and to the Jewish Center twice a week."

Fourteen months later, her appearance indicated that dramatic changes had occurred. Rather than the healthy-looking woman we first encountered, she was a frail and weakened version of her former self. She explained:

> I haven't been well—I pick up colds and flu easily. Ever since the earthquake, things have changed. I was knocked down with the shaking and was unconscious for almost two hours. After I came to, I took a cab to the emergency room. They saw something in my head, but said it wasn't cracked. I still have a lot of pain though. The doctor says it's natural at my age, but I think it's something else. I haven't been out for a long time. The last time I went to the Center, I picked up the flu.

By the next contact, she continued to complain of her earthquake injuries and her noticeable memory problems. She coughed continuously during the interview explaining, "The flu is still hanging on. I can't sleep at all because of the pain. I keep busy though. I have friends at the Center, but I can't remember their names." She was consulting with someone from the Center about moving to a nursing home. The interviewer observed that her medications had been organized into daily slots, but it was apparent that she was taking them erratically.

By Time 4, she had relocated to the intermediate care wing of a nursing home. She still complained about her injuries three years previously. "I still have a pain in my head from the earthquake, but I have no complaints." At the final interview at the nursing home 10 months before she died, she kept on a heavy overcoat throughout the interview even when she had to lie down on her bed because of severe chest pains. Although increasingly confused and forgetful, she was able to answer most interview questions. She reported, "I'm doing well for my age—just these chest pains bother me. I am very grateful for how long I've lived. I've lived so long I forget how old I am."

Pivotal Changes in Mental Status. Symptoms of cognitive decline such as forgetfulness and confusion often accompany physical declines or become accentuated with them. These mental status changes had a pervasive negative effect on the adaptation of very old people. For example, they were more common among those entering an institution than among those who remained in their homes.

The Piano Player

Mrs. Bellamy was 96 years old at the beginning of the study and was living with a divorced daughter. Initially she too was very active taking the bus all over the city to play the piano at senior centers.

> She described these activities, "I am always making friends—you have to because old friends die. I just sent out 100 Christmas cards to my friends. My health is pretty good, even though I've had cancer. It's still here, so it doesn't bother me." Problems with her memory were noticeable, so much so that her daughter had written for us a detailed description of her mother's past life and present circumstances.
>
> Fourteen months later, Mrs. Bellamy reported no changes in her life, but her daughter interrupted her to detail numerous changes. She reported that her mother napped more and had eye problems that limited her activities. By Time 4, she had fallen on a city bus and broken her hip, from which she recovered and could even walk without a cane. According to her daughter, her life changed dramatically because of more pronounced dementia. Her mental status declined progressively, and she died shortly before her one-hundredth birthday.

Not Quite the Same Person

Likewise, Mrs. Clark declined noticeably over time. She was taking care of her third husband, who was 98 years old. At the first interview, she was an attractive, alert woman, who supervised her husband's round-the-clock nursing care and even managed to swim frequently and then have lunch at a downtown club.

> "I wouldn't know what a bad day is. I like to spend a lot of time with my husband." By the next interview, she was impatient and irritable and cut off the interviewer, saying, "My blood pressure is rising, because I am under pressure all the time. I'm stretched to the breaking point in having to deal with my husband's demands. I don't like being confined to the house and having the nurses around all the time. There are too many personalities for me to deal with." Despite much evidence of affluence in the decor of her home, she was dressed in a soiled, tattered house dress.

By the third contact, her husband had died. Since she had problems with falling, her husband's round-the-clock caregivers stayed on to care for her. Unlike the previous interviews, she was well dressed, and gracious. However, her speech was slurred, and her sentences were left incomplete, as she drifted into reverie. "I am not quite the same person after all the things I've been through. My husband kept me stimulated." She then asked the interviewer to check under her bed to see if the little girl was still there. A chocolate mint on a lace doily had been placed there for her "visitor." The next and last contact with her found her looking frail and napping for long periods of time. She could walk with assistance and each day dressed as if she were going out. She reported, "Nothing has changed. I'm still here and everything is the same."

Mediating Effects. Understandably, persons with adequate personal competencies are those without mental confusion or demoralization. Their personal resources most noticeably lay in their effective coping with the activities of daily living and exercising a strong sense of control over their life. With such personal resources, individuals are able to sustain community living as long as they received adequate social supports. Consequently, their personal and social resources were important determinants of outcomes at Time 5.

Coping with Cancer and Chronic Conditions

Mrs. Rose is a good example of personal competencies in dealing with serious health problems.

She was 90 as she began participating in the study. Only recently she had to alter her active lifestyle because of a mastectomy and chemotherapy. "I've always had good health, and now I'm able to keep the cancer from spreading. I also had a heart attack a few years ago, so I never go out without my nitroglycerin. I have so many health problems. I have some stomach troubles from all the medications, my eyesight is affected, and I have a hearing aid." Despite these complaints, she was able to perform all the activities of daily living.

By the next contact, she described her health, "I tore my knee cartilage, so now I have trouble walking. I'm still on chemotherapy—the cancer is still there in my spine—from head to tail, but it has stopped spreading. I had the flu at Thanksgiving that took me four months to get over. But my health is good considering all that has happened to me. My worst problems are with my mobility." By the third contact, her eyesight had worsened and she could no longer read. She was troubled by urinary tract infections, and then she had a reaction from the medications.

By the next contact, her conditions had gradually worsened.

I tried to make cookies for Christmas, but realized I was too tired. That made me so sad I started crying. My legs hurt, my back hurt, and my feet hurt. My mind is not in tune with my body. Thankfully, my mind is still young. I wake up in the morning and feel like going downtown. Then I get up, and no matter how hard I try, I can barely walk.

It is interesting to note that, with each additional interview, she spoke less of her cancer and heart condition, and instead concentrated effectively upon the difficulties handling the chronic problems with her lower extremities. At the next and last contact, however, Mrs. Rose had been institutionalized and died shortly thereafter.

The Cascade Effect

By examining specific cases, we see that physical changes tend to interact with mental status, particularly after a hospitalization. Dramatic declines were noted after a seemingly easily resolvable event. In some cases, social network problems also arose usually because of conflict among family members.

At our first and second contact, Mrs. Newman was an attractive, well-groomed widow who initially led an active life surrounded by family and friends. She reported her health as excellent and easily maintained her own home, doing all the gardening and domestic chores. Most days she took public transportation downtown to a restaurant which she referred to as a "widow's hangout," where she met her friends. Her family was attentive, calling daily and visiting weekly.

Her contentment with life changed dramatically after she fell and shattered her knee. After an infection and skin graft, she was transferred from a hospital to a convalescent home where she received physical therapy. After a month, she was rehospitalized, this time in a psychiatric ward. In our contacts with her there, she was confused and disoriented. A few weeks later she was again transferred, this time to a board-and-care home, where she spent all her time in bed. She also became incontinent. To compound her problems, conflict among her children prevented them giving her solace and support. As Mrs. Newman herself concluded at our last contact, "Why should I have this kind of exit? I've tried to lead a good life. I've worked hard all my life, so my children could be comfortable." She also concluded that she would never return to her home, when she heard that her children were dividing up her furnishings.

Social and Physical Losses

Mrs. Walker, who was 93 years old at the outset, offers a good example of how physical changes interact with changes in the support network.

She lived with her sister and had two daughters in the area. At the first interview, she was slowly recovering from a recent bout with the flu.

Every year I have this darn flu—otherwise I'm okay. I have had a leaky heart valve for 80 years, so I take heart medicine. I have glaucoma and very bad eyesight. I don't stay in bed—I'm just disgusted with myself for not getting better. I still walk to the store and beauty parlor. When you are 93 and have been sick as many times as I have and have outlived two bad marriages, you learn to take care of yourself.

By the second interview, she described herself as a "prisoner" of her sister's house, because of her disabilities. She was not allowed to do as she pleased. Mrs. Walker had increasing incidents of falling. "I'm concerned with messing up my brain. No health changes though—doctor says there is nothing wrong." In the following months, she had even more falls and broke her wrist. She also had had hernia surgery and was in a convalescent hospital for six weeks for rehabilitation. Despite these problems, she described her health, "I would say it's good, because I have a good bowel movement every day. I am not concerned about my health. I am just waiting until my time comes. I do think I'll have to go to an institution one of these days, that is, if I don't die."

By the fourth interview, her sister had died, and Mrs. Walker was forced to move to a nursing home where her physical status declined precipitously. Her daughter described the rapidity of the changes.

Mom is 97 now. She has good days and bad days. They think she is having small strokes. Her troubles all began with her legs swelling. After being given diuretics, she could not read the instructions, so she took too many pills. She became dehydrated and started talking goofy. We took her to the hospital where she climbed over the bed railing and injured herself. She was discharged to an institution where she was disoriented. Now she can hardly walk and says she is tired of living.

A brief visit to Mrs. Walker found her belted into her wheel chair, with her mind wandering.

Conclusion

In this report on functional changes and later outcomes, we find that difficulties with their activities of daily living increased significantly. In following individual trajectories over the first four contacts, respondents could be categorized into three groups: 1) The *functionally fit survivors*, 38 percent, continued living in the community with only moderate disabilities; 2) the *chronically disabled*, 27 percent, survived with a high level of disability; and 3) the *increasingly disabled*, the remaining 35 percent, experienced the effects of rapid increases in disability. The latter group is of particular interest, for within the ensuing 15 months, most of the morbidity, mortality, and institutionalizations occurred among respondents in this trajectory.

What have we learned from this naturalistic account of changes in physical status of the very old? For one thing, the majority of survivors maintain stability in their health status at an adequate or even impaired functional level. For the 35 percent who experience increased disability, the model guiding this analysis depicts the effects of physical changes. Precipitating events such as an acute illness or an accident usually precede declines in functioning. Such a turn of events usually requires a hospitalization. When such changes are accompanied by mental status changes, a pivotal point is reached when already vulnerable individuals become more at risk. With this turning point in their lives, their already fragile hold on a modicum of independence is often undermined, and some can no longer maintain community living. There are mediating effects, however, that lead to a more positive outcome. If they possess the necessary personal competencies and sufficient social and economic resources to cope with their problems, they are better able to continue community living.

These findings indicate that a single event alone rarely undermines community living. Instead, a combination of events interact, so that only the most dedicated efforts by the family in conjunction with the health care system and the formal support system can reverse a downward spiral. For example, living alone by itself does not lead to institutionalization, but the combined effects of living alone, having an acute illness or incurring injuries from a fall, and needing a hospitalization, can do so. Relocation may be necessary particularly among the childless or those without extensive informal supports. Without family members as mediators, they have difficulty in re-establishing their previous support system after a hospitalization.

Mental status changes commonly occur with changes in physical status and, in combination, initiate an irreversible cascade effect. Hospitalizing the very old imposes a risk of iatrogenic effects that can be manifested in delirium, increased mental confusion, depression, or anxiety (Johnson & Johnson, 1983; Lipowski, 1983). Without an energetic support system and the belief that some mental declines can be moderated or reversed, it is doubtful that very old patients can return home.

Another turning point that undermines adaptation is the death or serious illness of caregivers. When a caregiver dies or becomes incapacitated, those without extensive support systems are faced with making transitions to another living situation or, at best, to finding substitutes for the loss of a significant relationship. In a population with few surviving spouses and as many as one-third without children, social needs can be high.

The second question addressed here concerns what can be done to improve outcomes. Certainly steps can be taken to reduce the prevalence of accidents, such as falls. Practical adjustments can be made in the living environment to minimize the risks that impaired mobility poses. For example, assistive devices, such as a cane or walker or bars in the bathroom prevent falls. Similarly, sleeping arrangements can be changed, so a person no longer has to negotiate stairs to get to their bedroom. Prescription drugs for very old people also need to be very carefully administered and monitored to avoid drug interactions from multiple medications.

Usually older people are relegated to the chronic disease group who are in need of long-term care, yet high proportions of the oldest old in our study are hospitalized annually because of acute episodes or accidents. Certainly more research is needed on the very old and the iatrogenic effects they experience with a hospitalization. The possible chain of events poses not only health risks and cognitive problems, but also they can undermine their fragile hold on independence. In spite of the declines in functioning, it is remarkable to find so little change in mood. Most survivors continued to express contentment and to perceive their health as good. By our definition of adaptation, consequently, many are able to sustain their morale and motivations despite increased disability.

Chapter 5

Late-Life Family Relationships

Over the course of the research, the activities in most families fluctuated with the changing situations of its members, but the actual family resources changed little. Those who had close family relationships at the beginning of the study continued to have them, those who were bereft of family involvements continued to be so, and those where family relationships existed mostly in their potentialities or their sentiments did not change. Such stability existed even in the face of dislocating changes. We also found fewer gender differences in family relationships than we had anticipated. This chapter describes the structure and functioning of the families of the oldest old and, where family relations are absent, we describe the processes many use to reconstitute family-like relationships.

Researchers no longer adhere to the theme of family abandonment of their elderly, an assumption what was resoundly rejected by Shanas' (1979b) survey in the 1970s. In its place, more positive images prevail, that depict older people as enjoying their prolonged life basking in the love and attention of added generations. In fact, when family researchers speak of changes in the late life family, they point to the enrichment of family life because more generations are alive concurrently.

The research literature on the American family concentrates on the family at earlier stages in the family cycle, when the "family" is equated with a household or a childrearing unit. Since older people in this country rarely live in two- or three-generation households, the family for them is not a domestic or household unit. In fact, as many as 24 percent in our study have outlived the family as a unit of social organization in which tasks are being performed and where social interactions occur. Consequently new models are needed to understand the late life family. In response to this situation, some suggest that shared households or even face-to-face contact are no longer necessary for family continuity, because sentiments alone can provide a strong sense of family allegiances (Troll & Bengtson, 1992). Even in the provision of social supports, actual contact is not viewed as a prerequisite, because family members can orchestrate a support network for its older members from afar (Litwak, 1985).

These diverse views reflect differing conceptual frameworks. One popular approach is a developmental perspective that mainly focuses on intergenerational relationships. This literature uses a psychological lens, or what Sprey (1991, p. 223) refers to as the "search for inner forces" in the family. Thus, love, attachment and solidarity are viewed as the primary determinants of social interactions and supports (Bengtson, Rosenthal, & Burton, 1990). Consequently, a whole series of social relationships and an impressive array of social organization are ignored. In contrast, sociologists and demographers are interested in changes in the family that are occurring with recent demographic shifts.

Another area of family research comes from the caregiving model, one that is based upon the assumption, like the popular views, that there are large numbers of older people who are needy and in a state of decrepitude. As a consequence, they require extensive help, usually from a spouse or child. Such a need-based model depicts the elderly in negative terms as those who cause stress and burdens upon their families. An unfortunate result of this strong emphasis upon the caregiver is the neglect of the elderly themselves and their views of their own situation (Barer & Johnson, 1990). This concentration of interests dominates research on the late life family even though national surveys indicate that only 25 percent of the older population have a child as primary caregiver (Kovar, 1986; Stone, Cafferata, & Sangl, 1987).

While the care of the elderly is an important practical issue, it makes few theoretical contributions. Probably, a more relevant model is one that follows the lead of Matilda Riley (1983). She suggests that the extension of life has stimulated a view of the family as a dynamic unit, "a latent web of continually shifting linkages that provide the opportunity for activating and intensifying close family relationships" (1983, p. 439). Such a model provides a useful framework for depicting the diversity and dynamics in the families in our study.

When the family is viewed as a dynamic unit, a range of family types emerge (Johnson, 1993). Some families are *multifunctional units*, where various members interact and assist one another. Reciprocity and interdependence are prominent, not merely between parents and adult children, but also between multiple children and other relatives. These can be compared, to *families as a unit of potential*. This most common late life family form mainly functions in terms of its potential resources. Members rise to the occasion when older members need help, but at other times, little assistance is extended. Thus, these families in Riley's words have "continually shifting linkages" within a latent network of relationships. Family roles are flexible and usually activated instrumentally when needs arise, or socially for special ritualized occasions. Essentially these family members remain intimate at a distance except when needed.

Relationships in other family types have little of substance in terms of contacts and reciprocity. However, many are *families as vessels of sentiment*, where members maintain little contact and reciprocity, but they adhere to strong sentiments and allegiances to "the family." Except for intermittent letters or phone calls, few interactions take place. Usually there are numerous photographs of relatives in evidence. These respondents often reminisce about their past family life, idealizing their parents and their happy childhood, and bemoaning the events that led to the current distance between relatives. Finally, *attenuated families* maintain few or no ongoing relationships most often because they have no children, and they have outlived the contemporaries in their family. Their only contacts may be the exchange of Christmas cards or an annual telephone call.

We will illustrate how, when faced with the typical needs of late late life, the American family system permits its members to sort out relationships, define what constitutes family membership, and essentially maximize, or in some cases minimize, family involvement. Given the individual's options in defining the membership of his or her family, it is necessary to ask, what maintains the family? Are family members activated out of sentiments, normative directives about obligations and responsibility, or out of the need for social supports?

Family Structure in Late Life

Major demographic shifts are affecting the structure of late life families. Increased life expectancy has added more members to the oldest generation, and declining fertility rates are resulting in fewer family members in younger generations (George & Gold, 1991). As more members of the oldest generation are living into their 80s and 90s when needs for support increase, family members may be asked to provide assistance at a time when its structural resources are shrinking (Treas & Bengtson, 1987).

The "beanpole family model" is also occurring because there are fewer kin in each generation (Bengtson et al., 1990; Knipscheer, 1988). Others speak of a "top heavy" family structure where there are potentially more care recipients than care providers in contrast to a "bottom heavy structure" that occurs in those times when fertility is high (Burton & Sorensen, 1993). Another potential consequence associated with a "top heavy" family structure is a diminishing number of horizontal relationships which results in the declining importance of sibling bonds (Hagestad, 1992). Thus, the weakening of collateral relationships in the late life family may be a source of negative effects on the oldest old, particularly among the childless.

Most evidence for a vertical family type is anecdotal, because no surveys with representative samples have collected such information (Uhlenberg, 1993). In fact, a Boston study found that almost as many older individuals had no direct lineal kin as had four generations in their families (Rossi & Rossi, 1990). With 20 to 30 percent of the oldest old today being childless, a considerable number are at the end of their lineage (Kovar & Stone, 1992; Preston, 1992). The question thus arises, do other relationships substitute for the absence of children (Johnson & Barer, 1995)?

In combination, these demographic factors raise important questions about variations in the family after the conventional designation of old age at 65 years. Does family size and structure vary because of increased numbers of descending generations or are their numbers offset by a high proportion without descendants? Do most very old people have three or four descending generations, as some have said, or, as a consequence of low fertility rates earlier in this century and the predictable losses over time, are they more likely to have fewer or even no descendants (Cornoni-Huntley et al., 1986; Treas & Bengtson, 1987)? Are those with more generations likely to get more help than those with truncated families?

The verticalization of the family was assessed by the presence of four or more generations (Johnson & Troll, 1992; 1996). As indicated in Table 5.1, the late life family is one predominantly of women, 70 percent in the 85 to 89 age range and 79 percent after 90. The proportions with surviving children and grandchildren do not vary significantly by age, with 65 to 70 percent having at least one surviving child. Two thirds have grandchildren, but the numbers with great grandchildren never reaches 50 percent even among those in their 90s. The fact that fewer than one-half in their 90s have great grandchildren most likely is related to late childbearing and low fertility in both the oldest cohort and the contemporary cohorts now in the childbearing ages (Baldwin & Nord, 1984).

Thus, these findings indicate that fewer than one half of the families of those 85 years and older could be called vertical in structure, if defined by the presence of four or more generations. In fact, these aggregate measures indicate that a high proportion, 30 to 35

TABLE   5.1
Family Size and Structure by Age (by percentage)

	Age 85–89 (n = 93)	Age 90+ (n = 57)
Male	30	21
Female	70	79
Added generations:		
Surviving child	70	65
Children in proximity	58	52
Grandchildren	65	65
Great grandchildren	32	44
Childless	30	35
Family losses		
Deceased child	29	35
No surviving sibling	55	65

percent, have no children at all and are at the end of their lineage. These patterns also seem to be consistent with the "beanpole structure" hypothesis. Family losses are prominent with increasing age and appear to offset the added numbers of descendants: 29 to 35 percent have at least one deceased child, and a majority have no surviving sibling, 55 percent in their late 80s to 65 percent in their 90s.

In summary, there is evidence of some shrinkage of family size with increasing age, particularly with the deaths of siblings and other age peers (Hagestad, 1992). Not only is there evidence of significant losses of family members by the time people reach their 90s, but also four-generation families are not in the majority. Nevertheless, almost two thirds in both age groups belong to three-generation families. Overall, these respondents tend to fall into two groups, those with multigenerational families, typically of three generations, and the truncated families with no lineal kin.

The Functioning of Dyadic Family Relationships

If the late life family consists of a continually shifting latent matrix of relationships, the study of specific dyadic relationships single out those that encourage or discourage attachment, sociability, and support (Johnson, 1988b). Shanas (1979b) has formulated the principle of substitution, which suggests that family members are available to older people in serial order. If one is married, a spouse is there to help, if one is widowed, a child fills the gap, and so on. This assumption carries over to other relatives, although there is little evidence that siblings and other relatives are substitutes in the absence of children (Johnson, 1983a). Consequently, if there are no overlapping and interchangeable functions, one needs to examine dimensions of each relationship. These dimensions include the strength of the norms of obligation and responsibility in each relationship and the extent reciprocal exchanges take place that benefit older people. When examining the characteristics of specific dyadic family relationships, one would agree with Litwak (1985), who argues that each family relationship is specialized in functioning rather than having interchangeable functions.

The functioning family of the oldest old is also likely to be affected by the sheer length of family relationships. Respondents

can have marriages of 60 or 70 years duration, parent-child relationships that are almost as long, and sibling relationships of 80 or
90 years. Watkins and her colleagues (1987) have found that even
with declines in fertility and increases in divorce, individuals
spend more time as currently married spouses and in conjugal
units than did earlier cohorts. Thus what is the impact of the sheer
length of family relationships? Do conflicts diminish with increasing age, so relationships become more placid and compatible? Or
are these relationships laden with stresses and burdens that very
old people place upon their family because their expectations are
not met?

Husbands and Wives

Only a small number of the respondents, 20 percent, were still
married at our first contact, 11 women and 19 men. In an analysis
of marital histories, we found only 7 percent had never married.
Consequently, a large majority had been married at some point,
and as many as 32 percent of these had more than one marriage.
Those currently with a spouse had been married a mean of 45
years. If those in their second marriage are omitted, that mean
increases to 59 years with a range from 46 to 70 years. It appears
that marriage is like old wine—it improves with age. As Table 5.2
indicates, of those married, 62 percent said that their spouse was
supportive in terms of instrumental supports, and all but one, 97
percent, reported high expressive rewards from the relationship.
Nevertheless, only 5 percent had a spouse as a caregiver. The interviews reveal little marital conflict and much companionship and
mutual supportiveness. In fact, women who were still married had
a special status that often elicited the envy of their friends.

These distributions reflect the findings from a large body of
research. Being married is the single most significant factor pre-
venting institutionalization of older people (Health Care Financing
Administration, 1981). With illness and the need for social supports, the spouse is the major provider of social supports (Johnson,
1983a; Palmore, 1979; Shanas, 1979a). Late-life marriages are pervaded by mutual needs. It is not surprising then to find a level of
interdependence and mutual support between husbands and
wives. After spending so many years together, most express strong
norms of responsibility. This interdependence is strengthened by a

TABLE 5.2
Dyadic Family Relationships of the Oldest Old (by percentage)

	Spouse ($n = 31$)	Child ($n = 102$)	Grand child ($n = 98$)	Great- Grand child ($n = 56$)	Sibling ($n = 65$)	Other Relative ($n = 118$)
Percent of sample in dyad	20%	68%	65%	36%	43%	78%
Social contact						
Weekly or more	20	44	19	—	4	12
Monthly or bimonthly	0	11	17	—	5	15
Less than monthly	0	14	29	—	25	36
None/not applicable	80	31	35	—	65	37
Instrumental supports						
Supportive	62	52	13	0	8	5
Nonsupportive	19	25	25	7	5	21
No relationship	19	23	62	93	87	74
Expressive supports						
Supportive	97	93	91	72	67	67
Nonsupportive	3	7	7	15	28	17
No relationship	0	0	2	13	5	16
Caregiver						
Yes	5	37	3	1	1	—
No	16	22	94	98	98	—
Not needed	79	41	3	1	1	—

high level of companionship, a quality that may reflect a more equal distribution of power in late life. Both husbands and wives share the status of survivors and more importantly, they share the risk of becoming dependent and in need of help from their spouse (Johnson, 1985). Apparently this combination of factors overshadows any previous conflicts in the relationship.

Parents and Children

At this point in family research, the prevailing views are worth noting. As a counterpoint to the much-heralded conceptions of solidarities between parents and children (Bengtson et al., 1990), a second conception is phrased in terms of constraints and facilitators to affectual bonds between parents and adult children. Hess and Waring (1978) have pointed out that numerous factors contribute to attenuated bonds, such as diminishing opportunities for mutual services, the competing demands in the lives of middle-aged adult children, and numerous psychological barriers to intimacy. In their view, ambiguity is evident because of the cultural directives in the average family. On one hand, the parent in late life says, "I never want to be a burden on my children," and thus they report having few expectations of their children's help. Children, on the other hand, feel some norms of responsibility at the same time they do not feel obligated to make sacrifices for them.

Our findings about the relationships between parents and their adult children parallel research findings of others. Most older people prefer to be independent from their children, particularly in maintaining a separate residence. This independent stance is carried over to social supports; many prefer to hire help rather than bother their children. When hired help is used, children function more as mediators than regular helpers, but most are very attentive in filling the gaps in the service network. Even where children are providing some supports to parents, they often express filial anxiety at the possibility that they should do more. It is likely that they fluctuate between filial attentiveness and filial anxiety (Cicirelli, 1981).

Table 5.2 indicates that 68 percent have at least one surviving child, and 44 percent of these are in at least weekly face-to-face contact with them. Over one half report a child is very supportive in terms of instrumental supports, and 93 percent are supportive in providing expressive supports. A child functions as a caregiver in 37 percent of the cases, while another 22 percent of the parents need a caregiver but their child could not help them. The remainder did not need help at Time 1. In contrast to the 37 percent of the children who functioned as a caregiver, other relatives rarely functioned in that role. The caregiver was a spouse in 5 percent of the cases, grandchildren in 3 percent, a sibling in 1 percent, and another relative in 1 percent of the cases.

While not in tabular form, we find that only 25 percent of the children actually shop for a parent, and only 18 percent help them around the house. Even fewer have a child they confide in or turn to when feeling down. Apparently a child plays a key role in the lives of the very old, but, in many cases, it may be as a facilitator of formal supports rather than an actual supporter. These proportions were much the same with the survivors six years later and add additional evidence that where caregiving responsibilities were taken over by the family, they most often rested upon an off-spring. The caregiving offspring in our study often lived in the same household as the parent, 30 percent at Time 1 and 41 percent at Time 5. Almost all other children who functioned as a caregiver were in weekly or more contact with their recipient parent, so that their activities were rarely long-distance arrangements.

Gender differences in intergenerational relationships mostly stem from differences in marital status. In the oldest generation, men are more likely than women to be living with a spouse, so their family life is likely to be dominated by the marital bond. Men in this study have just as much contact with their children as do women. However, gender-based differences in physical status do have an impact upon their relationship with children. Women are more impaired and receive twice as much instrumental support from children as men and are four times more likely to have a child as a caregiver (Johnson & Troll, 1992).

A reading of these interviews reinforces the statistical findings on the significance of children, but in a majority of cases, children provided expressive functions. In comparison to children, other relatives play a minor role in the lives of the oldest old as providers of practical assistance. The importance of the parent–child relationship suggests that it becomes a more positive force with increasing age. Perhaps because children do not necessarily provide hands-on care, the onerous aspects of caregiving are replaced by greater expressive support. The question arises as to whether this situation is unique to advanced old age. For instance, among younger old people, children do not necessarily contribute to their parents' morale, but rather most turn to friends for social and emotional benefits (Crohan & Antonucci, 1989). However, with advancing age and as friends die or become incapacitated, the potential for friendship involvement declines. As friends play a less important role, the advantages of having children increases. Children then potentially become the primary providers of both instrumental and expressive supports.

These somewhat mixed findings, we assume, relate to the fact that the support capacities in most families lie mainly in their potential. When a parent does not need help, a child stays intimate, but at a distance, and does not routinely assist a parent in his or her activities of daily living. As a need arises, however, most respond with dedication. It is possible that the parent–child relationship becomes stronger and less conflictual with the increasing age of the parent.

What we are suggesting is that the ambivalence noted earlier in the parent–adult-child relationship may be less apparent among the oldest old. Findings from our study indicate that differing constraints and facilitators may be operating among oldest old parents. Children are the key figures in maintaining their often disabled parents in the community. For the sample as a whole, only 12 percent of the parents live with a child, but among those in need of a caregiver, the percentage, as previously noted, is much higher. At the other end of the continuum, few are estranged from their children or have an attenuated bond. In those cases, conflict or distance between generations had usually developed over many years. In other words, poor relationships did not usually develop because of current circumstances.

Factors that led to problematic relationships in late life were apparent in the respondents' retrospective reports. Some men had been distant from children socially and geographically after a divorce. Some men and women were not close to their children because of their own earlier emotional problems or those of their children; in two cases, children suffered from serious mental illnesses. In other cases, the parent had remarried after a divorce, and the new relationship competed with their relationship with their children.

The facilitators to a close parent–child bond, when parents are in their 80s and 90s and children are in their 60s and 70s, also differ from younger old people. First, neither parent nor child have as many commitments that compete with the generational bond, as they had in earlier years. Members of both generations are likely to be widowed, and they no longer have work or childrearing commitments. Second, the flow of reciprocity has usually been reversed and altered in content. Other than a monetary gift at a birthday, very old parents rarely give financial aid to children, and instead of children extending financial aid to parents, the public domain has taken over much of the responsibility for older people. Consequently, children are able to concentrate on both the instrumental and emotional needs of the parent rather than resolving conflicts about money. Third, at the last stage of life also, parents have generally abandoned attempts to exert influence over their child's life by being judgmental about age-related value conflicts. These factors in combination lessen the opportunities for intergenerational conflict, and they tend to strengthen the affectual dimensions of the relationship.

Grandchildren and Great Grandchildren

We have identified several constraints to relationships with grandchildren and great grandchildren. For one thing, the function of these relationships is largely expressive, not instrumental. Grandchildren rarely provide assistance, and only 19 percent of the respondents are in weekly or more contact with a grandchild, far lower than the 44 percent of the oldest old who have weekly contact with a child. Such sparse contact can be traced to the situation of grandchildren. Most grandchildren of the oldest old are already adults and in some cases in middle age. Since many grandchildren do not live in the area, only 13 percent provide some instrumental support to their grandparent (Table 5.2). This support usually comes in conjunction with their parent's assistance. They may drive a grandparent to the doctor or shop for him or her when their parent is out of town. In one family, a granddaughter became a caregiver after her mother died, but few others respond by helping with specific tasks. Great grandchildren are usually very young, and most of our respondents are physically unable to take care of a baby or young child. Nevertheless, the oldest old view these descendants with strong sentiments even if relationships with descending generations have little functional content.

Lillian Troll (1994), in her an analysis of our findings on intergenerational relationships, found important differences in the basis for the relationships between the oldest old, their children, and grandchildren. She suggests that the members of the oldest generation in our study place more importance on their relationship with their own children over their grandchildren. This situation could stem from the fact that as grandchildren reach adulthood, they become more independent from their own parent. That parent then is freed up to strengthen the relationship with their oldest old parent, at the same time that they, as a middle generation, maintain a lineage bridge linking their parent to their child.

Troll also posits a distinction between particularlistic and generic relationships that helps us to understand intergenerational linkages. Particularistic ties are those dyadic ties with specific people, while generic ties refer to ties to collectivities within a family, such as their grandchildren as a group. With particularistic bonds, some individuals in the same category are treated on the basis of their personal characteristics such as the favorite child, or on the basis of the history of the relationship.

Our observations in interviews with the oldest old and in an earlier study of grandparenting (Johnson, 1988a) supports this conclusion. In our discussions with grandparents, they usually described each of their children by name and in terms of their individual characteristics and their life situation. When discussing their grandchildren, however, they referred to them generically as "my grandchildren," without singling them out as individuals or referring to them by name. Instead, they would talk about "the older boy" or "the one in Cincinnati." Similarly, cousins, nieces, and nephews are commonly referred to as a group rather than being identified by name. Such linguistic distinctions seem to indicate different qualities in the relationship, particularly as to the extent of closeness or distance in relationships.

Other Kinship Relationships

Other relatives were rarely closely involved in the lives of the oldest old (Table 5.2). Of the 43 percent who still have a surviving sibling, that relationship is dominated by sentiments rather than social content. Only 8 percent receive instrumental support from a sibling. Nevertheless, 67 percent report emotional benefits from the relationship. More telling is the fact that only 9 percent have monthly or more contact with a sibling. Likewise, nieces, nephews, cousins, and assorted in-laws are distant, shadowy figures, and few receive help from them. Although a large majority of these relatives are viewed with affection, only 27 percent have monthly or more contacts with at least one relative. Perhaps as a reflection of the distance from these relatives, the kin-keeping role is rarely performed by the oldest old (Troll, 1994). They no longer initiate and plan extended family activities, keep communication lines open, or attempt to preserve continuity in kinship relationships. While they had earlier played such a role, it had usually been passed on to a daughter some time in the past.

This brief overview on dyadic family relationships indicates that norms of responsibility and the provision of family supports come almost entirely from a spouse or children. Only in rare cases are family roles interchangeable, so that everyone has a reservoir of helpers. While few tangible benefits come from other relatives, the emotional benefits from all family members can be significant.

At the End of the Lineage

Except for only three individuals who have grandchildren but no surviving children, most of the childless in our study have no lineal kin. This suggests that the childless, who comprise almost one-third of the oldest old urban population (Bowling & Browne, 1991; Cornoni-Huntley et al., 1986), have such attenuated families that they are not able to find substitute family supporters. They are thus at risk of being "family deprived" and without family supports in late late life (Troll, 1994).

Researchers have consistently found that involvement with children does not necessarily enhance the well-being of older people (Troll, 1986), but as we have demonstrated, they are the primary supporters in old age. Since the very old have high levels of disability and disproportionately large numbers of them are childless, many potentially face critical gaps in their social support networks. In view of these facts, it is particularly important to know how the childless oldest old handle their social needs. Our analysis of the late-life family, to this point, indicates that children are the linchpins in facilitating social integration of the very old (Johnson, 1993; Johnson & Troll, 1992). If offspring are in proximity, they are likely to be in frequent contact with their parents. And those oldest old who are in frequent contact with their children are also more active with others.

The childless are usually less involved socially, a situation that can make them particularly vulnerable to the problems of advanced old age. As the following findings indicate, nevertheless, the childless are no more likely than the parents in our study to be depressed or demoralized, and they are no more likely to be impaired or to perceive their health as poor (Johnson & Barer, 1995). Thus, by the criteria of adaptation used here, the findings tentatively indicate that the presence of children may not be the major factor in adaptation of the oldest old, however much children function as supporters. In any case, the childless may face problems in advanced old age that are quite different from those faced by the parents.

The principle of substitution does not operate with the childless, where, in the absence of children, other relatives assist. Comparisons of the childless and the parents in late life indicate that the childless have notably fewer family resources (Table 5.3). Although not significant, more childless are unmarried and live alone. They have significantly less contact with relatives other than children; only 47 percent have monthly or more contact in comparison to 87 percent of the parents. They are also disadvantaged if they need a caregiver; only 36 percent of the childless have a family caregiver or one who could potentially fill that role, in comparison to 88 percent of the parents. More telling is the significant finding that 64 percent of the childless need a caregiver but have no one. In marked contrast, only 12 percent of the parents have these needs

TABLE 5.3
Family Responses by Parent Status among Oldest
Old (by percentage)

	Childless (n = 48)	Parents (n = 102)
Household		
Live alone	71	50
Live with others	29	50
Marital status		
Married	10	24
Not married	90	76
Monthly or more contacts		
with family member	47	87***
Caregiving		
Family caregiver or		
potential caregiver	36	88***
No one available	64	12
ADL/IADL help		
Help from family supports	12	52***
Help from formal supports	82	72

*** $p < .001$.

going unmet. Family assistance on specific activities of daily living occurs with 52 percent of the oldest parents but only with 12 percent of the childless. It is interesting to note that there are no significant differences in the use of formal supports. Apparently paid help is secured irrespective of family resources.

Consistent with these statistical findings, the childless respondents identified few family helpers, so not surprisingly, most of their daily activities took place outside a family context. Where the childless did sustain a relationship with a niece or nephew, they received little instrumental help from them. In some cases, the relationship was tenuous because of realistic impediments. For example, assistance from a niece or nephew was not always reliable, because such supports were dependent upon the extent of competing commitments in that relative's life. A work role, their own health problems, or demands from their immediate family took priority over responsibility for an elderly aunt or uncle.

In some cases, genuine conflict stemmed from unmet expectations. One woman continually complained about her nephew's neglect. She expected more from him, because she herself had taken care of his mother at the end of her life. Although this nephew arranged for her chore worker and her eventual institutionalization, she did not recognize this service as supportive and was, in fact, hostile toward him. Other respondents feared that nieces and nephews would exploit them if they were not vigilant. Some interpreted any assistance in mercenary terms, as motivated by expectations of money from their estate. "I only hear from them when they want money," or "When they see how much my house is worth, they come calling." One childless woman described how a niece and her husband began to sell her belongings while she had a prolonged hospitalization.

Where the oldest old had frequent and friendly contacts with nieces and nephews and other relatives, little practical assistance was forthcoming. Where relationships were friendly, intermittent visits and telephone calls were often the only interactions, because these relatives resided in distant suburbs. When residentially dispersed, frequent contact was difficult to maintain even if one was so motivated to do so.

The evidence suggests that relationships with nieces and nephews very rarely provided the attentiveness of the typical child of the oldest old. In only a few cases did the childless respondents have expectations for filial-like behaviors or even intermittent assistance and sociability from nieces and nephews. Such a pattern is consistent with the normative directives of American kinship, where relationships outside the immediate family are optionally maintained on the basis of personal preferences rather than norms of responsibility.

Constructed Relationships

Despite their scant family resources, the childless have developed several strategies to lessen the risk of having no lineal kin (Rubinstein, Alexander, Goodman, & Luborsky, 1991). In fact, a latent matrix of relationships is particularly prominent among some childless. Those oldest old, who had been socially involved with relatives, friends, and associates in their past often continued to maintain social anchorages in late late life. Their social skills are such that they are able to cultivate new relationships to replace those they have lost. To be able to do so, however, hinges upon adequate physical functioning and economic resources. Some of the childless are adept in constructing ties that substitute for the absence of children. To cite a few examples, close friends can become like a spouse or sibling. Relationships with nieces or nephews can come to resemble a parent–child relationship. A widower with no children can acquire a "lady friend" whose family he adopts as his own.

One maneuver is to acquire new family members by expanding or modifying their definition of family relatedness. These constructed ties (Rubinstein et al., 1991) in some cases are adequate substitutes for biological ties.

Mrs. Gordon, who was widowed at age 80 after a 20-year late-life marriage, has constructed ties with one stepson and his family. She had wisely invested her savings and now is comfortably well off financially. She is involved in both her church and Masonic activities, which keep her busy several days a week. Recently she sold her house and deliberately bought a condominium in a level area of the city to be assured she could walk to her church and neighboring shopping areas.

With her marriage, she had acquired two stepsons, only one of whom she considers her own son. She rejects the second stepson as a relative, because she concludes, "He is only after my money." Her "son" has two children and five grandchildren with whom she relates as a generous and understanding grandmother. She has paid college expenses for both her stepgrandchildren and is most explicit about her will. She plans to leave all of her estate to them.

In return, her acquired relatives are solicitous to her needs and are on call for emergencies, such as when Mrs. Gordon fell and needed to be taken to the hospital. Her daughter-in-law routinely drives in weekly from the suburbs to take her shopping. In contrast, Mrs. Gordon's only surviving biological relative, a nephew, is no longer considered a member of her family, because he lives out of town and has never been attentive to her situation.

Anticipatory Socialization

Having anticipated their future needs, most childless have prepared for the time they would need help (Johnson & Catalano, 1981). This preparation benefits them as long as they can maintain a modicum of independence.

Mrs. Abbott was 90 when we first encountered her. She too had been married twice and in her late-life marriage, she acquired a stepson, who remained only a stepson. She has taken an independent stance in anticipating future dependency, in comparison to Mrs. Gordon, who carefully constructed a new family to see to her future needs. Mrs. Abbott is adamant about her independence. Her stepson and his family reside in a nearby city, but she insists upon remaining "friendly at a distance" with them. In their intermittent telephone contacts, she assures them that they do not have to worry about her. The only relative with whom she maintains regular contact is an eccentric niece who lives nearby with her three dogs and eight cats. Mrs. Abbott grudgingly pays her niece's rent, but complains of the sacrifices she must make to do so. She dismissed the fact she never had children by commenting, "My family is not prolific."

She is a witty, talkative woman whose good spirits persisted over time. "All my days are good. I am always happy, because I make myself happy. I've always been an optimist, and I have nothing to worry about any more." At our first contact, her only health problems were "just old age itself." With no impairment on the activities of daily living, she maintained an active schedule in her church and in her apartment building. Although she had given up a leadership role in a senior group at a nearby university, she still went to the symphony and visits frequently with friends. "I've got church friends, bridge friends, and just friends." While her best friend had recently passed away, she decided after some thought that her new best friend was the secretary at her church. She was proud of her advanced old age and her wrinkled face, "I have worked hard for every one of these wrinkles."

By the third contact when she was 93, her cheeriness and good health continued, yet she was anticipating the future. Her once tastefully cluttered apartment was now stripped bare of all but the basic necessities. For example, an expensive dining table had been replaced by a card table.

> *I am selling out and going back to Texas. They are closing down my army hospital here, so I'm going to move to a retirement community near an army hospital in Texas. I am getting old and will need care. It's time for me to move to senior housing, and it's cheaper in Texas than here.*

She expressed no regrets about leaving her friends and belongings behind.

There are numerous other strategies these very old childless individuals use to find less tangible substitutes for children. Pets in some cases can be as significant in their lives as family members. One 94-year-old woman with no surviving family members had two interests in life: her dwindling real estate business and her two dogs and one cat. Another childless woman with many nieces and nephews throughout the country distributed her tea cup collection to each of them. "The cups have gone everywhere. I get letters of thanks from relatives from all over—Chicago, New York, Denver. Parts of me are scattered all over."

Being All Alone

Some childless oldest old are all alone. In fact, most of those 24 percent who no longer maintain family relationships are childless (Johnson & Troll, 1992). The deaths of siblings in at least three cases led to serious problems for the childless, because their sibling's children in these cases did not respond to their needs. Some respondents, usually the never-marrieds like Miss Marsh, had moved to the Bay Area to join a sister and her family. She had taught school until retirement 30 years previously. The real change in her life, however, came with her sister's death five years earlier, when she moved from her sister's home to share an apartment with an acquaintance. This arrangement ended when Miss Marsh's disability increased. Her roommate wanted to travel but was hesitant about leaving her alone because of her frequent falls. After a short and unhappy stay at a board and care home, Miss Marsh fell again and was hospitalized after which she entered an institution. Shortly before her death, she described to us, "I feel all alone now—I'm cast adrift."

Interestingly enough, those childless with serious problems are not necessarily more distressed than others with children. Some who complain of loneliness remark:

"Everyone is gone. I'm all alone, but it's up to me to make the most of it. I don't let it get me down though. I brush my fears aside."

"I am a firm believer in prayer. I can sit down to pray and in the process I solve any problem."

"Thank God I have lots of strength. I can deal with being alone."

Only a few childless are demoralized because of being alone. Mrs. Fry is one of those who lives out her life in a constant state of anxiety and depression. At each interview, she said, "It is a bad day—it would be even worse if I didn't take Valium." She complained about her health, her light-headedness, and her fluttering heart. While her sisters are still alive and within a few hours drive, she only sees them every three or four months. Her niece, who lives one hour away, handles her affairs. She checks in daily by telephone. Apparently she chides her aunt about her dependency and complaints.

Mrs. Fry's sense of isolation became intensified after the death of her "adopted brother" three years previously. At each contact, she dwelt upon her grief and recalled the stress of his sudden heart attack and death. Evidently a platonic relationship, he was her square dancing partner and travelling companion to dancing meets. She claims she made no friends at these dances. "We'd just get to talking to others and then the next dance would start, so we never got to know each other." Unlike those who intentionally cultivate new friends, Mrs. Fry is fearful of new situations where she could meet people. Over time her physical status remained stable, but her pervasive psychological distress increased.

A Multi-functional Family

In marked contrast to the childless, who often have attenuated or no linkages to family life, as many as one quarter of the sample are embedded in an active family life. These oldest old maintain close relationships in a large network of family members.

Mrs. Rawlings is part of a complex interdependent family system that meets her needs, as long as she herself is adaptable to her children's ever-changing situations. She was 86 at the outset of the study—a widow with four children. She was residing in the home of her son for 30 years. He was 65 years old, a Korean War veteran whose war injuries left him bound to a wheel chair. With all the assistive devices and his specially designed home, he was relatively independent and at Time 1 was actually functioning as his mother's caregiver. She was in constant pain with arthritis and walked with a cane. A daughter and another son lived nearby and both were very attentive to her needs. A second daughter lived in New York, but she called weekly and visited twice a year.

Mrs. Rawlings always conveyed a strong sense of contentment and cheerfulness. Her main worry was her son's physical condition and his progressive paralysis. She praised him for his devotion to her needs, in spite of his own disability.

> I'd starve without him. He shops, cooks and takes me out to dinner with his friends. My other children also help and give me things all the time. My daughter takes me to the beauty parlor every Saturday. My other son often takes me to visit my sister, who is dying. When I go, I see my brother there and all my nieces. I have my son to live with, so I don't have to go to a nursing home. We are a very close family. We help one another. I have everything here to make me happy.

By the third interview, her son's condition had worsened, but he was still her primary supporter. The relationship had become more reciprocal, as she was assisting him. "It takes him two hours to get dressed. I try to encourage him. He gets upset, so I go sit with him, and we talk." Her other son and her daughter continued to help both of them. Thus her family life remained much the same, only affected by the undercurrent of worry about her son's increased paralysis.

> I am needed here to help him dress in the morning. When he took a vacation, I stayed here alone. I can manage independently. My children called me every day. They all love me, and both my daughters and daughter-in-law say they have a room ready for me at their house. I appreciate that, but I want to stay here. My home is most important to me. I love to do little things around here. I love to work in the garden, and I love my family around me.

She did comment that only one grandchild visits her independently of his parents' visits. "My other grandchildren are not family oriented—that's funny because everyone else is so close."

By the fourth interview, over four years from the beginning of the study, dramatic changes in Mrs. Rawlings' situation had occurred. She had moved into her daughter's home and was adjusting to great upheaval created by her daughter's five dogs and a cat as well as three teenage grandchildren. This move was instigated by a deterioration in her son's condition as the result of a lung infection. Throughout his long hospitalization, she managed at home on her own, but upon his return home with 24-hour care, she was displaced from her custodial role over the house by his nurse. She worried that this woman was after her son's home and his generous government benefits. She was very distressed by this turn of events, but still looked forward to returning to her former living situation. "My son may own the house, but it's been my home for 33 years. His illness shouldn't have changed that, but he's not the same person he used to be. He is so different now, so we can't talk about it."

Always an effective adapter, nonetheless, Mrs. Rawlings reciprocated with her daughter, doing the laundry and dishes. She was most tactful with her grandchildren, never interfering with them. To block out their loud rock and roll music "I close my bedroom door and turn on my radio. We get along fine—I don't meddle. But I'll be very happy to get back to my home some time. I want to see my porcelain collection. I have over 60 pieces."

By the fifth interview approximately six years after the first, Mrs. Rawlings was still with her daughter, probably permanently. Having moved her belongings from her son's home, she was surrounded by her porcelain collection and her bedroom furniture. Since her son had by then married his nurse, she was resigned to her new situation and decided to make the best of it. By staying in touch with her son's cleaning woman, she said, "I get all the dirt. My new daughter-in-law tells her she likes me, so I guess we've accepted each other. I feel I had to, because my son needs someone to take care of him. As to my feelings, I just read a book and forget about losing my home."

Conclusion

Our investigation of the families of the oldest old unquestionably finds some discrepancies with the findings of most researchers on the late-life family. Certainly Shanas' optimistic view that virtually everyone has someone to care for them is not borne out by our findings that 24 percent no longer maintain ongoing family relations. The strong emphasis on intergenerational relationships in the literature is consistent with our findings on the importance of children to the oldest old. Such an emphasis, however, overlooks the large proportion in the cohort of the oldest old, who have no children. We also question the prevalence of the family as a caregiving unit, a topic so frequently studied today. This emphasis oversimplifies the nature of the late-life family and unfortunately obscures the fact that only 25 percent of the older population nationally have a child as a caregiver.

The family as a multifunctional unit with numerous members involved in the life of a very old individual is found among a quarter of the oldest old. More commonly, the family is important in its potential, where members shift their attention to the oldest members in times of need. Other families are sources of emotional benefits rather than units providing sociability and support. Finally the attenuated family is particularly common among the childless, so they must construct relationships if they are to have some family-like bonds.

In this analysis of the late-life family, we also examined family structure to determine whether the prolongation of life has resulted in a vertical family form because added generations are alive concurrently. Defining a vertical structure as having four generations, not the three-generation family common until now, we found that the proportions of families that have four generations never reaches 50 percent, even among those in their 90s. In fact, the number of childless is so large among the oldest old that in the aggregate, they offset the number of added generations. The family structures of the oldest old is bimodal with a large proportion with at least three generations, on one hand, and the truncated families of the childless, on the other.

To examine how the family functions, we have singled out the dyadic family relationship as a unit of analysis and then examined how sociability and support are extended to the oldest members. Since relationships in the contemporary white family are often latent but activated in times of need, then those dyadic relationship that are most likely to respond to the needs of older people should be identified. Since few oldest old are married, and other family members remain uninvolved except as a source of sentiments and rare exchanges of letters and visits, children are the most significant relationship. Thus, norms of responsibility are evident mostly in the relationship between parent and child.

In an examination of the proposition that family conflict may diminish with advanced old age, we find some evidence that it does. The few who are married report good relationships. Children as the linchpins of family support are also sources of emotional support to the oldest old. In fact, we suggest that the tension and conflict of the parent–adult-child relationship encountered earlier in old age may dissipate in late life. Most of the constraints have lessened such as the child's competing commitments, and the parents have fewer surviving friends who serve emotional functions, than found at younger ages. Grandchildren and great grandchildren are far less important practically in the lives of the oldest old, although strong sentiments are quite common.

The childless are particularly vulnerable, because they are without the support an offspring traditionally provides, yet many are enterprising in constructing substitute relationships. In the next chapter, we will analyze other network relationships that range from friendships, to pieced-together networks that also serve the needs of the oldest old.

Chapter 6

Social Networks: A Continuum from Sociability to Isolation

Early in the respondents' first discussions about their social networks, seemingly contradictory findings emerged. Most complained, "My friends were so old, they all died off. I'm the last one alive." "I don't know anyone my age. I've outlived everybody." They also complained about the few surviving friends who were too forgetful or demented to socialize. Some complained about the loss of their contemporaries as one of the great disadvantages about living so long. Most would agree with a comment by James Madison following the death of Thomas Jefferson, "Having outlived so many of my contemporaries, I ought not to forget that I may be thought to have outlived myself" (Quinn, 1995). Even with the insistence that they had no surviving friends, a large majority still reported having at least weekly contact with someone they identified as a friend. With this inconsistency in mind, we designed the second interview protocol with an extensive section about their friendships, the results of which have been published elsewhere (Johnson & Troll, 1994).

This chapter will review these findings and further explore the various nonfamilial relationships of the oldest old—those with friends, acquaintances, neighbors, contacts at community associations, and paid helpers. Great variations were observed in their social lives. As the following will demonstrate, some institutions in the urban community provide mechanisms to potentially keep older people in contact with others. The important question concerns the nature of social relationships beyond the family in late life and the benefits they bestow upon the oldest old. In this chapter, we will review the aggregate findings about friendships that serve the social needs of many oldest old and then describe a continuum of relationships from intimate to distant ones.

What We Know about Late-Life Friendships

Even though the average person defines friendship by subjective factors, someone they like, trust, and have the capacity to confide in, researchers usually collect information on objective factors such as frequency of contact and patterns of reciprocity (Adams & Blieszner, 1989; Lowenthal & Robinson, 1976). Among researchers and the general public, the term "friend" can be used to refer to a wide range of relationships from short-term, superficial ones to longstanding committed bonds (Matthews, 1986). Gender is also a predictor of friendships; older women not only report having more friends than men, but they also have more intimate relationships with them (Barer, 1994; Chown, 1981; Wright, 1989). With increasing age, individuals usually face a decline in the numbers of friends, and they are less likely to take the initiative in making new ones (Allan, 1989; Allan & Adams, 1989; Arling, 1976; Roberto, 1989).

Conceptually four features of friendship might affect these relationships among the oldest old. First, friends tend to be of similar age and status (DuBois, 1974; Matthews, 1986; Paine, 1974; Suttles, 1970), so as age peers, they also share the same potential physical problems. Thus, friends in late life have difficulty in maintaining frequent face-to-face contact with each other, a situation common to the people in our study. In fact, another study also found that the social networks of the oldest old tended to dissipate during the last stage of life (Bury & Holme, 1990).

Second, as a relationship with equals, more or less equitable exchanges are the norm (Allan & Adams, 1989; Gouldner, 1960;

Homans, 1958; Roberto, 1989). Given the difficulties in mobility in late life, the oldest old are often unable to reciprocate with friends. Therefore, unmet expectations commonly result (Walster, Walster, & Traupmann, 1978).

Third, friendships mostly bestow expressive benefits rather than practical assistance. In fact, friends are more important than children in improving morale (Blau, 1973), leading Wood and Robertson (1978) to conclude that when in need of someone to comfort you, one good friend is worth more than a dozen grand-children. Such emotional benefits may even be independent of the number of face-to-face interactions (Blieszner & Adams, 1992), a factor that is particularly salient for very old people who have difficulty getting around. Thus, friends may be a source of companionship and fun, in contrast to family relationships that usually entail responsibilities (Johnson, 1983b).

Fourth, friendships are voluntarily maintained on the basis of personal choices rather than institutional norms. There is some evidence that older people slough off unwanted relationships with an attitude of "good riddance" (Lowenthal & Robinson, 1976). Consequently if personal preferences change with increased interiority, we have found, a portion of those over age 85 willingly and selectively disengage from some relationships without negative effects on their morale (Johnson & Barer, 1993).

Patterns of Friendships in Late Late Life

The common refrain, "I am outliving all my friends" is accurate for 59 percent of the men and 42 percent of the women, who had lost a friend between our first and second interview. The frequencies in Table 6.1 indicate that, despite the high proportion who had lost a friend, over one half of the sample (53%) still had at least one close friend, and many more (78%) were in weekly contact with at least one individual they identify as a friend (Johnson & Troll, 1994). Moreover, over one half had formed new friendships in adult life or after age 65, while as many as 45 percent had also made new friends after age 85. New friendships were most often formed through contacts at community associations such as churches or senior centers. The only significant gender differences found were

TABLE 6.1
Friendship Patterns by Gender (by percentage)

	Men (n = 26)	Women (n = 85)	Total (n = 111)
Friendship involvement			
A close friend	38	57	53
Weekly contact	77	78	78
Satisfied with friends	54	43	45
Lost friend, past year	59	42	47
New Friend 65+	54	68	64
New Friend 85+	31	49	45
Source			
Neighborhood	31	65	57*
Associations	77	58	63*
Family	8	20	15
Work	31	10	15
Functions of friendships			
Confide in	—	15	12
Share a laugh	54	42	45
Household help	4	5	5
Transportation	8	14	13
Caregiver	—	4	3
Potential caregiver	8	—	3

*$p < .05$.

in the source of new friends; men were likely to meet them at associations and women in their neighborhood.

Even though large numbers report weekly contact with friends, friends are not usually sources of active support. Few receive instrumental help from friends on household tasks or money management. Transportation is the most common source of help from friends, but even then, only 13 percent mention that form of assistance. Only 3 percent have a friend who functions as a caregiver or even a potential caregiver. In expressive supports, friends are mentioned most often as those people with whom they share a laugh, suggesting that friends are those associated with having fun. Far fewer mention friends as confidantes or someone they turn to when they feel "down." Consequently, the findings are clear; the functions of friendships are mainly for recreational purposes rather than for practical assistance. Those with close friends are likely to be in better health and have more desire to socialize (Johnson & Troll, 1994). Those who make new friends also are healthier and more sociable, and they also are more likely to go to senior centers or some other community associations.

The predictors of friendship involvement change over the first, third, and fifth contacts (Tables 6.2 and 6.3). We found that at the first contact, gender and subjective well-being significantly accounted for the variance in friendship involvement. A mean of 31 months later, however, these variables were no longer significant, and most of the variance was explained by the level of dis-

TABLE 6.2

Major Study Variables, Means, Standard Deviations, and Range at Times 1, 3, and 5

	Time	M	SD	Range
Friendship activity	T1	2.81	1.31	1 = active/5 = inactive
	T3	2.89	1.39	
	T5	2.60	1.39	
Gender	T1	1.76	.43	1 = male/2 = female
	T3	1.75	.43	
	T5	1.78	.43	
Age	T1	88.70	3.13	85.00 to 96.00
	T3	91.23	3.19	87.00 to 99.00
	T5	92.9	2.60	
Education	T1	3.97	1.68	1 = 16 or more years/
	T3	3.92	1.71	7 = 7 or fewer years
	T5	3.92	1.72	
Perceived health	T1	2.13	.73	1 = excellent/4 = poor
	T3	2.25	.73	
	T5	2.32	.86	
Disability	T1	17.08	4.07	14.00 to 33.00 /
	T3	20.13	5.95	14.00 = no disability
	T5	22.25	6.78	
Affect balance	T1	16.60	4.32	8 items, 4-point scale
	T3	16.18	4.78	1 = positive, 4 = negative affect
	T5	15.2	4.5	

TABLE 6.3
Predictors of Friendship Activity over Time

Independent Variables	Time 1		Time 3		Time 5	
	b	Beta	b	Beta	b	Beta
Age	−.00	−.00	.04	.09	−.15	−.31*
Gender	−.64	−.22*	−.59	−.19	−.08	−.03
Education	.10	.14	.15	.20	.30	.41*
Perceived health	.04	.02	.08	.04	.55	.32
Disability (ADL/IADL)	.05	.15	.12	.44*	−.00	.23
Affect balance	.15	.50***	.05	.16	−.00	−.00
Standard error	1.11		1.18		1.19	
R^2	.34***		.33***		.29	

*$p < .05$; ***$p < .001$.

ability (Johnson & Troll, 1994). By Time 5, only age and education were significant.

It is possible that the survivors at Time 5 were more sociable at the outset than those lost to the research, so they were less affected by the typical constraints to late life friendship. In contrast, most of those who experienced losses of friends had already been too disabled to sustain friendships. They themselves had either become too disabled or had died by Time 5. In fact, an analysis of attrition found that a significant difference between survivors and those lost to the study was the decline in friendship involvement (see Table 2.2). Thus, the remaining survivors after six years were not only more sociable, but also they were more physically able to sustain friendships.

The Nature of Friendship in Late Life

Constraints to Late-Life Friendships

The high level of contacts with friends in late life takes place despite impressive barriers. Physical disability is the most prominent constraint; some are in too much pain, they may have limited mobility, or they are too fatigued to socialize. Others would like to see friends but cannot find transportation to visit them, or they cannot manage the stairs at a friend's house.

"My friend has no banister, so I can't go up her outdoor stairs with my cane, and she can't handle my stairs with her walker."

"My best friend's husband had a stroke, so he can't drive her over for a visit."

"My best friend moved away. We wrote until my hand got bad." Hearing problems also interfere with interactions; some do not attend events with more than a few people, because their hearing aids do not work well in groups. Since friends are usually of similar age, they too encounter the same difficulties. As we noted in Chapter 3, men in advanced old age have a particularly difficult time maintaining friendships with the loss of their wife. By their 80s, any friendships with fellow workers had long ago dissipated. If their wives had planned and initiated their social life, they felt particularly lost upon their death. One man spoke in detail of his loneliness, "Since my wife died, I'm all alone. I miss her so much that sometimes it makes me cry. Even when I moved to senior housing, I made no friends. I don't have the personal touch I had with her around."

Even when friends can meet, many very old people find it difficult to maintain a more or less equitable pattern of reciprocity. Since friendships are usually based upon equitable exchanges, they commonly cease functioning when individuals can no longer reciprocate. Most no longer entertain in their home or even have a neighbor in for a cup of coffee. Even those living in senior housing rarely visit each other's rooms, instead socializing in common rooms. Various reasons were discussed by respondents. Some residents do not keep their quarters clean enough to invite others to visit, they view their home as a retreat from all the socializing downstairs, or they do not want to be in the position of having to return the hospitality.

Relocation can also disturb long-term friendships. Some of those who moved to another community to be near their children, concluded that, at their age, it was not worth the trouble to seek new friends. Even in age-segregated communities, friendships are not automatic; the formation of new relationships requires the same social skills as needed outside such a facility.

Culturally heterogeneous settings do not encourage the formation of new friendships. For example, urban communities have changed with new immigrant groups coming into neighborhoods where some respondents have lived most of their lives. Already hard-to-maintain relationships become even more difficult with those of a different background. Publically supported age-segregated communities also can have a multicultural population. Some respondents are elitists (Matthews, 1986); they are unwilling to make concessions in the process of replacing lost friends. They do not want to make friends with those of differing socioeconomic status and cultural background, or those whose values and interests they view as incompatible with their own. For example, one childless widow was forced to move into subsidized senior housing after an economic setback. She avoided her fellow residents with disdain. "They are not my kind. None of them have a serious thought in their head. There's not one person in this building I could be a friend to."

Deaths of Friends. The deaths of contemporaries is such a common experience in the lives of the oldest old that their responses are often muted. When discussing her mood, one survivor said, "Really I have no complaints except that I am a survivor. All my friends are dying and I'm still living." Another commented, "I don't have any friends any more. As a survivor, it's rough watching them die. The worst thing is not knowing what happened to my friends back East—I haven't heard from them for so long." Nevertheless, there is a hint of resignation and detachment in their comments:

"I take it as it comes, no one lives forever."

"I don't like to see them suffer—it's just part of life."

"That's the way if is—it's not unusual at my age."

Sadness is a common reaction to the loss of friends, but even among the down-hearted, these losses are viewed as a natural part of late life. Some maintain that it is not worth making new friends and then having to experience the loss again. "It is time to learn to live by myself—I'm the last one of my group." Such losses of contemporaries are the most vivid reminders of their own finitude. "I feel left alone and more conscious of how old I am."

In some cases, friends' children make an effort to continue the relationship. They may invite the survivors to family parties. In other cases, a man who has lost his wife seeks out her friends for companionship. One terminally ill woman saw to her husband's future. As he explained, "My wife was ill for many years. After she died, one of her friends rescued me. My life would be very different now without her. She is the friend my wife picked out for me."

These factors in combination explain why most respondents complained of a thinning of their networks with the death or relocation of age peers. "It's hard to say who my friends are. It's hit-and-miss. My social life is slim pickings. I was friendly with a woman at church until my back got bad, and I couldn't go any more." Others conclude it is impossible to make friends in late life, so they never try to replace those who are lost. One woman reflected another attitude, "I don't want to get attached to people here in the building. I had a good friend and then she died. I don't want to feel bad about a death again."

Consequently, as networks decline in size, social life can continue only if individuals change their criteria for forming friendships. Some actually plan ahead. Assuming that they will live a long time, they form friendships with younger individuals. One resourceful never-married women commented, "Because my parents lived so long, I always knew I'd outlive everyone. Years ago I decided to cultivate younger friends, so I wouldn't be so alone." Most evidence suggests that friendships have a fragile sense of impermanence in advanced old age. One respondent traced for us her recent anniversary parties. "At our 50th anniversary, our children gave us a big party at the country club for 100 people. At our 60th anniversary, there was a luncheon here at the building's social hall for 24 people. At our 65th, our children took us out to dinner—there were 10 of us."

Facilitators to Late-Life Friendships

In our previous article (Johnson & Troll, 1994), we pointed out that friendships thrive in culturally homogeneous settings where equal status entails similarities not only in age, but also in socioeconomic status and ethnicity. For example, Mrs. Fitzgerald and Mrs. O'Hara had lived next to each other for over 50 years. They attended the same church where Mrs. Fitzgerald's son was a priest, and they participated in a neighborhood monthly prayer group. They volunteered at a meal program in the Tenderloin district for the homeless, and they were the only survivors of the "merry sherries," a group of friends who for years had met in late afternoon every Monday to share a glass of sherry. Upon the death of such a friend, the grief can be devastating.

Despite these obstacles, the sociable individuals in our study continue life-long patterns, because they possess the motivation and skills to make new friends that replace those they have lost. The ability to reciprocate with a friend is also a catalyst for continuity in social relationships. For example, one busy widow is active in her church and a senior center, and she is a member of three bridge clubs. Only after almost everyone died or became incapacitated and she herself had increasing difficulty getting around, did these activities cease.

Redefining Friendships. Those who want to continue socializing with friends tend to make some concessions. First, instead of face-to-face contact, they become satisfied with writing letters and making phone calls. Phone calls are particularly important in the lives of the very old. Commonly, a specific time of the day is set aside for telephone conversations with friends. One woman talks to one close friend every morning at eight and a second at nine. No plans are made for the day until these calls take place.

Second, if not satisfied with that form of contact, others realize that, if they are to have friends, they must change their criteria that define friendship. Where such a process takes place, a range of relationships of varying degrees of intimacy replace their lost friends. These include casual friends or acquaintances, club friends or church friends, and even paid helpers. The following examples indicate how there is a blurring of the criteria for friendship, once one goes beyond the qualities of a close friend. If they define friendship expansively and all-inclusively, they are rarely without friends.

Along this continuum of relationships, *close friends* are usually described as relationships where each is familiar with and interested in the other's life. Good communication is the most frequently mentioned criterion of a close friend. "She is someone who listens, one I can tell things to that I would tell no one else." Such communication persists, because strong sentiments prevail. Close friends are often identified as old friends who share memories of the past. "If you have known someone for a long time and have gone through so much together, that makes a good friend. That's why when you get older, you never quite make a new good friend." Some respondents consider themselves good friends with others, because they are accommodating. As one woman commented, "I have a best friend—I met her five years ago. I'm a good pal—I help her shop and I go with her when she visits her retarded son."

In contrast, *casual friends* are acquaintances, those whom one knows superficially. Usually they are available by the mere fact that they live nearby and can be easily contacted. Some are fellow members at their senior center or church, while others are neighbors one greets on the street, "My neighbor is nice—I guess I could call her a friend." Respondents describe these relationships as having shallow communication, because casual friends are usually unfamiliar with one's background and previous life.

Third, *club friends* are also casual friends, but they are identified by the setting in which the relationships were formed. With great specificity, some distinguish the source of the friendship—"bridge friends" or "church friends." Generally they are not seen outside the social context that brings them together. One conclusion commonly heard, "If you go to senior centers or bridge clubs, you always have friends. I make new friends every week." Another respondent was in the early stages of Alzheimer's Disease, yet she continued to go to senior centers and considered everyone there as her friend. The sociable individuals participate in the many planned activities in senior housing and usually report, "I have a bunch of friends," or "It's a cinch to make friends." In contrast, others remain in their rooms except at meal times. When asked if they had new friends in an age-segregated facility, they gave qualified responses, "If you call people I see each day friends, then I guess I have friends."

Fourth, *neighbors* are usually distinguished from close or casual friends. In some cases, it would be difficult to remain in their home, if a neighbor was not available to fill the interstices between family and formal supports. A neighbor might stop by on her way to buy groceries and bring back a needed item. They might mow the lawn or bring in the newspaper. Neighbors are also particularly helpful in time of emergencies, calling the children, the doctor, or just staying with an individual until other help arrives. While some neighbors are also counted as friends, in other cases, a neighbor holds a unique status as a stop-gap part of the support system.

Fifth, *helpers* at times become friends, particularly to the housebound or bedfast respondents or those who have few remaining relationships in their informal network (Barer, 1992). "Oh yes, I have a friend. I can't remember her name, but she is the one who brings me my meals." Another woman was isolated and lonely at our first and second contact, but by the third time, she had been linked to a volunteer network. Her mood had significantly improved with the additions of these new "friends." Another woman described her network as consisting of three friends—the one who brings her meals, the nun who comes to give her communion, and the woman who comes to set her hair.

Range of Sociability

To have friends and to be satisfied with the relationship rests upon how one defines friends and the expectations one has for them. Those oldest old who retain high expectations for a "give-and-take" of a reciprocal relationship are bound to be disappointed when one of them can no longer reciprocate. Those who come to terms with situations where constraints supersede facilitators to friendships can adapt by revising their expectations and accepting altered social networks. Thus, determinants of friendships rest upon choices of individuals, who develop and maintain relationships according to their preferences, needs, and life-long patterns of sociability.

Patchwork Networks

Enterprising individuals with scant family resources can devise a network consisting of casual friends, club friends, and helpers. These pieced-together networks comprise an important support system for the very old, particularly those who have few family resources.

Mrs. Steinmetz, a widowed, childless World War II refugee, had few surviving relatives. Nevertheless, she had an assortment of individuals who functioned as friends and helpers. Each morning she met three other women for breakfast at a diner across the street from her apartment. All were foreign born—Mrs. Steinmetz from Germany, one from China, and one from Peru.

> *I met them there and we just got to talking, so we decided to meet regularly.*
> *The talking helps me a lot. Then I have a woman who owns the dry clean-*
> *ing store next to the diner. She helps me. Another woman comes every week*
> *to see what I need. She promised me she would take care of me, so I don't*
> *have to go into a home. Then I also go to temple. Some friends pick*
> *me up.*

A 90-year-old woman, Mrs. Creighton, had two children but was estranged from her daughter and her grandchildren, while her son rarely visited her. As a final affront, when she had a mastectomy at age 85, her male companion left her. Nevertheless, she was most enterprising in concocting a new and supportive network.

> *I have Amy, who I met on the street while she was walking her baby;*
> *Elizabeth, who owns the dress shop where I buy my clothes; Flora, who is*
> *Elizabeth's customer, who I met while shopping there; Patrick, who fixed my*
> *phone and sometimes shops for me; and all the people in my cancer support*
> *group—they are now my family. When I'm not feeling well, I also have a*
> *neighbor who shops for me.*

As her cancer spread and her needs for support rose, members of a volunteer association also joined her new friendship circle.

> *Sally comes to read my mail and pay my bills, Jane takes me shopping, and*
> *Karen cleans my house. Nurses who give me chemotherapy treated me to a*
> *birthday celebration with flowers and cards. I am so happy with all my*
> *friends, I don't want to die and leave them. I am so neglected by my family*
> *and here these strangers come into my life and love and care for me. I am*
> *mother to them all.*

Mrs. Wallace, a 90-year-old former waitress, lives on the fringes of Nob Hill, a neighborhood where she worked for years. She had been married three times, divorced twice, and most recently widowed. She was independent until a stroke created problems in mobility.

"Since that happened, I'm worthless—I have fallen 15 to 20 times." As she became more impaired, she had a diverse support group.

> *Joyce, my late husband's cousin, treats me real nice. She comes from the East*
> *Bay to get me for holidays. Otherwise, she only comes when I need her. When*
> *I had my stroke, she came every day for 11 days. Her son is a banker here in*
> *the city. He takes me out to lunch a couple times a month. I see my husband's*
> *nephew once in while. One lady friend lives down the street. She calls every*
> *day at nine and gives me a bath once a week, and does my shopping and*
> *laundry. The manager of the building and his wife look out for me. My neigh-*
> *bor, a cab driver, knocks on my door every evening as he comes home from*

work to see if I need anything. I go to a day-care center. The storyteller there is my best friend along with my hairdresser—I've been going to Lucy for 25 years.

Friendships in Age-Segregated Housing

In other cases, physical changes and problems with mobility are bothersome impediments to the socially inclined, but age-segregated housing usually has mechanisms that prevent feelings of desolation.

Mrs. Evans along with her husband had already adjusted to an expensive high-rise building at the beginning of the research. She took the lead in encouraging the move once her osteoporosis became more crippling and her vision deteriorated. With a back brace not evident under her clothes, her attractive and youthful appearance belied these problems. Although her husband was less enthusiastic about leaving their home, she had no regrets.

Life in a retirement home with 300 people is never dull. I'm a groupee and do we have groups here! It's so easy to get acquainted and to find those with similar interests. We moved in so we wouldn't have to be dependent upon our children, and we feel so secure for that. And we have all the benefits of being around so many people.

With each contact, her spine was degenerating and her eyesight worsened to the point she was legally blind, but her social activities did not change. She continued to take the lead in organizing interest groups, exercising on the building's long hallways, and making new friends. She did report,

I have become more hesitant about seeking out those who are 8 to 10 years younger. I can see they think we are too old. We socialize too much anyway. We decided to limit getting together with friends to two nights a week. We are still booked up for dinners with the people here. And the administrator counts on me to do things, so I can't let him down. With my poor eyesight though, I can hardly do anything else but be involved with the activities here. I can still get around, thank goodness. With everything taken care of, I even have someone who comes every morning to help me put on my stockings.

Friend of Many

A few respondents have large networks of friends, because they are conscientious about maintaining contact. Such individuals also maintain patterns of reciprocity similar to younger people. They still entertain and socialize. Understandably, they are competent in retaining a social life when many their age have detached themselves from the responsibilities friendships bear.

> At age 85, Mrs. Bryce could look back on a distinguished volunteer career as a leader in many community associations. Throughout the study, she devoted her energies to peace groups, and she proudly attached a dove on a spring that bobbled from the top knot of her upswept hair. Widowed for 14 years, she retained a large house with an extra apartment, and she had been renting out rooms to students for many years. She also opened her home to numerous groups and entertained a constant flow of house guests. Her living room was filled with pictures and cards from the many former students who had lived there. She swam in the chilly bay weekly and went out to dinner frequently with her male companion. She also had friends of many years standing and enjoyed reminiscing about such experiences with one of them, also in the study, about hitchhiking to Big Sur while they were in college.
>
> Her son lived back East, and she had a distant, conflictual relationship with her daughter, so she described her friends as her family, "My extended family consists of those who used to live here. They go on and get married and have children. Some of their children are now getting married and having children. We always keep in touch—I send 300 Christmas cards a year, and sometimes that is not enough." In the end, when she was terminally ill with cancer, a few of her former renters moved back in and alternated in taking care of her.

The Impact of Relocation

Whether relocating to low-income housing or to an expensive retirement community, some form of a social network must be recreated. Some feel cut off from the outside world. There were complaints about former friends not visiting them, even those who lived a few miles away. Even more formidable is finding one's own niche in the informal structure of the facility that already is rife with cliques, exclusive seating arrangements at meals, and prejudices against those who are different. Then too, the formal structure aims at establishing a sociable environment that forces sociability upon sometimes resistant residents. One respondent complained, for example, about her first assigned table at a retirement home, "One woman at my table is paralyzed and can't speak or understand what others are saying, another is deaf, and a third is too forgetful to talk to."

Mrs. Hauge was 86 at our first contact. She lived independently, absorbed in activities at the nearby YWCA and at the Norwegian Club a short bus ride away. As she described her days,

> I practically live at the Y. I go there three times a week, play bridge, do the exercises, and see many friends. On Tuesdays, after the Y, I go out with my friend. She is like me—always wants to be on the go. On Wednesday, I have another friend who still drives. She picks me up and we so out shopping and for lunch. On Thursday, it is Golden Age Day at the Norwegian Club. The Noriega 17 bus goes by my house and then straight there. On Friday afternoon there is bingo at the center. There is a man there who is interested in me and wants to take me out, but I am too busy for that. On weekends, my younger son comes and I cook dinner. Then every few weeks I stay home and clean the house. I love people, I love to play bridge and bingo, and I love to sit with my friends for lunch. I go out so much. I do a lot of dancing at the Norwegian club. I love to be around people my age, particularly if they are Norwegian.

A year later, the pace of her activities was much the same, but she complained of increasing fatigue and the need for more sleep. She also put her name on the waiting list at a Norwegian retirement home in the suburbs near her oldest son. By the next contact, she was recuperating from two eye surgeries.

> This is a big turning point in my life. It's such a helpless feeling not being able to see. It's a slow process. I just sit in the chair watching TV. My sight is slowly coming back—that perks me up a little. It's lonesome when you get to be this age. There are just a few things to look forward to. I want to see to play bridge and to go out. I feel lonely unless I talk to my friends.

By the fourth interview, she had moved into the retirement community shortly after her ninetieth birthday party. Because of her fatigue, she had turned down a big party including her friends and settled for a family dinner. Even this very sociable woman had difficulty adjusting to her new situation.

> I accept the people here as they are. Some are very nice, others a little cooler. When I say "hi," I usually get a response. Then they turn away and ignore me. It was strange when I moved in. I knew a few people here, but they didn't even show me around. It seems that once you are here, you get in the habit of being alone—it's as if we are all strangers to each other. When I ask people at the table to repeat what they said, they just tell me to get a hearing aid. But I'm thankful to get a nice meal. At least I'm keeping my body going. I'm all by myself here. I didn't feel that way when I lived by myself in the city. The mornings go pretty fast if I go to the exercise class, but the afternoons are pretty dull. They are losing money here, so they've cut out the afternoon programs. I guess I'm too tired to do much anyway. It's too hard to be friendly, because people don't remember what you say. I am too limited to do what I used to do, so I just follow the crowd.

The Exploited

Mrs. Grady had lost her son and husband a few years previously. Her main asset was a house that, with inflated property values in the city, was worth $500,000. Over the course of six years, her arthritis worsened and she could no longer go to church or visit her friends.

"Friends all died some years ago. Sometimes I go a whole week without seeing anyone. A lady from church called me a lot, until her throat cancer got bad. My niece lives in Fremont. She has to make a toll call, so she can't call every day." Over that period, Mrs. Grady had intermittent bone fractures and a stroke, all of which required hospitalizations and temporary stays in convalescent homes. While incapacitated, the everchanging personnel in her network did not always look out for her best interests.

To review the events over six years, a niece who originally helped withdrew assistance when her marriage failed and a divorce was pending. A neighbor helped her until they had a dispute about the neighbor's dog. After breaking her ankle, however, Mrs. Grady said, "I mended fences with my neighbor. It's not worth breaking off a relationship. She comes in to talk to me now." She seemed to have solved her support problems when she took in a young woman who assisted her in housework and drove her on errands in exchange for a rent-free apartment. "She is kind of sweet and has a good sense of humor. We laugh a lot." Unfortunately, by the next interview, that woman was no longer there.

I used to talk to her. Now I feel bad that it didn't work out. She just stopped helping me, so I had to ask her to leave. She wasn't paying rent. My brother's daughter doesn't seem to care about me, even though I raised her for five years. She put my brother in a nursing home and ignored him. She would do the same to me.

The final insult from her family occurred after she had a stroke and was in the hospital and a convalescent hospital for a time. Her niece and her new husband assumed she would die, so they moved into her house and stripped it of most of her possessions. "When my neighbor told me what they were doing, I went to a social worker who found me help so I could go home. They wanted me to die—that upset me. I thought they were my friends, because they were nice to me. I don't trust them any more."

The Disappointed

Mrs. Tracy is an example of one who was unable to adjust to losses of friends when her physical incapacity prevented her from making new friends.

She was an affluent widow who remained in her home where she has lived for 55 years. She had many friends in the neighborhood and throughout the city. She grew up in a large prosperous family and still has many surviving cousins as well as two sons in the area. While active with her family, her main rewards come from her friendship circle. At the first contact, she complained about her poor eyesight that prevented her driving. Nevertheless, she had many friends who drove her to her numerous social engagements. "I'm very sociable and see friends every day. I go out a lot—play bridge maybe three times a week. I go wherever I'm invited. My motto is, 'Be interested in things and don't think about yourself all the time.'"

Just over a year later, she complained of some health problems. "My doctor tells me I look young, I act young, and I have all my marbles, but my body is wearing out." Yet she continued to be active with friends. "Fortunately I always have had younger friends. Most of my close friends my age are gone. Neighbors pop in—there's always someone around. I've never had trouble making friends. And I've always been a happy person." When she had her 95th birthday party, 100 family members and friends attended. In an interview shortly after that, however, she was discontented. "I feel miserable most of the time. I can't drive, I have leg cramps, heart fibrillation, and a lot of indigestion. I still go out once a week to play bridge, but my other two bridge clubs folded, because most of the members either died or became mentally off."

At the fourth contact, she reported hospitalizations for pneumonia and a slight stroke. She was noticeably less active because of transportation problems and her friends' declining health. "It's so boring. So many friends are sick, and those who still drive don't want to get in the habit of always having to pick someone up. I'd like to see more friends, but they are either sick or they don't drive." By the fifth contact, she seemed depressed,

My life has changed a lot, and I can't do anything about it. My friend, who drove me places, moved away. Now there is no one who can help me get about. I still play bridge but only once a month. Our group gets smaller and smaller. It is so sad to lose friends—one after another. In the past six months, I've lost three friends—people I've grown up with. I try to convince myself I can still do things. I used to be so active and now I have to stay home.

Her feeling of isolation increased, even though she saw family members frequently. In fact, this cheerful vibrant woman at the first interview had become tearful and complaining after six years. Unlike others, who changed their social preferences as their physical limitations increased, Mrs. Tracy was fighting a losing battle, as physical and social factors interacted to reduce her much-desired social involvements.

Loners versus the Lonely

The loners form a special category. They are the ones who had never been active socializers, and they have little desire to make friends late in their lives. For example, one man described himself as a loner, "I've never had many friends. I don't need them. They'd just annoy me." Others explained why they had no friends, "I was never a joiner." Some reported it was a life-long preference.

"I don't like everybody—that's why I see so few."

"I don't want people hanging around."

"It's not good to be talkative with people. You lose your freedom and get tied down with their affairs."

Others are lonely, because they are the unfortunate victims of circumstances. Miss Baldwin, a retired teacher, recounted how she left a large family in the Midwest in order to join her sister in the Bay Area. After her sister died, she delayed returning to her home town until it was too late to re-establish ties with nieces and nephews. As her friends died or became disabled, she saw few people. "I didn't know how bad it would be to be so alone. I do have church friends, but I only have God to talk to." She reported that her best friend was her radio. "I have nobody. After the earthquake, I just picked up all the broken glass. No one called, and no one came to check on me."

Some consider themselves as loners, because they are without primary social relationships, yet they are around people for a large part of their days.

Mrs. Renaldo is a childless, divorced woman living in a downtown hotel. At 85 years of age, she was impoverished, in poor health, and devoid of family and friends. Throughout her long life, she experienced continual assaults upon her well-being. As a child, she lived in the same area before being dislocated by the 1906 earthquake. Her mother, a single parent, took her on a nomadic life, and a while still a young child, she was raped in a boarding house where they were staying. Limited education, unskilled jobs, and a short marriage continued to make her life difficult. Recent assaults upon her life include several bouts with cancer, being physically attacked in the dangerous area where she lived, and a final assault, being knocked down by a bus.

She reported that she had no friends. Despite seemingly devastating events, she found fulfillment in her days by "helping the less fortunate." For many years, she enjoyed her role as a volunteer at the senior center a block away from her residence.

I keep myself busy. I love to be around seniors—I do anything I can to help unfortunate people. I get my main meal free at the Center because I volunteer, and I bring the rest home for dinner. I don't need groceries so I don't need to carry things from the store. I like to go to the Center to see people and help them. We don't have much to say to each other, but I like to help.

At our third contact she was recovering from a mastectomy, remaining in her single room with home visits from the VNA and a home care worker. She lamented, "I can't volunteer yet. I'm not strong enough." At our fourth contact, we located her at a Catholic long-term care facility, some distance from the center of town. She was most discontented and missed her downtown neighborhood.

My whole life changed when I came here. Even when I feel so weak, I take the bus downtown. It takes me a whole hour to get there, because I have to transfer. I have to do it. Even though I'm in excruciating pain walking on the street, I miss the area where I volunteered for so many years.

When we saw her at our last interview she had become more reconciled to her new living situation, although she resisted interacting with the other residents. However, she was happy to have a new volunteer job.

On Tuesdays and Thursdays I volunteer here. I can only do jobs sitting down, so I peel apples in the kitchen. It's very hard when you get weaker. I feel so bad that I'm not strong enough to do other things. Volunteer work makes you feel good inside and eases up your pain.

The Abandoned

Very few respondents have been truly abandoned by family, friends, and formal supporters. Where it does happen, a combination of factors seem to interact at a fast pace. For example, a sudden loss of resources may occur in conjunction with an illness or declining cognitive abilities, and the social welfare bureaucracy is too cumbersome to identify someone who has lost a safety net.

Mrs. Filbert, who at 93 lived in a downtown hotel, had recovered from a stroke and could walk with a cane. "I'm in good shape—I'm not a goner yet." She had a chore worker who helped her go to the bank, shop, and do laundry. She reported that she had no viable family relationships, "I used to visit them every year, but they all died, so I had no one to stay with. Now I have a whole cemetery of family in Wisconsin." Because she wanted to be buried back there with them, she used her meager savings to make arrangements with funeral homes in both areas. Once the welfare office discovered that expense, they labeled it as an asset and removed her from supplemental income. With only one meal included in her rent, she was left with only $100 a month for other food and sundries, making her the neediest person in the study.

After suffering from a second stroke, she became very anxious about being evicted from her room. She avoided the manager, who might realize she could no longer come down for the daily meal and then transfer her to a nursing home. In the end, she became increasingly confused, and she looked malnourished. Because she had so little help, her white hair hung limply to her waist and her yellowed fingernails had grown to look like talons.

Conclusion

Since the family in late late life for some is not a regular source of solace and support, the wider social network assumes more significance. Turning first to friendships, this chapter addresses seemingly contradictory findings. Most respondents complain about having outlived their friends, yet over one half report the presence of a close friend and almost as many still make new friends. Friendships are important in the lives of the oldest old, we found, although that relationship changes its form in late life. As to the constraints on friendships, the deaths of friends result in a shrinking social network, just as the high level of disability makes socializing with friends difficult. Relocation, a common event in late life, often places respondents in culturally heterogeneous settings where differing values and interests hinder friendships from developing.

Nevertheless, just as they adapt to attenuated families, the oldest old are resourceful in finding substitutes. The sociable among them often develop new criteria for friendships that do not rest upon homogeneity or even face-to-face contact. Often those formerly viewed as acquaintances in late life become labeled as friends, when one's old friends are gone. Others reorder their priorities and decide that having an active social life is no longer as important as they had once thought. For practical purposes, people like Mrs. Steinmetz devise patchwork networks from various sources. Likewise, Mrs. Creighton, who was at odds with her own family, found friends who became helpers. They came from stores where she shopped, from a telephone repair man, and from volunteer groups.

While we have itemized the many complaints of those who move to age-segregated housing, some respondents thrive in such settings. Mrs. Evans, who calls herself a groupee, delights in having 300 people immediately accessible to her. Mrs. Hauge, in contrast, feels at a loss in such a setting even though she led a very sociable life before relocation. Mrs. Bryce still retains friendships with former roomers of such closeness that they became caregivers in her final illness. A few respondents with no children to look out for their interest are lonely and exploited by distant relatives. While some continually complain, like sociable Mrs. Tracy, who can no longer physically socialize outside her home, others have been life-long loners who, in late life, feel nothing is missing from their world. Only a very few like Mrs. Filbert have been truly abandoned having no safety net of formal or informal supporters. This chapter has demonstrated a range of social networks from those that include a host of friends and acquaintances to those networks that are sparse. Often these networks take forms compatible with the preferences of the respondents and consistent with their life-long patterns of sociability.

PART III

Processes of Adaptation

Chapter 7

Managing Daily Routines

Our model of adaptation makes a distinction between problem-focused, situation-specific coping strategies and a more generalized sense of control (Rodin, Timko, & Harris, 1985). The former is mostly applicable to dealing with the activities of daily living, while the latter explores the perceptions about one's capacities to deal with the typical challenges of late life. This chapter will describe the first response, the coping process observed in the performance of daily activities. Following Pearlin's stress model, we conceptualize coping as "the individuals' actions on their own behalf to avoid or lessen the impact of life problems" (Pearlin & Schooler, 1978). The coping responses to specific problems or situations have three functions: 1) to change the situation, 2) to manage the meaning of the situation, and 3) to keep the symptoms of distress within manageable bounds. Stress researchers are interested not only in the impact of life events such as widowhood and relocation, but also the effects of persistent strains, such as those stemming from the chronic illnesses common among older people. Finally, daily hassles are also a source of stress, those less dramatic irritations arising from the daily round of activities.

While very old people must deal with chronic strains, the major sources of stress from dislocating life events had usually occurred some years in the past. Even when they face potentially stressful situations in late life, withdrawal and detachment are the more common reactions at their age, rather than anxiety and agitation. The oldest old are by no means without problems, nonetheless. As discussed earlier, the major problems stem from the many ripple effects of their disabilities. Problems handling the activities of daily living tend to lead to the daily hassles, the minor problems that are far more accurate than life events in predicting psychological and somatic symptoms (Lazarus & Folkman, 1984).

As the following will illustrate, the oldest old are continually faced with daily hassles stemming from the most mundane matters. Who will change a light bulb for them, who will take them to the doctor, or who will help them shop for clothes when they can no longer read price tags? Even ordinary expenditures result in dilemmas unique to this age. For example, one 90-year-old discussed her broken vacuum cleaner and posed the question, should she buy a new vacuum cleaner when she might not be around very long to use it?

This chapter describes how the oldest old cope with the problems of daily life and, in most cases, remain in control of their lives. We begin by describing their daily regimen and the round of activities on typical days. Then we will describe the various coping processes used to confront the predictable daily strains and hassles encountered during a typical day. Most are able to develop a sense of control with the belief that they have the power to influence outcomes. In the process, they are able to keep stress within manageable bounds.

The Daily Round of Activities

The process of coping with the daily regimen includes four types of responses. First, respondents simplify their physical environment in order to make it more easily manageable. Second, they regulate their time and ritualize ordinary daily tasks so as to make them predictable, meaningful, and compatible with their level of functioning. Third, individuals reorder their priorities by changing their criteria of what makes a good day and then adjust the daily regimen to make it congruent with their functioning. Fourth, some project a new status and create a new role that compensates for their losses.

In studying how daily life is experienced in late life, we asked questions about the monotonous but necessary activities of daily life. "What do you do on a typical day? What are your sleep patterns? Do you eat three meals? Do you see someone every day? How does your health affect your daily routines and how you feel? What makes a good day and a bad day?" In reading their quite detailed responses, we find that ordinary daily activities are effectively managed through a wide variety of coping strategies.

Individuals in our study orchestrate their days around the scheduling of their meals, the times for taking medications, exercise, grooming, television, and for some, prayer. The typical day begins early, and most activities in personal hygiene and household maintenance happen in the morning. Going to a senior center is common for 41 percent, and they usually go for the noon meal and some socializing with others. By afternoon, the typical respondent seeks more passive activities; many take a daily nap. Few plan activities outside the home in the evenings. Fear of crime, transportation problems, and fatigue keep most respondents at home. The oldest among the respondents are likely to go to bed early, often after watching television. *Wheel of Fortune, Jeopardy,* and the early evening news are among their favorite shows. These programs challenge their alertness.

Establishing a Daily Regimen

With difficulties walking and with the aches and pains common in late life, incidental chores, however simple, become the focus of the day. One man summarized this pattern, "My days are filled with doing the most unimportant things. What used to take me three hours now takes me three days to do. It's all much ado about nothing." Understandably there are both active and passive approaches to handling the daily regimen. The days of one woman are dominated by activity, "I make things happen. I must have something to do. When I finish one thing, I start on another. I never sit idle—never!" Another woman living in senior housing stands in contrast in her passivity, "It's all I can do to go downstairs to eat lunch. Then I come up and brush my teeth, put my feet up, and that's my day."

Mrs. Murphy described a fairly typical day that began with matters of personal hygiene.

I'm a good half hour in the bathroom before I can start my day. Then I have breakfast and read the paper. By then, much of the morning is taken up, and then lunch takes me two hours to prepare and eat. Everything is scheduled. After lunch, I must take a nap or I'll fall asleep before dinner. In the evening, I eat dinner, watch the news, and then go to bed. There are no evenings for us old folks. We never go out at night.

Miss Grieg is a striking woman who stands erect and dresses elegantly every day, still looking like the successful banker she once was. When asked about her typical day, she described how she established time markers and a rhythm to the days that were orchestrated around what she calls "my daily program"—meals, health behaviors, and prayer.

I used to do so much, but now just getting across the room is a major accomplishment. I may look well, but I'm in pain practically all the time. The most important thing about my day is taking care of my health. I get up at 5:00 and pray for two hours. Then I make my own health concoction for breakfast—one tablespoon each of nuts, seeds, bran, and oats, four prunes, and lots of water. I cook it for 15 minutes. Usually by then, I've been standing for too long, so I move around—making my bed and cleaning up. While doing these things I listen to Svendahl at 7:00 and Paul Harvey at 8:30. If I'm on my feet too long, I lie down. By 11:00, I finish things and get dressed, but that depends upon the pain. I time myself on everything—that's my program.

A regular schedule can become symbolically significant, conveying the sense one is control. One man stressed the importance of putting on a tie and shirt every day. In fact, very few of these respondents appeared at interviews in night wear, even if they were ill. Another woman described her day:

I set my alarm for 6:45, for if I don't start early, nothing much happens. It is distressing to lose so much time, but I have to take a two-hour nap in the middle of the day. On Mondays I do housework, Tuesdays I keep for visiting friends, Wednesday I swim, Thursday I keep for paperwork, bills, and such, and Friday I go to a lecture series.

Diet is an important focal point for organizing the day. Food preparation and mealtimes help structure the day. Also methodical in programming his days, a well-known musician gave a minute-by-minute account of his schedule. He was meticulous about describing not only what he ate but the fact that he ate the same foods every day at precisely the same time. He was emphatic about how important it was to establish a routine and follow it compulsively.

> *I eat the same thing at the same hour every day. I get up at 6:30 and have tea—my tea is a mixture of molasses, honey, lemon, and boiling water. I also have toast with margarine and a thin layer of peanut butter, avocado, and a little wheat germ. At 10:00, I have juice with a pill, a honey graham cracker, and a banana. At noon, bong, exactly at 12:00, I have a thick soup with meat, vegetable, and a starch, and fruit. At 4:30, I have a snack of Sanka, with 2 percent milk and a cookie. At 7:30 sharp, I have a light dinner. I don't want much—it's the regularity of eating that's important.*

Simplification of the Physical Environment

To cope effectively with their physical disabilities, a process of simplification and constriction of boundaries around their physical world often occurs. In doing so, they retain essential activities and household objects but omit nonessential objects that are difficult to maintain. In devaluating those areas of life that are problematic, some women give up ironing sheets for the first time in their long lives. Homes have been stripped of all extraneous objects to make housekeeping easier. Some avoid clutter by putting away mementos of their past. Others put away knick-knacks that take too much time to dust, or they give a chair to Goodwill rather than having it reupholstered. Other changes involve rearranging furniture so that there is always something to grasp onto or to break a fall. Essential parts of their lives are retained, while unimportant ones are discarded, making the physical environment more manageable.

Many have difficulties with impaired mobility. To cope with this problem, respondents use canes and walkers for support, as they do their daily tasks. One woman referred to her pronged cane as her "pony" and to the walker as her "Cadillac." Hand railings are often installed in bathrooms and on stairways. Hearing aids and amplifiers on telephones improve their hearing, and magnifying glasses permit them to read. Usually a confined living area has been arranged. A chair is set aside close to the television, with a nearby table to hold a telephone, medications, books, and knitting.

Coping with limitations in mobility outside the home is more challenging. When walking outdoors, some respondents use grocery carts filled with bags of cement to stabilize themselves. Others who are still able to walk independently exercise caution. One woman shops at a distant grocery store, because it is at the end of her bus line, so seats are available on her return trip with her shopping bags. When crossing intersections, others wait through stoplight changes, so they have the advantage of a full red light. One man who still drives plots out his itinerary and maps the streets, so he will not get lost. Another drives around the block rather than make left turns into traffic.

Ritualized Regulation of Time

If one defines rituals loosely to cover, not only religious and life course rites, but also a broad range of activities of daily life, it is readily apparent how much very old people ritualize the ordinary but very necessary activities of daily living. A primary function of any ritual is to endow meaning to experiences and elevate ordinary activities to a higher level of importance. Moore and Myerhoff (1977) refer to these functions as secular rituals, those that structure and interpret social reality and endow it with significance. By explicit, repetitive, formalistic behaviors, they suggest, implicit statements are being made. These memoranda to themselves are usefully applied to situations that are ambiguous or difficult to control. Such difficulties are commonly encountered in late life, but with an orderly plan of action, the situation is usually more controllable and predictable. The mundane, humdrum, commonplace but necessary activities become significant according to some, because "I'm still alive, I have all my marbles, I can get out of bed each day, and I can take care of myself."

The optimal outcome is the explicit recognition that they have successfully executed their daily regimen. Implicitly this sense of accomplishment signifies that they still have some control over their lives. In extensive research, this sense of control has been associated with better health and morale (Rodin, 1986). Perhaps these actions on the part of individuals to establish an order over their lives can at least in part explain why they continue to sustain a sense of well-being in the face of functional declines.

Understandably, these rituals also involve the regulation of time. In reading respondents' descriptions of their typical days, we are impressed by how carefully time is regulated. By careful scheduling, they can handle daily tasks yet avoid having either too much time or too little time on their hands. In order to accommodate to the disproportionate hours needed for personal care and household maintenance, a daily plan is carefully determined. In fact, respondents themselves said they never accepted an offer of a cup of coffee from friends their age because of the time it would take for them to prepare it. Monotonous routine tasks tend to become a primary focus of the day, and through regimentation and ritualization, these activities are elevated in importance.

This structuring of the day satisfies the need to impose an order and a schedule to days where not much happens. It is one means to regulate the day as one might have earlier regulated his or her work life. As one woman commented, "I don't want to be at loose ends. I have to do a lot just so I can keep even—so I won't fall behind. It would be easy to sit back and not care about anything, but that would be a terrible step backward for me."

From Active Social Days to Passive Days

Like the physical environment, the boundaries of the social world are redefined, as the oldest old reframe their optimal level of social integration. They intentionally narrow the boundaries around their social world, deliberately limiting the number of social relationships about which they feel involved and concerned. Through a process of selective withdrawal, they can ignore potentially bothersome events (Johnson & Barer, 1993). At some point, even the most active individuals find the need to alter their daily activities to be congruent with their physical status.

As we will see in a later section, those who are unable to adjust to more passive days are likely to have more problems with morale. Those who had long led relatively solitary and inactive lives had no such difficulties limiting activities because of physical demands. In fact, just as the respondents narrow the boundaries around their physical world, they also tend to redefine their optimal level of social integration. They reduce their social obligations and retain only those involvements that are important to them.

For example, one woman in her mid-90s described her day in detail.

I have very little free time, because I need a lot of time to rest. I get up at 7:00 and have breakfast and clean up the kitchen. Then I lie down to rest and listen to music or a talking book—I can get them free because I am legally blind. Some days I see no one, but I always get dressed. A cleaning woman comes every two weeks, a young woman comes twice a week to write letters for me and do errands, and my daughter comes on Saturday. That's my social life. I watch TV from 9:00 to 11:00 at night sitting right next to the screen. My favorite thing about the day is resting. I fall asleep a lot over the talking books.

In contrast, Mrs. Shapiro made a great effort to stay socially involved and aware of the outside world, not only with friends and family, but also through the media.

I get up at 7:00 and make my breakfast and listen to the news. I have a three-room apartment and a TV and telephone in each room, and in my living room, I have an answering machine and a VCR. I do everything to keep up. I have stopped giving dinner parties except for my family, but I still see close friends every Friday and Saturday. Then I go to the Nutrition Center five days a week. Afterwards my friend and I stop to have a cup of coffee, then we walk to Stow Lake and sit and watch people. After that, we walk to 19th and Judah and take the streetcar home. By then, it's about 3:30, and I watch Oprah and Donahue. I'm tired after dinner and turn out the lights at 9:00.

Projecting a New Status

Others spend their days involved in activities that create a new status and role, one that enhances their feelings of importance. One method, particularly for those without family and friends, is to reach out to celebrities. By writing letters to those they read about in the paper or see on television, they receive appreciative thank-you letters. These letters are commonly kept in a file and brought out for future reference and for visitors to see.

Miss Mahoney is an 88-year-old Irish woman who lives downtown in a single room occupancy hotel (SRO). Once a corporate secretary, she had moved downtown 50 years ago to take advantage of the theaters and restaurants. As the area deteriorated, she was going through a bout of alcoholism. By the time she got back on her feet, she felt she had no options but to stay on. The dreary SRO hotel where she lives also functions as a half-way house for mental patients.

Despite her surroundings, she is cheery and proud of the life she has created for herself. She maintains she is still down-hearted about the deaths of her last siblings, but said, "I am definitely alone, so I know I have to make the best of it." And make the best of it she does by being politically aware and active in a community consisting mainly of single room occupancy hotels. She volunteers at a thrift shop connected to her church and attends all events at nearby community centers. She is a frequent letter writer to city leaders, so she is invited to receptions in their honor when they visit the neighborhood. She showed us a copy of her letter to the mayor, commending him for having his mother beside him at his inauguration. He responded with appreciation. Her thick file of correspondence with then Mayor Dianne Feinstein consisted of form letters in response to her letters. "I am a pretty good friend of Dianne's. She looks out for me—look at the letters she writes to me."

Mr. Killian, a recently widowed, childless immigrant from Ireland also went over his thick file of correspondence. His letters were mostly to the editors of local papers, and they focused upon national issues. The opinions in his letters seemed to attract heated responses from other readers that were also filed.

In describing his days, he said, "When I get mad at what I see on television, I sit down and write to the big shots. They can't shut up an Irishman unless they gag me. What's keeping me alive right now is the pursuit of Reagan." He catalogued a string of vitupretives about then President Ronald Reagan and even his wife, Nancy. One of his letters to the editor of a local paper drew a response from another reader who criticized him for insulting the President. Another time, after seeing John Houston on television, he wrote him asking how he remained so active in his eighties. This drew a response that was carefully filed along with a response from a Supreme Court justice who said he agreed with him on some legal point. It appears that these activities help to ease his grief at the loss of his spouse, whom he described as "The finest woman I ever knew."

Another man, Mr. Shaw, age 86, had never married and had no family and few friends. He lived in senior housing where he created a useful and rewarding role for himself.

The interviewer reported he looked like the Wizard of Oz, except for the prominent burr holes in his skull from surgery on an injury from a serious fall. He had been an assistant buyer for an oil company for years. As a new resident in a senior housing facility, he attempted to feel at home there by helping others. When he became upset seeing a stack of newspapers not being delivered to the residents' doors, he drew upon his experiences in his distant past. Without being asked, he set up an active paper route in the building. Every week he placed a free paper at each resident's door.

I've always been in the newspaper business. I had two corners downtown from 1912 to 1918—during World War I when Woodrow Wilson was president. When I noticed papers were disappearing in this building, I did a study to see who was taking them. I began a record book and started delivering a paper to everyone every week. I go to bed at 7:00 on the night before they are delivered and then get up at 2:00 in the morning to wait for the delivery.

By the next contact, the free paper he had delivered had gone out of business, but he was now paid to deliver the major Sunday paper, "I do 43 papers every week. I'd like to get it up to 50—it would look better. The residents think I am doing a good job. I'm proud of that."

Defining Good Days and Bad Days

When asked what makes a good day and a bad day, some respondents replied that every day was a good day because:

"I lived through the night."

"The sun is shining."

"I am so thankful to be still alive."

These questions single out those who feel they take personal responsibility for their own days. "You make your own days by sheer willpower. For me, every day is a good day. There are no bad days. I thank God for all days." Taking responsibility also indicates they are independent and in control. Mrs. Fontaine fills her days with activities that keep her mind alert, "I do all the crossword puzzles every day. I love them. On Sunday, I do the two big ones—they take all day." Another was content because of life in general. "I enjoy every day. I'm thankful I can do things for myself. I don't have to rely on anyone. Every night when I go to bed, I take inventory of the day. Everything falls into place—that's the truth."

Good days were also related to one's expectations, "Nothing bothers me. That's why I have lived so long. I'm not the type that needs a lot to make me happy." Some feel a good day is when they are doing something special, like taking a bus to Reno or going to the horse races. Others claim one of the greatest advantages to living so long is that they are free agents—they no longer have to do things they do not want to do.

Good days often center upon health:

"A day free of pain."

"When I don't have to climb hills."

"When I have energy to wash dishes."

A "good day" is linked to being able to cope with their physical status. Mr. Caldwell, at 92, simply stated his view, "The distinction between a good day and a bad day depends on how vigorous I feel." Others say a good day is when they can do everything for themselves, or when they can get out.

A 90-year-old woman, a former public health nurse, feels a good day occurs only when she has complete freedom over her life.

> I sleep when I feel like it. I worked a lot of night duty, so I still stay up most of the night. I watch TV, I play my harmonica maybe for two hours. I read like a fury—eight books in three weeks! Nothing bothers me. I don't let problems touch me. I learned that from my hard life. I don't live by any rule. I do anything at absolutely any time. I have no friends anymore, no job, nothing to make me angry.

Conversely, the main ingredient of a bad day is a physical complaint. "I don't like it when I have no energy," or "I don't like having to rest so much." A bad day can also refer to the day of each month set aside for paying bills or cleaning up the house. Others blame the weather for a bad day.

> When it's foggy, I get aches and pains from all the "itises"—arthritis, bursitis, tendinitis. A bad day is when I don't feel like going for a walk. If I don't go for a walk, I force myself to go up and down the stairs four times. I'm a hard disciplinarian. I know I'm wearing out and if I just lie down, I will become more and more depleted.

Others comment that a bad day is when,
"I have shortness of breath."
"I have seizures."
"I can't sleep because of the pain."

Second to health status as determinants of the days are social factors. Social involvements make a good day, when a friend visits or calls or when they hear from their children. Over one half of the sample identified a good day as when they have rewarding social relationships. "A good day is when someone visits." Certainly not all the oldest old are sedentary. For some active people, a good day is when they go square dancing or when they are able to entertain friends. A man caring for his wife reported, "At this age, I don't have bad days, I have boring days. We don't have much elbow room in this apartment, and we're always together. The days are too long."

Third, how respondents experience the day is usually a reflection of their mood. In fact, questions in this area elicit responses that reflect depression or demoralization. One such response was, "Every day is bad as far as I'm concerned. These are not the golden years—they aren't even silver." One homebound woman, described her day, "I just sit here and look at the four walls."

A Glimpse at the Varieties of the Days

While the daily regimens are variable, there is a thread of continuity in the following examples. Considering their physical capacities, there are few failures in the ability to manage their days because of lack of competence, but there are many compromises. Some cope by maintaining continuity at least symbolically. Others reduce the arena and the scale of daily activities. Others make compromises by taking their physical capacities into account, while some are stern taskmasters, driving themselves beyond their capacities.

Continuities in the Rituals of Marriage

Some individuals go to great lengths to retain continuities in their daily life. For example, wealthy Mr. Jackson has live-in help, but he still functions as a caregiver for his wife who has Alzheimer's Disease.

> She won't let anyone help her dress for cocktails and dinner. Through our long marriage, we always had cocktails before dinner. It was the high point of our day. Every evening now I help her take a bath, I get her dressed and put on her best jewelry. We have our drinks and eat dinner without much to say to each other any more. Then I help her undress and get to bed. I don't like to do it—I don't know why I do it. I guess I'm just hanging on to something of the past.

Another couple also have carried on a long tradition. "For over 50 years, we have played three games of double solitaire every night before bed. The children think it's silly to cling to that, but it is a special time for us to be together. How lucky we are to have each other."

Continuities with Relocation

Others retain continuities in their lives even though they are going through major changes. Mrs. Davies is one such person; she is able to maintain her social involvements in spite of changes in her health and after a relocation to senior housing in the suburbs. At age 90 initially, she was a vital and healthy woman, living independently in her own apartment. Since being widowed fourteen years previously, she had volunteered five days a week at her neighborhood senior center. She was obviously well known. "I'm there from 8:30 a.m. to 2 p.m. every day. I sell coffee, set the table, help serve, and clean up."

Around her 93rd birthday, she began to have health problems. She was hospitalized for an infection in her leg. When she fully recovered, she resumed her volunteer work. "I get up at 6:30, take care of my apartment, and then go to the Senior Center. I leave the house nice and clean. I take a nap after I come home. Since I have my main meal there at noon, I eat a light breakfast and have a light dinner at home." Subsequently she began falling and was once hospitalized after hitting her head. While in the hospital, a pacemaker was inserted because of an irregular heart beat. Following these changes in her health, she moved to a suburban senior residence near her son and his family.

> At first it was kind of strange. There's no work to do here as I did in my own apartment and at the Senior Center in the city. Everything is done for me— meals, housecleaning, laundry. I did everything for myself before. But everything here is good. I have a busy schedule. They have a lot of activities—social meetings, lectures, happy hour, sing-alongs. I enjoy the community singing and the different entertainments on the weekends. Even with my little aches and pains, I can't complain. I like to sit around and talk with the ladies. I've always liked socializing.

Recreating the World on a Smaller Scale

At 85, Mrs. Miller was described by the interviewer as a tiny wren-like woman whose voice was much louder than her body frame and weight would indicate. She gave very precise and detailed descriptions of her days.

> *I get up, go to the bathroom, wash my face, put in my teeth, make the bed, put on a kettle of water, make breakfast—oatmeal and bran, and prune juice with potassium. I sit and read over coffee and sometimes watch TV. Then I get up, wash the dishes, wipe them, put them away, and straighten out a few things. I figure out what I'm going to have for dinner. I try to be out of the house as much as possible. After lunch I go out and stay out until 4 or 5 o'clock. I do the laundry once a week, and on Wednesday my daughter takes me out to the supermarket for heavy things. I'm not one for sitting. I don't like to sit.*

Initially she planned a bus trip each day to some tourist spot, such as Fisherman's Wharf. At each stop, she took a long, energetic walk. In the ensuing years, Mrs. Miller's physical condition deteriorated, but she did not complain, "Everything ain't comin' up roses but I'm managing." Always a staunchly independent woman, her only concession to aging was having a cleaning lady in to do the heavy things. "I still have to dust though before she comes. She doesn't even move the phone when she cleans." Mrs. Miller did not change the content of her activities, but she replicated them on a smaller scale. Even after hernia surgery and another hospitalization following a fall, she continued her daily outings. Whereas she once walked an energetic three miles, she subsequently took three short walks a day, when combined, equalled her former distance. By our last contact, she reduced her exercise routines further, but did the same type of activity. She walked around the block, or if the weather was bad, she walked the hallways of her senior residence, even taking the elevator up one floor where the halls were longer.

She approached another activity, reading, in the same determined and systematic way. As her eyesight worsened, she read the daily paper with a magnifying glass. By the age of 90 she described what she called "light reading." "When I'm trying to read, I have to put the book down when everything gets blurry. I pick it up and read some more and then put it down and pick it up again later. I can't look at things too long or I see those wavy lines. I'm used to that already."

At 91 years of age, Mrs. Miller's description of her typical day replicated her earlier account. She still organized her days methodically, so they were microcosms of her former life. "I eat breakfast, and I always make my bed, but everything takes a little longer. I'm slow to get dressed." Rather than taking buses around the city, she reported, "I have plenty to keep me busy around here. I need to keep my clothes rotated in my drawer so they don't wear out so fast. I wear the ones from the left side and then replace them with clothes on the right side. I keep what I have in good shape—night gowns, underwear, sweaters." With increased home help she explained, "I have to be here Monday and Wednesday afternoon when the girl comes to clean and do the laundry. Tuesday is usually a free day. I always watch the evening news and on weekends I read the Sunday paper." Mrs. Miller could not go to bed until everything was in its place. "The other night I made applesauce. While it was cooking, I fell asleep in front of television. The pan was so burnt and the stove a mess, I stayed up until midnight cleaning up."

Compromises of a Former Vaudeville Performer

Mr. Foreman's daily life is a good example of creative compromises. He is an 88-year-old man who had never married and had once been a Vaudeville performer.

He looked trim and fit with mischievous, twinkling blue eyes. He lived alone in a well-maintained home with his poodle, Daisy. So as to keep active, he had recently undergone hip and knee replacements. Much of his days were spent on health-promotion activities. "I have a banana every day for the potassium, I go to the YMCA to swim laps, then I'm home for lunch. I nap after that and then have cocktails at 4:00 or 5:00. I usually go out to dinner with my best friend. I don't have any relatives, but my friend's big Italian family has adopted me. My favorite activities are swimming and singing."

At the second and third contacts, he reported a slowing down, even though he maintained the same pattern to his days. "Instead of swimming 20 laps, I swim 5. I still sing and do a show once in a while. I take a nap and then have a Margarita. Since you were here last, I took a three-week trip to Egypt with my friend to see the pyramids." By the fourth contact, his health seemed to change; he had lost 30 pounds, he walked with a shuffle, and he looked much older. Yet he reported that he was still active,

> Yesterday I was up on the roof cleaning out the gutters. That was awful—I had to a hail a neighbor to help me get down. I have had a slight stroke and have fallen twice, so I can't do what I used to do. Despite everything though, I feel pretty good. Now I swim only three laps. My memory is worse, so I can't learn new songs like I used to. I got tired of all the time it takes me to clean this place, so I threw out all my rugs.

By the fifth contact, he reported both good and bad news. "I was in the hospital for five days for shortness of breath—I am down to 50 percent lung capacity. Now it's even more important to swim and I've joined an aerobics class at the Y to help with my breathing. What really keeps me going is Daisy. She gets me out—she likes to take long walks. I still take care of my house. It just takes longer. Yesterday I pulled weeds in the back yard and boy, do I feel it today. Instead of singing, I listen to music—Don Giovanni is keeping me entertained today."

In Control over One's Days

Mrs. Smith was 86 at our first contact and had moved to San Francisco a few years previously upon the insistence of her son.

Her late husband had been an army officer, who had to move frequently. She was proud of her own competence in setting up a new home every few years over a 40-year period. Even in her 80s, she was quite enterprising in getting settled in a new community and meeting the "right sort of people." At each place she had lived, she joined the Episcopal church and the American Association of University Women. Shortly after her move to the Bay Area, she broke her ankle, so she delayed joining the usual associations until the cast was removed. "I wanted to make a good impression." Her son and his wife had selected a condominium on the border of the most affluent area of the city. It had a swimming pool, and her residence had a second bedroom that she called her playroom. An array of her hobbies dominated the room— a half-finished painting, Christmas decorations she was using in a class she taught at a senior center, hot pads she made for a church bazaar, sewing and knitting in process, and a garden on a tiny balcony.

At the first contact, she described her days,

I get out each day. After you leave today, I'll go to the Senior Center where I teach, then I'll go to the health spa on the way home. I'm just getting back into shape after a bout of pneumonia. Last week I had eight gals in for dinner and bridge. Every Monday I go to the finance committee meeting at my church. I find out then who is sick, and then I visit and bring flowers. Once a week I water flowers at the church. I have no problems, because I don't make problems.

By the next contact, she described a hospitalization after a shellfish reaction. The only changes in her routines were giving up some activities at night, but she was making up for it by doing more during the daytime. By the next visit, just under three years into the study, she had redecorated her condominium, she swam daily, and she continued her impressive round of activities. "Fifty people at church consider me a best friend. My daughters are here four times a week." By the fourth interview, however, she reported being limited by her health problems with pain and shortness of breath that forced her to make changes in her activities. "I have not been good at anything lately. I was in the hospital for four days because of my health." But still she was more active than most respondents. "I don't drive as much but still go out a lot using cabs. I have so many projects. Here are booties I'm knitting for the church bazaar. I still teach at the center, and I still have my bridge group."

By the fifth interview, she had given up her car symbolically the day after celebrating her 90th birthday.

I don't have health problems—I just have old age. My days are the same. I go to the university group, the church, and the center. But now I only sub-

stitute in a bridge group. My memory is not as good—I'll either have to play bridge more or give it up. I swim three times a week. For the first time in my adult life, I am not on a church committee. They are giving the best committee spots to younger people. I guess that's fair, and anyway I'm very busy. Right now, my main project is taping my family history.

Even with the subtle changes in her daily activities, it is apparent in her discussions that she remains the same in her coping strategies and her sense of control over her life. "Sometimes I feel like doing nothing, but I tell myself, 'For heaven's sake, get yourself going.' The most important thing is to get up and swim."

Body-Centered Days

One example of a daily regimen was less successful because of physical problems.

Mrs. Franklin's daily routine is dominated by coping with her incontinence, a situation that worsened over the six years in the study. At the last contact, she was forced to withdraw from most social activities. Always a sociable woman, she faced the dilemma of wanting, on one hand, to continue participating in the many activities in her senior housing yet, on the other hand, risking embarrassing situations caused by her bladder problems. Initially, when in her late 80s, she participated in a variety of social programs and lectures, with a particular interest in environmental issues and global affairs. She also enjoyed the sociability of having meals three times a day in the residential dining room with friends that had similar interests. "I love being surrounded by people—I never have to feel I'm alone."

A year later she complained of the time she must spend changing her pads and soiled clothes and washing them in the bathtub. Just dressing for meals was a major undertaking. With each contact, Mrs. Franklin became more withdrawn and isolated because of her incontinence. Her days no longer centered on her favorite times, meals with her friends and the special programs, but instead she explained,

Just taking care of myself now takes a lot of time. I'm just trying to exist. I don't do anything any more. I have to be very sure that my garments are changed enough and that the pads are large enough to absorb the unwanted urine. I'm incontinent day and night and that means there's a lot of washing to do and that takes a lot of time. I haven't had fun for a long time. I wish I didn't have the incontinence because it keeps me more or less homebound. As my body consumes my days, I get more selfish and self-centered. As my interest in the world diminishes, only the immediate things occupy my thoughts. I'm quite withdrawn now. I have no aspirations. It seems as though my day is gone before I know it.

Solitary Days

Mrs. Jones is also an exception to the successful copers. She is an isolated, lonely demoralized widow with no surviving children.

She has painful arthritis, heart trouble, and hypertension. Her days are passive, she concludes, because all her medications make her very tired. Each daily task, she explains, "tuckers me out" and must be followed by a period of rest. "I do a little at a time. It's usually about 11 a.m. before I am dressed. I keep up my house and water my plants, deal with the mail, and pay bills. I'd like to see people, but I rarely do. It's impossible, because I have to lie down so often." Her depleted energy is most evident in the routine she has established for grocery shopping.

I manage to drive to the market once a week, but it's hard. I go at noon when it's not so crowded. Even then, walking the aisles and standing in line wears me out. I get very tired when I shop, so I come home, I drive in the garage, come in, and lie down before I take the groceries in. Later I take a few things out of the bag at a time and carry them to the kitchen. Sometimes I just take the meat out and leave the rest in the car for a while.

Her loneliness persisted with each contact. "I used to be a happy person, but it's hard to be happy when you are all alone." She maintained her husband had been her best friend, so she had never needed friends. "He's gone and my son is dead, so I have no one." On two occasions in the course of the six years, Mrs. Jones spent time in a convalescent home recovering, first from a broken ankle and later from a slight stroke. Each time she returned home to her lonely status. "When you live alone, there's no one to get on your nerves. One day goes and then there comes another. You have to learn to be satisfied with what you've got. I need more communication with others, but I can't go out."

Conclusion

Hopefully, these descriptions of the typical daily round of activities have conveyed how individuals organize their daily life. Overall most carry out the humdrum but important business of getting through each day with a sense of accomplishment and good spirits. Most have found the means to cope with impressive stressors and hassles that would daunt younger people. Nevertheless, these individuals in their 80s and 90s cope effectively by establishing a daily regime with their time carefully regulated. They also ritualize everyday life to elevate their activities to a higher level of importance and to convey a predictability to their world. Among the numerous techniques are efforts to simplify their social and physical environments, reorder their priorities, and even find a new status in corresponding with celebrities.

Each individual has some unique way to organize daily life that usually is consistent with his or her abilities and the demands encountered in late life. For some, continuities in their days is important, even if such attempts are inconvenient or unrealistic. Dressing for dinner and even having to dress his demented wife is symbolic of a past life for Mr. Jackson and thus still important, just as playing double solitaire every night is significant to another couple.

Others must structure their days to tend to their physical needs. Incontinence, as Mrs. Franklin has learned, makes her days so centered on her body that she feels too self-absorbed. Others recreate their world on a simpler scale, like Mrs. Miller, who replaced her long walks and sightseeing with meticulously rearranging her lingerie drawers. Mrs. Jones' passive and solitary days stand in contrast to the former Vaudeville performer, Mr. Foreman, who compromises but still performs his daily activities with enthusiasm and verve. Finally, Mrs. Smith is noted for her control over her days retaining the activities of far younger people.

These descriptions came from close questioning at each interview about what the very old do each day. While such a topic is not usually covered in most research protocols, for the oldest old who are still living in the community, the information conveys much understanding about their adaptation. How they structure their days determines how they can accomplish the activities of daily living and continue to survive more or less independently. These vignettes portray the ordinary and uneventful aspects of life as a long-term survivor. In many cases as we were interviewing the oldest old, the ordinary seemed to become extraordinary, given the social circumstances and physical limitations of many respondents.

Chapter 8

Discourses on Self and Time

We began our study of adaptation among the oldest old by posing simple, straightforward questions such as, What competencies are needed to survive and sustain community living? As the chapters on the family and social networks indicate, such resources are important but comprise only one route to survival and well-being in late life. In fact, much of the spontaneous portions of the interviews concerned, not objective experiences about surviving day-to-day, but the cognitive and emotional processes that seemed to be more central in interpreting their experiences.

Consequently, in investigating the lives of the oldest old, the research techniques of anthropology were particularly appropriate in exploring the uncharted interior world of the oldest old. Little is known about the daily experiences of very old people and the meanings they evolve about the exceptional demands they face—persistent pain, problems with mobility, loss of vision and hearing, the recurrent deaths of contemporaries, the onset of old age of their children and, in 30 percent of the cases, the death of at least one child. Understandably, it is not unusual to encounter those who feel a sense of aloneness, or feeling that they are in a social limbo, because they are "off time" in dying—a feeling that "Everybody dies but me."

As we have noted in previous chapters, it is puzzling but reassuring to learn from our research that the onset of disability does not necessarily lead to demoralization and despair. In fact, most of the respondents assess their health as good and retain a sense of well-being and pride in their special status as long-term survivors. Over repeated contacts, the objective findings indicate family resources remain relatively stable over time, at the same time their physical status worsens. More dynamic processes are occurring, not necessarily in the actions of the respondents, but in the discourses they carry on with themselves, and with us, that explain themselves in terms of their long-term survivorship. These processes need not be based upon reality but rather, on the individual's perception of reality. For example, very old individuals may be in pain, housebound, and without support, yet they can alter their definitions of their personal adequacy and competence by restructuring their conceptions of their situation. The question thus is posed, By what means are they able to sustain well-being despite seemingly insurmountable odds?

This chapter describes the discourses respondents carry on about their experiences of living so long and how they evaluate the formidable challenges they face. The processes of reconstituting their self-concept is evident in these discourses, as respondents come to terms with being not only "an old old self," but also "a healthy self," one whose health is good despite their disabilities. These oldest old also view themselves as "a detached self" who is removed from areas of their life that were formerly bothersome or demanding. Finally this chapter will include a discussion of their time orientation and the means by which conceptions of time are manipulated to be compatible with their long-term survivorship.

Definitions of Self

In our analysis of the adaptive strategies used by the oldest old, we are focusing on self-formulations that are specifically applicable to advanced old age. We view the self as an umbrella concept overarching an array of thoughts, feelings, values, and attitudes. This all-inclusive self includes a set of conceptions about who they are, who they were, who they would like to be, and who they do not want to be (Baltes, 1993; Ryff, 1993). Others conceptualize a series of possible selves that represents an individual's ideas about who they might become (Markus & Nurius, 1986). For example, Ewing's (1990) theory of multiple selves is particularly useful in interpreting our findings. She suggests that the self representation is continually constructed and reconstructed within specific contexts. Since the self is culturally shaped, it is infinitely variable (Ewing, 1990). Moreover, the self as it arises out of a social and cultural context is continually subject to change. A self-concept is also infused with emotions in an ongoing process of self-evaluation (Rosaldo, 1984). Self-awareness can be constructive, or in rare cases, it can be destructive, as very old individuals confront problems in their final stage of development.

These conceptions of plasticity in personality are in agreement with Baltes' (1993) view, and ours, that the aging self is a resilient part of a new framework of evaluation. We will demonstrate how, as the oldest old cope with practical problems, they also use cognitive processes that can minimize the threat of physical, social, and psychological losses. In this progressive reformulation of self, aspirations change, expectations are revised, and the social world becomes more delimited (Johnson & Barer, 1992; 1993). Where the process of aging is successful, the very old are effective in using the self system as a protective shield against negative effects.

Unlike self-conceptions of younger individuals, few oldest old conceptualize their self-concept in terms of a social role, "the good mother" or "the dutiful wife." Instead, with the realization that they have little control over many areas of their lives, the oldest old shift their focus to concentrate upon basic existential concerns about life and death. In fact, most have come to terms with imminent death by viewing that possibility without fear or trepidation. In a narrowing social world, altered goals often lead to feelings of detachment, increased introspection or interiority, and even a feeling of remoteness from the typical worries and concerns of daily life.

The oldest old have revised their self-orientation in four domains. First, they develop conceptions of themselves as very old. Second, although very old and usually disabled, the self-concept belies the reality of their age; they tend to view their health as good or excellent. Third, some respondents view themselves as detached from some aspects of the world around them. They describe how they narrow and delimit the boundaries of their social world and voluntarily disengage from problematic roles and relationships. Fourth, these oldest old tend to revise their temporal orientation and see themselves as living mostly in the present, "one day at a time." In the process, they de-emphasize the past and recognize that they have little future. The self-concept is often fused with the feeling that they are an accident of time or a captive of fate, a status when time becomes inconsequential.

The Old Old Self

The self-concept is useful in explaining oneself within the context of being a long-term survivor. An illness or the loss of a last contemporary often brings the realization, "I am very old." At that point, a reconstituted self emerges, that of a survivor when age peers are dead. Most are proud of having lived so long, and they shun the notion that they should act inappropriately younger than they are. When asked at one interview what it means "to act your age," most replies can be summed up with the following. They can act young as long as they do not dye their hair, wear short skirts, and flirt with members of the opposite sex. Despite a realistic stance about their age, they want their self-concept to be defined on their own terms, a definition that usually means a self that is younger than their very old body.

If their chronological age is not congruent with how they feel and how they function, then individuals become concerned about how they will be defined by others. Coming to terms with being very old but still feeling young often raises fears that others will see them as too old. "Others may think I am old, but I don't feel old." Another respondent explained, "I don't tell people my age. If they knew, they would start treating me differently."

Not only are respondents concerned about others stereotyping them as old no matter how young they feel, but some also conclude that those around them may be attempting to take away their personhood. For example, children with the best of intentions commonly try to influence their parents to adopt a life-style in keeping with being very old. Some respondents react with resentment about such an intrusion. "My son tries to take over my very personhood—I must be on guard. He insists I wear a hearing aid and walk with a cane. I refuse to change who I am. I am not a decrepit old lady." When children persuade their parent to give up driving or to move to senior housing, these pressures can be a threat to their well-being. One respondent used metaphors to describe her life after her daughter insisted she give up her car, "I am past that point when I can change my life. Now others are taking over. My wings are clipped. I'm a bird in a gilded cage. I will just dry up of old age and blow away." Some pose a counterattack to such a threat. "Other people cause me to age. There are some who think I'm forgetful, but I have a good memory. Each night before sleeping I remember all 50 states in alphabetical order."

In contrast to those who reject a self-concept as one who is very old, others accept a self-representation as that of a very old person with relief, with the feeling they can now sit back and relax. As one woman described her relocation to senior housing. "Now I am free of the hassles of running a household. I am also free of those involvements that used to trigger irritations. In fact, I can't even remember any more what used to bother me." Many also conclude that they have become an observer of life, a reactor, no longer an actor. Others indicate they can become more egocentric. "I am at the stage where I no longer worry about my children and grandchildren. I only have to think about myself, and that gives me peace of mind."

The Healthy Self

Manipulating the self-concept can also be useful in adapting to pain, illness, and disability. The individual is an active problem solver who cognitively regulates the perceived world, evaluates his or her health, and uses coping strategies to lessen the impact of their aches and pain. In other words, individuals have a lived-in body that is continually sensed and experienced as a source of information about their health. In this scheme, such information is central to their changing sense of self. We found that respondents devised four categories of meaning to evaluate their health, each one of which reconstructed the meanings of their symptoms in such a way that moderated their emotional impact.

Most common, first, are responses such as "My health is good for my age." This reference point offers positive comparisons on the basis of opinions of family, friends and their physician's physical assessments, who assure them they are better off than others their age. Second, "I am healthy because I still have my mind" reflects the propensity to compare themselves with demented elderly. By doing so, they focalize their symptoms and health complaints on one area of their body quite distinct from the core self. Third, "I am healthy because I take care of myself." Having personal control over their health was traced to their good health habits, positive outlooks, and their active life-style. Fourth, "I can't do anything about it. It's just aging," or "It's in the hands of the Lord." Such resignation to external causality is attributed not only to the "wear and tear" theories of aging but also to trust in the supernatural, fate, or natural forces that are beyond one's control.

Positive Comparisons. After posing a general question about health, we went on to ask how their health compared to their age peers. Most respondents gave favorable and even glowing evaluations of themselves in comparisons to others their age. This process of positive social comparison is a well-known coping technique that uses a distinct reference point to others their age. "I am healthy for my age, because I am healthier than my friends." Even more telling is the conclusion, "I am healthy because I'm alive. All my peers are dead." Moreover, no matter how disabled a respondent may be, he or she usually knows someone else who is in worse shape.

"I see people younger than me who are in worse shape."

"I think I'm excellent for my age. The lady who lives across the street is 12 to 14 years younger and she can't walk."

Those with limited mobility or even those confined to their beds or wheelchairs can usually find someone worse off than themselves, who can be used as a source from which to make a positive comparison.

"I'm much better than some. Many are bedfast, but I can get around in a wheelchair."

"I'm better off than many people I know. Others need help to get to the bathroom."

"I'm better off, because I can breathe lying down."

Their doctor's positive and encouraging remarks also promote a self perception of health.

"My doctor says I have great health for my age."

"The doctor told me, '20-year-olds don't recover the way you did.'"

"When I said to the doctor 'I'm old,' he patted me on the knee and said, 'Don't be silly.'"

Moreover, an emphasis on what seems ordinary to younger people is crucial in evaluating the competence of very old people. By still performing their activities of daily living, they are acting like a younger person. Freedom of movement around their home or outside of it, however limited it may be, serves not just practical functions, but it also acts as a symbol of vitality and youthfulness among the oldest old. Perhaps more than any other criterion, independent mobility such as the capacity to move, walk, and travel unassisted is considered a special achievement.

Mind/Body Dichotomy. A second strategy is one that fits a particular Western concept of self, that is to establish a dichotomy between the mind and body. By making this distinction, one's self-presentation is that of an active self that lives in a disabled body. Even with loss of control over physical functioning, having an alert mind is an achievement. One strategy is to distance themselves from their body, its symptoms, and the ravages of old age. Consequently an alert mind is equated with being in good health.

"I have good health because I still have my faculties."

"Mostly my knees bother me, but my mind is perfectly good."

"I have all my marbles so I'm healthy even though my body is wearing out."

A second strategy is to focalize their symptoms on one area of the body, and by doing so, symptoms become separate from the mind or self-image.

"All my aging is taking place in my right eye."

"I have spells, I have headaches, but it's really all due to my bowel condition."

"I've never had misery in my body—just in my feet."

A third strategy involves the invocation of metaphors in which the body is seen as a mechanical or natural entity separate from the mind and self. "My body is like an old jalopy; one day the water-pump, the next day the radiator."

Sense of Control over Health. Positive self-assessments are also linked to personal initiative in exercising control over their physical status. As we discussed in Chapter 7, respondents usually enumerate their daily self-care routines in obsessive detail when discussing their health. The more disabled respondents have difficulty with maintaining hygiene and cleanliness because of poor eyesight and difficulty bathing. When they accomplish these tasks without assistance, feelings of personal pride and autonomy surface in their discussions. "I do my hair myself" or "I can still dress myself."

A sense of control also comes from establishing dietary and exercise regimes, use of personal remedies, or the ability to treat oneself when ill. Some respondents are skeptical about remedies offered by professionals. "At this age, you have to be cautious about advertised medicine," or "I'm a non-drug person. I control my bad spine with hot baths, showers and heating-pads." Monitoring and anticipating the body's idiosyncracies is another source of self-control, "I listen to my body."

"Keeping busy" is also a sign of good health and well-being, "I still play ping-pong, do gardening, and I anchored the cabinet for earthquakes." "I'm alive because I have so many responsibilities." In the face of declining functioning and increasing physical symptoms, staying active is an accomplishment. "My diabetes and high blood pressure don't stop me—you should have seen me dancing." Keeping busy also offers a distraction from typical symptoms of advanced age. "If I keep busy, I don't have time to think about my aches and pains."

Forces beyond One's Control. Good health is also traced to natural or supernatural forces over which one has no control. Natural influences include the weather, "When it rains, I get some pain in my shoulder." A dramatic natural event occurred with a diminutive respondent, "A sudden wind blew me down. Before that happened, my health was great." Understandably, rapid changes in the natural and domestic environment particularly affect a vulnerable population like the oldest old. Nevertheless, the identification of external causes of pain and distress serves to displace responsibility or blame onto an agent other than oneself.

The supernatural is also invoked to rationalize the lack of control over one's health. Here the "Lord," "God," or the "Almighty" is seen as a benevolent being who prevents disease, eases pain, and speeds recovery. For example, "I stumble around but I don't fall. God will take care of me," or "I attribute my good health to the Mormon Church." The timing of death too can be placed in the hands of the Lord. "The Lord has taken me this far; He will carry me to the time He wants me."

Finally, old age itself can be construed as a category of causation over which one has no control. Consequently, declining health is seen as inevitable and beyond their capacity to change. This stance is reflected in such seemingly negative comments: "I think I'm going downhill, that's all," "I'm not concerned, because that's part of growing old."

The Detached Self

With the realization, "I am the only one left," individuals come to terms with the reality of being true survivors who have outlived their contemporaries. Some respondents identify two types of alterations with this realization. First, they conclude that their attitudes about their lives and the world in general are more flexible. As a result, their worries and concerns have become diluted, and fewer aspects of their life cause them to worry. Second, most describe a levelling of their emotional life. As a result, as will be discussed in the next chapter, the intensity of emotional experiences diminishes in late life, a change that is particularly evident in their last year of life (Chapter 11).

The self as detached is congruent with our conception of a continuum of social network types where some individuals willingly accept a disengagement from some areas of their social life. Such a retreat is congruent with the realities of late life, when there are fewer opportunities for face-to-face contacts with others. Because of their functional limitations and depleted energy, they are less able to socialize or even enjoy social interactions. Respondents simply state, "I don't have the same desire to keep mixing and going out." This sense of a detached self does not necessarily lead to loneliness. In fact, as we will describe in the following chapter, loneliness is an emotion rarely encountered among the oldest old. Consistent with our findings on disengagement, we conclude that those who reach such an advanced age, redefine their goals and expectations in order to come to terms with their reduced stamina and their many losses. Five strategies were observed.

First, many oldest old increasingly retreat into an interior world and exhibit interiority (Neugarten, 1977; Schulz, 1985), one of the few personality changes observed in later life. Effective copers come to terms with social losses and increased isolation by selective withdrawal and retreat (Johnson & Barer, 1993). Such withdrawal is usually viewed as an advantage. "I have reached the peaceful age of quietude." Making a conscious choice to be alone is one way of rationalizing the lack of social contact. It was not uncommon to hear statements such as, "I'd rather be alone. There are no people I'm interested in. They all talk pills, their doctor's bills, how many times they went to the bathroom at night, or how they slept. Who cares?"

Second, through redefining their social needs and viewing their narrowing social world as a positive change, individuals manage to adjust to their increased detachment and disengagement, often welcoming time spent alone. When asked about forming new friendships to make up for lost ones, typical responses were "I don't want any more friends. I want less," or, "I enjoy my privacy." Problematic relationships can be avoided with some sense of relief. The positive aspects of being alone are stressed, and being alone is not necessarily equated with feeling lonely, isolated, or desolate. An age-linked preoccupation with self-protection and survival also can justify disengagement. A woman aged 102 stated, "People impinge on you at my age. I need more time to be with myself."

Third, others retain the closeness of relationships through memories, that is, keeping others alive in their thoughts. This is often accomplished by remaining in familiar surroundings. A 95-year-old woman expressed how much her home meant to her. "I get up and walk around the house and look at all my pictures—people that I've not seen for ages. I look at the pictures and think about them." Awakening memories of family and friends provide a feeling of being with them, and these memories seem to reduce the need for constant social reaffirmation.

Fourth, still others repress their feelings about being lonely so as to control its effects. Common explanations are: "I talk myself out of feeling lonely," or "I don't allow myself to get those feelings." One man justified his aloneness by saying that he was "semi-retired from life."

Fifth, by redefining their social expectations, individuals come to terms with being alone in much the same way that they ultimately confront their impending death. With time and experience, they adapt to their situation. As one person said, "I like being alone—that is more important at the end of life." Another respondent commented about adjusting to the death of her husband, "Time cures loneliness. Since I have lived beyond the most painful times, the sense of loss wears off."

As these strategies demonstrate, in spite of substantial losses in physical functioning and deaths of family members and friends, most oldest old neither need nor desire constant companionship. The absence of others is not necessarily experienced as a negative condition, for many enjoyed being alone at this stage in their lives. Our findings suggest that with advanced old age, the desired level of social involvements tends to decrease, and individuals develop the capacity to be alone. Thus they may cherish peaceful solitude rather than experience the discomfort of loneliness.

In conclusion, theories of self provide one explanatory scheme to interpret psychological aspects of adaptation, that is, as a source of their identity as a survivor. The self concept is viewed as resilient and capable of responding to changes in physical status, in the social context, and in their beliefs and feelings. The main problem with this prerequisite, however, concerns how to exploit the rich possibilities the literature on the self offers. If one defines the concept of self too diffusely, it becomes meaningless.

The Meaning of Time in Late Late Life

In the discourses of the oldest old, their conceptions of time obliquely but frequently figured into their explanatory scheme. Surprisingly, these respondents did not dwell upon reminiscences about their past, nor did they refer in detail to their future. In fact, their conceptions about the time left to live was rarely mentioned. Instead, most continually referred to themselves as living very much in the present, taking one day at a time. We suggest that the oldest old perceive, define, and manipulate the temporal dimensions of their lives as an adaptive strategy to deal with the usual difficulties of late life.

A review of the literature on time indicates that this ubiquitous dimension of life is little explored or understood, even though time is a central concept in the developmental aspects of aging and in the individual's social constructions of the aging process (Hendricks & Hendricks, 1976). In Chapter 7, we described one domain of temporality, *regulated time,* that structures daily routines and their functioning on the activities of daily living. Time has discrete segments that establish a rhythm to the days and a pacing of their activities. With methodical care and planning, the mundane activities can become a productive busyness that gives daily activities greater significance.

A second domain relevant to this analysis, *symbolic time*, is a personally constructed temporality signifying the sequential experiences of individuals and the social and cultural context in which they live (Geertz, 1973). Hence, time exists in the significance it has for the individuals who recognize and define its qualities. In other words, time exists as a system of meaning within the consciousness of individuals.

While the issue of time is of central methodological interest to gerontologists, it remains an elusive property conceptually (Fry, 1985; Hendricks & Hendricks, 1976). In fact, we take time so much for granted that only when we pause to examine it, does the complexity of the concept loom large. St. Augustine stated this conclusion most appropriately. "What is time? If no one asks me, I know; but if I want to explain to he who asks, I know not" (cited in Hendricks & Hendricks, 1976). The conception of time is distinctly human, for only we in the animal kingdom give the world of events a self-reference and maintain notions of the past, present, and future (Becker, 1971). Time also pervades conceptions of aging. In fact, the very definition of age uses a temporal rather than a social or functional criterion. Researchers on the aging process, as participants in our culture, tend to have a culture-bound view of time as a linear, objective, measurable ordering of events like a clock. Older people are also assigned to age groups, which have become increasingly specific in recent years—the young old, the old old and, most recently, the oldest old.

In conceptions of adult development (Neugarten & Hagestad, 1976), the life course is commonly considered as being shaped by biological determinants into a beginning, middle, and end. This constitutes a linear passage which is methodically segmented into temporal sequences and stages. Individuals are viewed as moving in step with their cohort, as if life were an obstacle course through which one should traverse—hopefully with a minimum of trouble (Dowd, 1986; Lasch, 1979). Such obsessiveness about time has been consistently associated with the work ethic of Protestant Western cultures. This view makes the status of the elderly particularly atypical, since they are no longer in the labor force.

Life course conceptions of time focus on being "on time" or "off time," and usually conclude that staying the same or going through transitions "on time" is the key to adaptation, particularly when it entails activity and social integration, rather than passivity and rolelessness. Conversely, being "off time" is viewed as fraught with problems. Such assumptions are less productive, when applied to the oldest old, for they are "off time" in dying. More productive is the view that the life course is open-ended and continually recreated by individuals who shape and rework the past, the present, and the future (Gergen, 1977; 1980; Seltzer & Troll, 1986).

Anthropologists, who take nothing at face value, point out that such a lockstep, normative perspective on time is by no means universal (Fry, 1985; Ostor, 1984). Cross-culturally, time can be cyclical; it may be reversible, plural, or even unmeasurable. In other words, the concept of time is quite varied in its meanings and uses throughout the world, because it is inseparable from culture (Hall, 1983). As Edmund Leach (1961) pointed out, "We create time by creating intervals in life. Until we have done that, there is no time." We suggest that the oldest old do shape their time orientation to take their unique situation into account.

As we noted in Chapter 7, time is also related to rituals that mark off not only stages in the life cycle, but also the daily regimens. Rituals occur in a temporal context through a patterning of events and in such a way, provide certainty and predictability to the lives of the oldest old. As Myerhoff (1984) has so eloquently pointed out, with the ever-growing prolongation of life, the aged face vague role expectations and conflicting attitudes about their status. Nevertheless, she also suggests that rather than isolation and anomie, older people can exploit their rolelessness and enjoy the advantages of being beyond social obligations. They are likely, in her view, to be deft manipulators who, in the absence of public rituals, create their own private rituals with enthusiasm and even obsessiveness.

Memory and Time

In the study of the oldest old, their conceptions of time are particularly relevant. At the practical level, memory problems are prominent, so time is frequently confused on a neuropsychological basis. Even in persons who do not have the symptoms of mental decline associated with dementia, there is a pervasive and progressive loss of the facility to recall and preserve a temporal accuracy about their past. Such deficits not only affect the recollection of recent events, but also act to confuse access to more remote life events. In fact, in some cases, we abandoned attempts to draw an accurate chronology of their lives, simply because time sequences are reported in confusing ways. Some respondents do not conceptualize the immense duration of their lives, such as a 92-year-old woman who reported, "I was married twice, 7 years in my 20s and 7 years in my 70s, so I was alone for 20 years in between."

Time for a very old person also is segmented differently than for younger people, "I've lived so long; I tend to think of the past in terms of decades rather than years." Some respondents stated they will answer no questions about time. As the centenarian said in Chapter 1, time questions were out of bounds. She insisted that at her age, "time is out of mind."

Shifts in Time Orientation

The very old tend to shift their time orientation from the past or the future to present time, as they concentrate on coping with daily activities. Their comments include, "My life is lived in the present. Tomorrow is unknown, and my past is behind me." "Time is now. Continuity is no longer important. What is important is to be happy today." The advantage of this shift was pointed out by one man, "Everyone should start anew—take a new path. Forget the past, wipe your slate clean, and live in the present." In contradiction to the oft-cited uses of reminiscence among the aged, memories of the past are not spontaneously discussed. Unlike younger old people who might benefit from the therapeutic aspects of reminiscence, many of our respondents by choice ignore or de-emphasize their past, so that the sharing of recollections is neither important nor perhaps possible. A literary view of this orientation comes from novelist Paul Bowles (Gussow, 1995) who, at 84, described his time orientation. "I live in the present. There is no future." (And the past?) "I remember it as one remembers an unchanging landscape."

In those instances where the past looms large in consciousness, its meanings tend to be reframed. Memory can be very selective, "I only remember pleasant things," or I "whitewash the past." Selective remembering consists of putting a frame around the areas of attention and selectively reflecting upon some past events, while ignoring others. Some of our subjects feel dissociated from the past; a woman who had been widowed for 35 years said that memories of her marriage seemed like a dream.

The future is generally considered as nonproblematic. The very old have outlived worry, because in some respects, "There is no future; my future is behind me." Many respondents feel that they have already experienced all possible tragedies, and they conclude that they have nothing left to worry about. In fact, no one in this sample described time "as running out."

"I don't worry any more. Worry has a future. I have no future."

"I don't give a damn any more. That's a wonderful thing about getting old."

"Life gets easier all the time, because no one expects anything of me."

With no future or at best, an abbreviated future, their own mortality is viewed from several vantage points. For the philosophically inclined, it can provide "new eyes to see the world" and new understandings of the meaning of life. One woman eloquently stated, "By coming to terms with death, I can now begin to enjoy life." While some worry about a long and painful process of dying, death itself brings forth no fears. Consequently, a rejection of a future other than the immediate future of getting through the coming day, seems to be an important step in approaching death.

This shift in the time orientation can result in the very old placing themselves in a limbo status beyond time. In this situation, fate rather than purpose or volition takes control of their lives. Through living in a social world which is outside conventional time, they exist in "a detemporalized time" (Geertz, 1973). Hazan (1980) describes how older people create a new world outside time where previous accomplishments and failures become inconsequential. Golander (1995) in her research on a geriatric ward in Israel describes how older people establish a boundary between the past and the present and the future, so that time becomes arrested into "limbo time." Consequently, a future orientation that involves planning and progress is eliminated. Numerous comments describe this status, "just marking time," "putting in time," "living on borrowed time," "I'm beyond time," or, "I am an accident of time."

Linda Mitteness (1995), in her analysis of time and the tempo of life when dealing with chronic illnesses, notes contradictions in time. She suggests that the suddenness of events such as the flare-up of symptoms occur in the context of a fatigue-related slowing down of one's days. With increased impairment, there is a speeding up of the life course, "I feel old before my time," yet a slowing down of daily life, "It takes me forever to do anything." The time orientation varies. For example, in the nursing home, time stands still as individuals wait to die. With some illness, time is in dispute between doctor and patient, such as involving a diabetic's decision about when to seek treatment. In other cases, such as incontinence, time is heavily regulated.

Conclusion

These discourses of the oldest old signify an active interior world, a world where the oldest old constantly think about the meanings of their lives as very old people. These discourses were commonly shared with us and offer productive clues as to how they can sustain their well-being. Atchley (1994) suggests that in aging research, the concept of self can be a central organizing concept linking the quality of life and the individual aging. While that proposition is undoubtedly true, it is difficult to test (Bengtson, Cutler, Mangen, & Marshall, 1985). If the self is viewed as resilient and dynamic, as it adapts to changing conditions, then it potentially becomes a shield against the adversities of later life. In this analysis, we have drawn upon the pragmatics of self suggested by Baltes (1993) and Ryff (1993) where the self is part of a dynamic process that arises out of and is influenced by experiences. Consequently the self is continually changing as an individual's conception of their identity responds to their environment.

Those who survive into late life have a unique status, for, on one hand, they are near death, but on the other hand, they have the specialness of having lived beyond the normal life span. With the realization that they are alive when their contemporaries are dead, these respondents tend to develop conceptions of themselves as very old. Although very disabled, they tend to view themselves as healthy for their age. And they also see themselves as detached from problematic aspects of the world around them.

As active manipulators of a self-concept molded to be compatible with their status, they also apply these skills to deal with time.

Most respondents live very much in the present and skillfully avoid bothersome memories of the past or worries about the future. In discourses about their lives, they speak of being "off time" in dying, yet beyond time. This process of molding a self concept and altering the subjective experiencing of time, we maintain, is one factor that controls the emotional consequences of events impinging upon the oldest old. In the next chapter, this linkage between interior psychological processes and the realities of the objective world will continue in an analysis of the emotional life of the oldest old and how they define their subjective well-being.

Chapter 9

Sustaining Well-Being: The Content of Emotional Life

In this chapter, we continue to explore the intriguing finding: individuals continue to express contentment over time even when experiencing rising disabilities. We conclude that in terms of their emotional life, most survivors are doing well. Since there are few social or environmental factors that can account for this stability or even improvement in their level of contentment, it appears that an important determinant of adapting to physical declines comes through psychological processes. Thus we pose the questions here, is there something unique about advanced old age? Do new personal strengths arise out of the vulnerabilities the very old face? Given the circumstances of many, why are not more of these very old individuals depressed, lonely, and anxious?

In the previous chapter, we described in some detail how respondents carry on discourses about their lives that interpret and explain their long-term survivorship. We have suggested that this process helps control the emotional consequences of the inevitable losses they face. It is common to observe from their discussions how they redefine and reinvent a self-concept that takes their survivorship into account. They also detach themselves from mundane and bothersome social ties and develop a practical conception of the finite time remaining in their lives. Furthermore, in evaluating their health, most consider themselves in good health even if they have numerous physical problems. They also emphasize a time orientation that focuses on the present, and in doing so, they minimize the effects of troublesome aspects of their past and potential worries about their future. This chapter first maps the subjective well-being of the survivors over five years and analyzes the respondents' discussions about emotional dimensions of their lives. Hopefully this material will go beyond the current emphasis on subjective well-being as an outcome variable and explore its key attributes in the context of the ongoing experiences of the oldest old.

Background

One of the most persistently studied outcome variables in aging research is some measure of subjective well-being—interchangeably referred to as morale, life satisfaction, or happiness (Maddox & Wiley, 1976). Most studies identify predictors of well-being such as education, marital status, health and, even in some regression models, the availability of transportation (Larsen, 1978). Psychological concepts of personal efficacy or a sense of control have been associated with a higher sense of well-being (Abler & Fretz, 1988; Rodin, 1986). Use of the self-system is also seen as a mediator between physical and mental health (Heidrich & Ryff, 1993). Missing from this large body of research, however, is a better understanding of the emotional state as a unit of study in itself (Ryff & Essex, 1991).

Despite the wide use of instruments measuring emotional states as outcome variables, the findings on the relationship between some version of well-being and age are decidedly mixed. This vast literature has inconclusive findings on whether older individuals grow progressively unhappier as they age. Large-scale epidemiological studies report lower rates of depression with increasing age (Newmann, 1989), while clinical studies find an increased incidence (Blazer, Hughes, & George, 1987). Paradoxically, others have found a lower incidence of depression but a high rate on symptom scales (Newmann, 1989). It also appears that the milder mood state, such as dysphoria, is found less in older than younger people (Gallo, Anthony, & Muthen, 1994). Whether these discrepancies are related to measurement deficiencies is uncertain. Ryff (1989) suggests that earlier conceptions of positive psychological functioning were based upon limited theoretical understanding. If that be the case, then the instruments to measure these emotional states may miss important aspects of positive psychological status.

To add to the confusion, the terms mood, affect, and emotion are used interchangeably to denote the ubiquitous subjective feelings encountered in daily life at any age. The fact that this phenomenon has no single identifier probably reflects the lack of precision in its definition and even the absence of common agreement about basic categories of emotions. Despite the great interest in subjective well-being, there is little evidence that gerontologists connect these observations and theories to the state-of-the-art findings about emotions at any age.

During the past 25 years, researchers and theorists clarified some of the ambiguities (Ekman, Serenson, & Friesen, 1969; Izard, 1977; Scherer & Ekman, 1984). For example, it is now generally accepted that irrespective of cultural variations in the display of emotion, universal, biologically based feelings may be observed. Although some controversy remains, there is now agreement on some basic emotions: *surprise, sadness, disgust, fear, contempt,* and *anger.* Moreover, these basic emotions are associated with specific facial expressions that activate various muscles to produce universally recognized markers of feeling as well as distinctive changes in the autonomic nervous system (Ekman, Serenson, & Friesen, 1969).

Until recently, emotion theorists and researchers have rarely studied how emotions change during the aging process. On one hand, some reports indicate that emotions decrease in intensity during old age, while others point to the crucial role emotions play in adaptation (Levenson, Carstensen, Friesen, & Ekman, 1991). For example, there is persuasive evidence that emotions continue to play a crucial role in later life in the linkage between social ties and morbidity (Berkman & Syme, 1979) and in bereavement (Schliefer, 1989). Most information on emotional states of older people remains indirect or anecdotal (Levenson, Carstensen, Friesen, & Ekman, 1991). Schulz (1985) in his thoughtful review of the scant empirical literature concludes that older people have a higher level of stored experience than younger people, a situation that might trigger greater intensity and duration of emotional responses and a potential increase in negative emotions.

Recent research is addressing this gap in the literature by exploring the extent to which emotions diminish in intensity with aging. One possibility is that emotions become increasingly central with aging but are better controlled or suppressed (Lawton, Kleban, Rajagopal, & Dean, 1992). A laboratory experiment found that, compared to younger people, older people control their emotions more, integrate them more into their lives, and describe them as more central (Carstensen & Turk-Charles, 1994). As the following will indicate, the emotions of the oldest old seem muted and, in most cases, relatively well controlled. Nevertheless, Carstensen and Turk-Charles (1994) suggest that emotions are more likely to be differentiated and mixed among older people so that, for example, depressed feelings may elicit concurrent anxiety and hostility.

Subjective Well-being over Six Years

Three sources of information were collected about emotions. First, a modified Bradburn Affect Balance Scale elicited responses at each interview on eight emotions—loneliness, anger, lethargy, feeling interested in something, depression, feeling of accomplishment, boredom, and, uneasiness about something without knowing why. In our study, where respondents were accustomed to an open-ended interview format, they spontaneously fleshed out the meanings of their forced-choice responses. Second, one structured question was always asked about happiness. "Taking all things considered, would you say you are: very happy, sometimes happy, or rarely happy?" Finally, at one contact, respondents were asked to discuss emotions they had experienced recently. The respondent-elicited information about their emotions have obvious advantages over forced-choice instruments in identifying the circumstances in which the emotion occurs.

Figure 9.1 plots changes in the Affect Balance Scale in five contacts over six years. It demonstrates a steady improvement in well-being over six years. While there are no significant changes between each contact, these oldest old report a significantly better mood at Time 5 when compared to Time 1. Since we do not know the norms of this scale for the oldest old, it is difficult to interpret why respondents become more contented over time. Of course, we

Mood (Mean Scores)

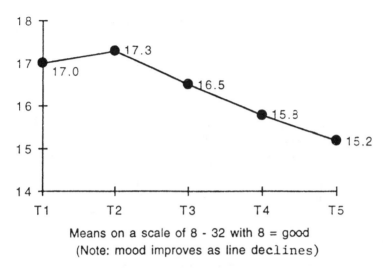

Means on a scale of 8 - 32 with 8 = good
(Note: mood improves as line declines)

FIGURE 9.1   Comparison of mood over six years

have considered that this may be a "halo" study effect—participation in the study has enhanced their sense of their special status as a survivor.

Table 9.1 presents the distribution of emotions among the 48 survivors in response to the Affect Balance Scale at the first, third, and fifth interview. Only one emotion significantly changed over six years; the survivors became less angry. On the other emotions, the proportion who were sometimes or often lonely, bored, or uneasy remained much the same over time. More changes were noted in emotions involving lethargy and depression but in an unanticipated direction. The survivors at Time 5 are less likely to be lethargic or depressed than they were at the outset. Likewise in their positive emotional states, the proportion who were sometimes or often interested in things and who had feelings of accomplishment in the past remained much the same. Consequently, these findings indicate that, at least on those specific emotions tapped in the Affect Balance Scale, most emotions remain steady and unchanging. These findings are consistent with our impressions and respondents' comments, that their emotions have "levelled off" over the years.

TABLE   9.1
Affect-Balance Responses by Survivors on Eight
Emotions at Times 1, 3, and 5 (by percentage who
sometimes or often experienced the emotion in the
past week, $n = 48$)

Emotion	Time 1	Time 3	Time 5
Angry	39	21	14*
Lethargic	53	54	35
Interested	51	46	48
Depressed	40	41	20
Accomplished	40	37	25
Bored	29	26	35
Uneasy	33	30	20
Lonely	38	41	38

The Content of Subjective Well-Being

Affect Balance

As they were responding to the forced choice questions from the Affect Balance Scale, we recorded the respondents spontaneous comments. First, respondents felt significantly less *anger*, down from 39 percent to 14 percent over five years (Table 9.1). Generally, the responses had a bimodal pattern. Either they never got angry, or they were frequently angry. A few described how anger neutralized the impact of other emotions. "I get angry a lot—that keeps depression at bay." Others could not explain their anger. "I'm getting to be a cranky old lady—I get angry for no reason at all." Others identified common sources of irritation.

"The most unimportant things annoy me—Right now, I am angry at my neighbor for parking in front of my driveway."

"I am angry at my landlord for raising my rent."

"I'm angry at my doctor for keeping me waiting."

Others deflect their anger from their immediate situation to the wider society—the state of the world, the programs they watch on television or current politics. One person targeted the supernatural as a source of her anger. "I'm angry at the Lord for letting me live so long, leaving me alive to suffer so much."

In contrast, others concluded that they have outlived that feeling and rarely became angry now that they had reached advanced old age. They report that they have better control over their anger than they did when they were younger. "I don't allow myself to get angry." Even with the frequent discussions about anger, it is possible that this emotion diminishes in advancing age as they detach themselves from bothersome situations. "It is so monotonous. I never blow up anymore. I just live and let live." "I have nothing anymore to make me angry." Memory loss also helps deal with anger, "I was angry yesterday, but today I forget what it was about."

Second, *lethargy*, or the feeling "they couldn't get going" was a less common emotion over time, down from 53 percent to only 35 percent. This feeling was often taken for granted as part of the aging process and was commonly traced to being in pain (Table 9.1).

"A bad day is when I can't get going."

"Some days I'm so damn lazy. I don't even want to make my bed, let alone clean the house."

"I accept being tired all the time, that's old age, but my mind is active."

Third, 46 percent to 51 percent said they had been particularly *interested* in something in the past week. Sources of interest were family happenings, a grandson's trip to Israel, new pictures of great grandchildren, a family birthday party, or world affairs. A new acquaintance or even the interviewer's visit was the focus of their interests.

Fourth, the numbers feeling *depressed* or very unhappy, decreased, 40 to 20 percent. Rather than discussing the source of unhappiness, respondents usually discussed this emotion in terms of their attempts to moderate its effects.

"I cry and get over it."

"I get a little depressed at night but I know daytime is just around the corner."

"I get depressed until I count my blessings."

Others were resigned, "I accept the fact that I'm 89 and I have to suffer." Still others may trace their feelings of depression to events such as the earthquake or worrisome news on television. They also reported how they coped with depression. "Everyone gets depressed. I do my best to handle it—I just communicate with myself and reason it out." "I'm inclined to be depressed, but it doesn't last long. I talk myself out of it."

Fifth, fewer, 25 percent at Time 5 in comparison to 40 percent at Time 1 had feelings of *accomplishment* over time. Accomplishment for the oldest old often came from completing ordinary tasks such as hemming a dress, paying monthly bills, being able to open a can of fruit or peeling an apple, getting the car fixed, doing the laundry, or walking outside alone. One woman said, "I've accomplished something when it is out of the ordinary, like making my bed in a shorter time—when I don't have to sit down in between." Another felt good after writing 40 thank-you notes following her 90th birthday party. In fact, a sense of accomplishment comes with any act of completion.

Sixth, 26 to 35 percent complained of *boredom*, but most concentrated their comments on how they surmounted that feeling. "I look out the window and watch the birds fly by." Others described how they were too busy to be bored. "There is too much to do. It takes my whole morning just watering my plants." Others described boredom as a constant state that is tolerated. "Boredom is my middle name, but what can one expect at this age?"

Seventh, when asked if they were *uneasy* about something without knowing why, 20 to 33 percent said they were sometimes or often. Some respondents described this emotion in terms of being alone. "I get scared at night. I'm afraid someone will break in." "I worry about getting older and having to be alone." Fear of being alone in some cases intensified fears of death, "I feel uneasy knowing when I go to sleep, I might not wake up," or "I'm uneasy about the unknown." But most respondents demonstrated some tactics to deal with persistent feelings of uneasiness.

"I take a pill."

"I call my daughter."

"I have that inner turmoil sometimes, but not on sunny days."

Eighth, 38 to 41 percent experienced *loneliness*, but this feeling was often described as controllable (Table 9.1).

"I'm too busy to be lonely."

"How could anyone be lonely when they have a radio and television."

"Some days I'm lonely, but then the day goes by and the next day comes and I'm not lonely."

Happiness, Sadness and Resignation

When asked general questions about their level of happiness and about the emotions they most commonly experienced, the majority of the respondents in our study concluded that their emotions had reached a plateau in their late life. Some explained that their emotional life was modulated by their cumulative experiences, so they had already been through so much emotional turmoil that they had little else to fear. In other words, their store of experiences lessened the impact of current sources of emotional reactions. They also trace their diminishing affect to the fact that they have less to worry them, because they encounter fewer people. Thus, their environment is devoid of stimuli that formerly triggered irritations.

"I'm just trying to exist and survive—that's all I do."

"I have no regrets. I forget the bad things in my life."

"I've even lived beyond worrying about my children."

In their self-reported responses to "all things considered," only 30 percent were unhappy. Those who reported they were happy traced their overall level of contentment to a generic factor inherent in their character or personality.

"I've always been a happy person."

"I've never let things get me down."

"After rain, there is always sunshine. That keeps me going." Others assume personal responsibility for their happiness, "I'm happy because I won't let things get me down. I won't argue with people." Small pleasures also can bring even more contentment to an already contented person. "What makes me happy is walking into a room with sunshine streaming in the window. Or when I'm having lunch with friends and the conversation is going lickety split."

Happiness was also traced to love of family.

"Love is important, because I am happy in my love of family and my good fortune to have them nearby."

"Every day I thank God I have my son."

"I'm happy because I still have my husband. If one of us is sick, the other looks out for him."

In comments about love as a source of happiness, some were all inclusive, "I love everybody." A few stressed immediacy, loving a helper, "I love Peggy like she is my daughter." Others love their children for their sacrifices, "I love my son for giving up his vacation and returning home to take care of me." Strong positive emotions were reported upon seeing a great grandchild, "I felt love when I saw the new baby—she is so beautiful." Only a few bemoaned the fact that they had no one left to love, "There is no chance to love, because no one is around." Others missed heterosexual love, "Since my husband died, I don't have that closeness of love."

Respondents who reported that they were "sometimes happy," concluded that happiness was an inappropriate term to describe their mood. "I don't like the word, 'happy.' I'm grateful for my family. I'm grateful that I can get out of bed each day. I can stand up. I can go to dinner. I can sleep. I wouldn't call that happiness—I'm just grateful." Another respondent concluded that the only one who is truly happy is a person who is romantically in love for the first time.

Others report a blurring between positive and negative moods.

"I'm not really happy but I'm not sad either."

"I enjoy some things, but I can't say I'm really happy."

"My mood comes and goes. Sometimes I'm happy, and other times I'm pretty low."

It is interesting to find that so few traced a mood state to regrets about the past, and then it was a relatively minor complaint. "I wish I had traveled more." More often they established distance from their immediate life by linking their well-being to current affairs.

"I'm not feeling at all happy about what I see on television."

"The world situation is the only thing that bothers me. I worry about what the future will bring to my grandchildren and great grandchildren."

If happiness is most often traced to strong social ties, unhappiness is likely to be attributed to poor health or limited functioning.

"I'm a bundle of nerves because of my health."

"How can I be happy when I'm in pain all the time."

"What makes me unhappy is the state of my health."

Some unhappy respondents were belligerent to the interviewer, "How can you even ask such a question when you see the state I'm in? I'm mad all the time because of what is happening to me. I took my body for granted for so long. Now poor health interferes with my whole being." As might be expected, increased dependency often accompanies poor health and is also cited as a source of discontent. "I'm not happy. I hate to depend on others. I can barely take care of myself." Only a few responses traced unhappiness to impending death. "I cry a lot when I'm alone. I get to thinking about death." A man with no surviving family members concluded, "I used to be happy but I'm not now. I have nothing special to live for. I can't do anything any more. The time has come for me to die."

Others discussed their sadness with resignation as an emotion they experienced in relation to specific circumstances, such as "when my best friend died" or "when I visit my husband's grave." Others describe feelings of sadness associated with the realization they have no one left, "I get quite blue, because my family is gone and so are my friends." This respondent like others, then adds a counterpoint, "But then I only feel blue when I'm tired" or ". . . when it is foggy." Thus, most retain sufficient control over their feelings of sadness, so they are able to avoid depression.

In their open-ended discussions of emotions, some mentioned anxiety about their increased disabilities, and related to that, the fear that they might have to go to a nursing home. Others expressed anxiety about family members, such as a daughter who has cancer or a son who is unemployed. But here also, respondents are likely to deal with the negative effects cognitively. "I get anxious about my health, but I realize I'm basically a secure person."

"I let things take their course, and my feelings have levelled off."

"When you get to be my age, you expect bad things to happen— like when my best friend committed suicide. I don't dwell on it, because there is nothing I can do about it."

Others are philosophical. "I try to avoid being sad. Life goes on. I don't want to see so many deaths, but I accept it as part of life." "I don't let myself get sad. If it comes on, I say, 'Now wait a minute. God, the great creator, has made a wonderful world for me.'"

Impediments to Well-Being

Most respondents concluded that, despite their many problems, they have become less emotionally reactive with increasing age. In response to questions about their worries, they implicitly use cognitive processes to moderate possible negative effects, such as forgetting unpleasant events in their past or manipulating the meaning of the troublesome situation. In exploring the types of problems the oldest old discuss, we noted in Chapter 3 that they differed from younger respondents whose ages ranged from 70 to 84. They worried less about their spouse and children, and they were less likely to report economic problems.

In fact, they were more likely to say they had outlived most worries about their past. Some even said that they had outlived earlier health problems such as recurrent migraine headaches. Nevertheless, 90 percent at the first contact described events or generalized feelings that undermined their well-being. And similar to other areas of their lives, they welcomed the opportunity to discuss their complaints with us.

When asked about the most difficult things they were currently facing, the most common responses again were about their physical status and the concomitant constrictions their increased disability placed upon their lives. Some complained about not getting out as much as they wanted to, because they had to give up driving, or they could no longer take a bus. Others complained about their inability to do the most mundane chore, like making their bed. Dealing with pain was also a source of complaints, "Every day is a bad day when I'm in pain." The effects of physical problems also resulted in a general ennui, "A bad day is when I can't get going. It's an unpleasant feeling—not being able to function."

Even more common were complaints about how the deaths of family and friends affected their well-being. Some experienced multiple losses in a short period of time, "My husband and I are so feeble—we can't deal with losing two sons in one year." "I lost 14 friends in the past year." Even the loss of pets becomes particularly significant in late life, "I damned near died when my dog died last year. How can I get a new dog when I'm 90?" Some linked these losses to loneliness, while others concluded, "I have nothing left to worry about—everyone I care about is in the cemetery."

Although sadness was readily associated with the loss of others, only a few associated a negative mood with a family situation—a grandson's divorce, a son's heart disease, or a daughter's economic problems. In such cases, the respondents concluded that they could no longer influence outcomes and hence were unaffected. Likewise, specific sources of discontent with their lives were rarely mentioned, such as a noisy neighbor or a slight from a friend. Finally, out of all the respondents, only three traced their unhappiness to regrets about the past.

Of the 10 percent who stated categorically that they never had any problems, this positive trait was traced to their basic personality, "It's my nature—I've always been easy going." Others associated their problem-free life to their shrinking social networks, "I've lost my husband and my daughter and friends. It's bearable, because that is what life is all about." Still others make a distinction between real problems and merely minor difficulties, things they refer to as annoyances or irritations.

A thoughtful 90-year-old woman concluded,

> If I had died at 65, I would have had a truly happy life. I would have thought I was the luckiest woman in the world. Since then, I have had lots of tragedies. My husband died after a long and painful illness; my stepson committed suicide; I became completely alienated from my daughter, and most of my friends have died. Now I cope with tragedy with a sense of detachment. I feel I've managed all these losses. I can handle any new tragedy.

Minimizing the Emotional Consequences.

Our review of open-ended discussions about their emotional lives adds additional confirmation about the resourcefulness of the very old. They are active agents in moderating the effects of negative emotions and enhancing positive emotional states. Perhaps greater tolerance for negative events increases in advanced old age. "Having lived through the best and the worst of life, there is nothing more to react to," typifies one conclusion. Equanimity can be achieved through putting their emotions into the context of long-term survivorship. As long-term survivors, they accept the likelihood of social and physical losses and have minimal expectations for the future. In fact, most had never expected to live so long. Consequently, by positive comparisons with their deceased or disabled contemporaries, they are doing better or, at best, as well off as they can expect to be.

These discussions of mood states are permeated by personal commentary about how the respondents cope with specific situations that undermine their well-being. Few negative comments stood alone without adding some clarification. Although loss is the overriding experience that can undermine well-being, most reports of negative experiences were followed immediately by descriptions of how they coped with the effects. The dialogues respondents carry on with themselves, some maintain, helps them dilute feelings of sadness and demoralization. This "talking cure" redefines their emotional reaction. For example, with the deaths of close relationships, the respondents commonly expressed relief. "I've learned to be philosophical about death. After the initial shock, I conclude they are at rest—they are no longer in pain." Others cope effectively by deflection. "I shed a few tears and think about the good times we had. And then I sit down and write their family."

Two general types of responses were noted. First, some oldest old confront their problems head on. As we have noted earlier, these oldest old are methodical and practical in meticulously planning how to deal with their negative feelings. Anxiety about having an automobile accident leads to making a map of the safest routes to take. Worries about money are addressed by careful budgeting. Frustration about housekeeping is lessened by simplifying the home environment and discarding belongings. One woman went so far as to change her appearance,

> After my daughter died, I was depressed. My doctor recommended I see a psychiatrist. How could I tell my innermost feelings to a stranger when I am 90 years old. Instead I put a rinse on my hair, bought new clothes, and stopped looking in the mirror. I felt like a new person, a younger person.

As a second mechanism, discontent is controlled through discourses with themselves, those cognitive searches for explanations which either alone or in combination with direct actions were used to solve problems. For example, Mr. Atkinson detached himself from his unpleasant situation.

> I get ideas that bother me just sitting here alone—just negative stuff about death. I know it doesn't mean a thing. I know the good Lord won't hit me on the head—he would give me warning before taking me off. But even knowing that, I get afraid and can't sleep. In the middle of the night, I feel I'm going to die. I get up and wander around the house, thinking it through. Then I go back to bed and go to sleep. It's just fear, but I get over it.

Similarly, a woman commented, "I have to come to grips with my limitations and get my satisfaction in different ways. Like I loved my home, but I couldn't keep it up. When I moved into this apartment, I tried to recreate the environment but on a smaller scale." Others speak of how they deflect their worries by sheer determination. "After my husband died and I sold our business, I felt lost. I'd cry every night, or I did until I found I could control my grief by thinking about my parents."

More respondents are successful in deflecting problems, not by repression or selective forgetting, but by changing the meanings of their negative feelings. These individuals conclude, "Whatever comes along, I know I can handle it." "When I get unhappy, I tell myself, 'It's up to you'. You create your own sunshine and rain." One woman found benefits by thinking about the worst thing that could possibly happen to her; then everything else could be well tolerated.

According to some, it is also possible to moderate the emotional consequences of their complaints by strategies of retreat, detachment, or resignation. For example, an isolated man says, "Nobody makes me a problem and I make nobody a problem." Others intentionally retreat emotionally, "Whenever I have trouble, I withdraw into myself to heal myself." Another woman approached her fear of death, "Last year I thought I was going to die. I started giving things away. By now, I still haven't died, but I'm more contented now, because I know I won't last long."

Some respondents capitalized upon their diminished affect. They concluded that in their advanced old age, they have improved their capacity to cope, because they care less about what happens. Namely, they take their lives less seriously, "I know when my eyesight is completely gone, I'll be six feet under." "At my age, I'm finally able to throw sad thoughts off—it took a year after my wife's death." There is also the attitude that there is nothing one can do to address major problems, "As you get older, you get more adjusted to things. I don't get upset anymore. I am more content, even though I am not happier." Resignation proved effective to a disabled, housebound woman, "My worst problem is waking and realizing how helpless I am. But when you get to be this age, you just accept it." In a few cases, religion is a useful resource to cope with problems. "I have a lot of faith in God. I trust God to take me at the right time. He has kept me alive, and when I die, I know eternity is coming. That will be the best time in all."

Some Examples of Unhappiness

Although we did not assess psychiatric states by clinical means, all interviewers were familiar with the signs and symptoms associated with clinical depression. These include despondence, self-recrimination, suicidal ideation, decreased appetite, insomnia, obsessive thought, and inability to function. By interviewer judgments, it appeared that clinical depression was rare. Some respondents identified by the Affect Balance Scale as unhappy, continually complained about their situation. They also complained about sleep problems, poor appetite, and overall lethargy, but not to the extent as seen in clinical depression. For example, Mr. Foster had always led an active life, so when his mobility became limited, he became most unhappy.

> I feel blue once or twice a day. I'm trapped. I can't go too far from the bathroom, or I'll wet my pants like a baby. Last night I fell down, and I couldn't get up. I sit and watch television, and there is nothing there. The screen might as well have been blank for all the interest I have in it. I can't do anything.

Those who complain about the length of the days may stay in bed until noon. One man who felt abandoned by his children retreated, "I don't think there is anyone who cares about me. I'd never be dependent upon my children. If I get cancer, I just want to roll over and die." Sometimes depressed feelings are intermittent. One woman reported,

> I fall asleep every afternoon. I can't help it—the house is so quiet, and I am haunted by my memories. I've lost all my friends; six died in the past year and two went to nursing homes. I only eat to fill the time, because I have to eat before taking my nine pills. Otherwise I'd sleep.

Another describes her depression as a temporary state.

> I don't know why I'm waking up now every morning feeling depressed. I'm not usually like that. I do know there is a lot to be depressed about—the world is a mess. I keep telling myself I should see more people. But then, I don't feel up to it, so I stay in bed until afternoon. I know it's better to get up, but there seems to be no reason to. At times I get to feeling sorry for myself, but I tell myself I'm being foolish. Inside I say, "What's the good of it. Life is supposed to be like this when everybody is gone."

In some cases, a depressed mood or demoralization is traced to a life-long personality characteristic. For example, Mrs. Sutton had always been active socially, so when her children insisted she no longer drive, she felt socially deprived. She complained at each interview about how lonely and isolated she felt, what poor help she had, and how foggy and cold it was. These complaints persisted in spite of the fact that she still went out several times a week and had frequent visitors. Her telephone rang frequently during the interviews. In fact, once when we called to set up an interview, her complaints over the phone were drowned out by what sounded like a convivial party at her house. Nevertheless, as time went on, she became such a negative and petulant person that she no longer could retain live-in help. Ultimately, she was forced to enter a nursing home, where she died after two months and only four months before her 100th birthday.

Conclusion

With any age group, the evaluation of emotions is fraught with conceptual and methodological issues. Such problems are compounded in studies of individuals 85 years and older. While various instruments measuring morale, life satisfaction, or subjective well-being offer outcome variables, very little attention is directed to the emotional states of older people.

One of the difficulties in interpreting responses to emotional status at any time in life is deciding the temporal extent of the responses to instruments or interview questions. Are such responses indicative only of feelings at the time of the interview, or can they indicate more pervasive, chronic patterns? Our research compensates for this problem through repeated interviews where successive reports can be compared and contrasted, to suggest either change or stability in emotional life. At least five findings can be gleaned from the descriptive material in this chapter.

First, the oldest old survivors not only maintain a sense of well-being but also they are likely to improve their self-ratings. Apparently, over time they are likely to transcend those factors that undermine well-being.

Second, few in the study were so demoralized as to exhibit the symptoms of clinical depression.

Third, respondents commonly attributed their positive mood to their resignation or coming to terms with the realities of late late life. Hence, a levelling of their emotions has occurred.

Fourth, in this chapter and the previous one, the positive aspects of selective withdrawal and detachment are readily apparent. Through a reduction of activities and a constriction of their social life, the oldest old studied here live in a world with fewer irritants or stressors that potentially undermine well-being.

Fifth, the variations in character traits are also apparent in these discussions. Some individuals most likely have always been relatively contented, while others are prone to unhappiness. Then there are some who complain constantly but balance the negative by mentioning some positive feature of their life. We have labelled this type of response as the "tapioca effect." One respondent entered a nursing home because of sensory losses and painful rheumatoid arthritis. When interviewed there, she complained continually, "I'm ready to go. I'm sick of being in such pain. I can't see television any more or read. I want the Lord to take me." But then after a time, her face brightened and she added, "You know, today is Wednesday and I will have tapioca pudding for dinner."

Chapter 10

Profiles in Survivorship

To this point, we have placed an emphasis upon the pervasive losses in late life. These experiences include the loss of functioning because of ever increasing disabilities and the losses through death of family members and friends. Consequently the activities of daily living become increasingly harder to manage. Despite these challenges, many survivors are able to cope with daily hassles and exercise some measure of control over their lives. More importantly, they are able to control the emotional consequences of these losses by manipulating their meanings, a process that may account for the finding that their well-being did not diminish over six years, but instead actually improved.

In this chapter, we present varied examples of adaptation that illustrate how most oldest old are able to mobilize their personal and social resources to meet the demands of late life. Case studies were selected to demonstrate the multilayered variations in adaptive styles. First, some respondents illustrate how effectively they can reconstitute their self-image as very old and as finite, and as different from their younger selves. They then go on to effectively act upon this evaluation by coping with daily activities and in developing a sense of control over their lives. Second, others may react to long-term survivorship by surrendering autonomy over their life and accepting with relief some dependency upon others. Third, a transition from engagement to disengagement is appropriate for some in late late life; namely at the personal level, each tailors his or her concept of what is successful. The outcome can take numerous forms. Some disengage from problematic relationships, others give up social engagements and retreat into family life, while others retreat into a spiritual world of prayer or revery. Finally, it is appropriate to conclude with a worst-case scenario of one who is ending her life with few personal or social resources except for the strong will to survive.

Coping and a Sense of Control

Two women illustrate effectiveness in meeting the typical challenges of late life. They both respond with actions that manage their daily living. At the same time, they continually sift through the meanings about their declining health and seek to lessen the emotional consequences of increasing deficits.

An Actor and Reactor

Mrs. Albert is a particularly good example of adaptation as both an actor and reactor.

At the first interview, she was 86 and had been widowed for 30 years. Her husband had been a popular obstetrician and is still remembered fondly in the community where she has lived in the same house for almost 60 years. Her son and daughter live some distance away, and her relationship with both of them is intimate, but geographically distant. She sees her son every other year and her daughter several times a year. In most respects, she effectively adapted to increasing disability over her six years in the study, at the same time she continued to maintain an active social life. She is notable for her effective mastery over her environment and for her overall contentment with her life.

Her *health status* at the outset was good, although she reported, "I'm a little under the weather after a long flight from the East." She exercised fastidious control over her health. In selecting a new doctor, she decided she wanted a woman in her 40s, "Someone who will see me through to the end." When the woman she chose proved to be rather aloof, Mrs. Albert acted, "She might be someone who wouldn't remember me if I called with an emergency in the middle of the night." Consequently, she deliberately cultivated a relationship with her, always asking about her daughter and referring her friends to her.

Subsequently, she developed difficulty walking and went through an unsuccessful procedure in the hospital to improve the blood flow to her legs.

With her increasing mobility problems, she secured more help with gardening. She enjoyed participating in the research, and at each contact, she prepared for the interview by making a detailed list of topics she wanted to discuss. Much information on her list concerned how she maintained control over her health by exercise, a schedule of medical and dental visits, and a good diet. She also pointed out the therapeutic effects of having a Bloody Mary each day before lunch and a martini before dinner.

During the next year, she had more health problems. "My health is definitely worse. I have less energy. My heart doesn't pump enough blood, so I have atypical angina. I feel like a stuffed doll much of the time." She experienced several blackouts at dinner parties. And she also had a bladder infection and then a reaction to the medications treating it. After these difficulties, she worried that she would never see her sister again or visit her hometown in Connecticut, the area where she had spent her formative years. Without hesitation and despite her declining health, she planned an arduous trip back East to visit her sister, relatives, and some surviving friends. "It was like a pilgrimage. It might be my last opportunity. It helped me tremendously." When a friend tried to convince her that she shouldn't undertake such a trip, she reacted with anger, telling her it was none of her business. Also her fatalism was evident in her decision not to undertake the expense of repairing earthquake damage to the foundation of her house. Such a feeling of imminent death proved to be unnecessary, however, for her health improved during the next year. "Life is a series of compromises. I can't walk up hills. I don't go out at night anymore. My hearing is worse, so I avoid noisy restaurants."

At the fifth contact at age 92, she said in response to health questions, "I'm steadily going down hill." After a third blackout, again at a dinner party, she had a three-hour wait in the emergency room. As one in control over her life, she consulted with her doctor, and they both agreed that she should not subject herself to the discomfort of another emergency room visit. She was to tell her friends and family to do nothing. "I tell them I've had these before; that they should just wait a while, and I'll be all right." At this contact she decided against having a tooth extracted, that was causing considerable pain. "Is it really worth it? The shock may shorten my life." Thus, her mastery over the changes in physical status was impressive, extending to her even making her own decision about life-threatening incidents.

Her *social network* was dense with friends, and her calendar was full most of the time. That schedule also was closely planned. When she went to social functions, she called ahead to find out where to park. She had some social activity almost every day, and when home, she had many telephone calls from friends. Over time her friendships remained the same in number, but she altered their form to accommodate to her increasing disabilities. She began to avoid large parties because of her hearing loss. She no longer entertained at meals and instead had friends for drinks or tea. Yet her friends remained very important to her, and she readily provided a sympathetic ear to those with troubles. She also organized support groups for friends with serious health problems. "The only change is I leave the initiative to my friends, about socializing. I accept invitations if I think I will enjoy it. I am not giving up on that." After six years, she had increasing difficulty shopping, but she still attempted to entertain occasionally.

Her family life differed greatly from sociability with her friends. With her children, she maintained, she had a warm relationship, "We are devoted to each other without being wedded to each other." She sent money at Christmas to her children and grandchildren and welcomed their periodic visits. When her son also developed some health problems, she described her mixed feelings.

I find I'm not concerned. I mean that I don't think about it night and day. Life is a series of adjustments. I love to see my children, but I love to see them go home. When they visit, they try to take over. They want me to plan my memorial service and to take care of burial arrangements. I accept that as something that has to be done. What I don't like is their wanting me to become an old woman, like using a cane and wearing my hearing aid.

Clearly Mrs. Albert prefers sociability with her age peers over generational bonds.

Her closest relationship remained with her sister in the East, as she reported, "I feel the time ticking away. I want to see her as much as possible." As time went on, however, frequent flights became increasingly difficult, so instead she sent her sister a plane ticket each summer.

In order to sustain her *mood and motivations*, Mrs. Albert devised a number of strategies. She had the memory problems typical of those her age and effectively compensated for this loss by writing everything down. She also described having increased problems with directions, like distinguishing her right from her left hand. To cope with these problems, she assigned herself projects to keep herself mentally acute, like updating her address book, organizing her correspondence, and filing letters from her husband when he was serving overseas during the war. While updating her address book, the numbers of friends who died were impressive,

I hated to see all those names crossed off—that's why it was time to fill in a new one. I think of that, of course—every day I feel a little sad. Who wouldn't when seeing all those who are not around any more. But this is counteracted by euphoria. I have happy fantasies. I also get pleasure out of accomplishing something. Oh, I have bad days that are without purpose, when I feel at loose ends. Then I get anxious because I'm not functioning.

Nevertheless, Mrs. Albert usually described herself as contented or at times happy.

When upset, I call upon my memories. And I still have very happy reunions with my sister. I really enjoy life. I have my projects, so I feel I can accomplish something. I wouldn't change my life. I sometimes think I could just

fade out when I'm not feeling well, but at a convenient time, of course. Death has always been a part of my life. I don't fear it. It's just something that has to be faced.

She shifted her discussion to her new address book as symbolic of the strong urge to get things straightened out. "An up-to-date book will help my children after I die." She then went on to discuss how she had more difficulty recently in controlling her anger, but then concluded, "I'm a strong-willed person—that's what keeps me alive." Her list of topics she wanted to discuss in the interview included her thoughts about her mood,

When I'm alone, I have an active feeling of happiness—a heightened appreciation of Spring and birds' songs coming in open windows. I also have an appreciation of close friends, confidences, making the right decisions on clothes, helpers, achievements. I get pleasure also thinking this all out as I prepared for the interview.

All Dressed Up and Ready to Go

Like Mrs. Albert, Mrs. Carter is an effective adapter who, as her physical status changes, reconstitutes who she is and how she wants to be.

At age 86 initially, she remained contented and socially active over six years despite a series of serious health problems. Divorced for 38 years, she was living with her adopted son, who worked nights at a local hotel. Throughout the interviews, she dwelt upon raising her son alone, supporting him by working two shifts as a nurse. She retired from nursing at age 75, and since then has worked in real estate. In her past, she had managed a dress shop and a yarn shop, experiences that may account for her great enthusiasm about shopping. She is a good looking woman, always attractively dressed, who looks much younger than her age.

In her *physical status*, she is proud of the fact that her doctor can't believe she is 86. "It's because I have so much energy and my health is excellent." As the interview ensued, however, we learned about her numerous health problems: she was legally blind because of macular degeneration, "bad knees and arthritis," a heart condition, high cholesterol, and high blood pressure. She passed it off by saying, "I take a bunch of medicines for all that." She also added, "I've had back pain for so long I don't think about it any more." A year later, she reported that she had had a major pulmonary thrombosis affecting 80 percent of her lungs, which brought on a heart attack. Even after a month in the hospital, she described her health as better than most her age. She had also adjusted well to her poor eyesight by getting special adapters for her stove and a magnified lamp for reading.

A year later, she had knee surgery but easily regained most functioning. She also wore a Life Line in case something happened while her son was gone. Although she said her health was excellent, she confided, "My doctor said I should rest more because of my heart. I am only getting half the amount of blood to my heart. He worries, because I feel tired all the time. Of course, I take a monstrous amount of medications." She had had cataract surgery, but the doctor advised against surgery on her other knee. By the fifth contact, her only physical complaint was an allergy. Then later she reported, "I'm in pain all the time, and the doctor still worries about my heart. He put a monitor on it and warned me it was skipping all the time. He said that could be the end of me. Now he wants to put in a pacemaker, but I don't think I need it." Despite these problems, she was undaunted. "My son asked why I was so dressed up yesterday in the morning. I told him that I wanted to look nice and be ready to go at the drop of a pin in case a friend calls and says. 'Let's go somewhere.' "

In her *social involvements*, Mrs. Carter devotes herself to her relationship with her son. They go out to eat several times a week, and she occasionally goes with him when he eats out with friends. Although she claims all her friends are dead, she has an active life, her phone rings all the time, her neighbor drops in often, and she is a confidant to many. "All cry on my shoulder. I love people, and I love to help them." Only after her pulmonary thrombosis and her heart attack did these activities diminish, but then it slackened mainly because she had so many doctors' appointments. After her recovery, however, she began inviting her niece's children for visits during their summer vacation. After her knee replacement during the next year, she was looking forward to taking a cruise with her neighbor. She also was devoted to her cat of 17 years. In subsequent contacts, she had restored much of her social involvements, going out with friends several times a week. Even with her heart problems, she looked forward to a week at her son's vacation place in the mountains. Her favorite activity in the city was roving around the shopping malls.

Throughout all of her serious, even life-threatening health problems and the pain and disability of her chronic conditions, Mrs. Carter's *psychological adjustments* were exceptional. She was effective in minimizing the health threats she continually faced by repressing the serious implications. "I no longer think about it." Even when her doctor tells her she could die any time, she says, "I think he is wrong, because I feel so much better now." At each contact, she reported she was happy or at best, contented. She also pointed to her assets. "I have a good mind, and I'm pretty balanced." Later she commented,

> I'm happy most of the time, because I have a good support system, a loving son, and financial security. I don't let anything worry me. I take one day at a time, and I'm thankful I've lived so long. I don't dread death. When we're ready, God comes for us. If I've lived a good life, I know a better life is ahead.

Surrendering Autonomy

With rising disability, some realistically turn to others for help. In fact, most welcome with relief a more secure life under the attention of another, particularly if they had been trying unsuccessfully to care for themselves. Assuming a dependent status, nonetheless, is at odds with the normative criteria of our culture. Probably no value orientation in our culture is more incongruent with the situation of older people than the strong emphasis upon independence and mastery. At the normative level, our cultural directives strongly endorse independence as a desired goal and dependence as a negative situation to be avoided. Basic dilemmas are particularly prominent in the clash between such a cultural directive and the realities of their lives.

The loss of autonomy and need for help are so common among those in their 80s and 90s. Reid (1984) in his research on older people in institutions describes the dilemma between independence and dependence that can be usefully applied to noninstitutionalized older people as well. Patients he studied express little desire to exercise control, because they fear that such efforts might reduce their level of care. Passivity bordering upon apathy is one means to secure and maintain a predictable environment. While most patients initially struggle to maintain control, at some point, they come to terms with their failure with a sense of relief. At that point, others take over. The oldest old in our study likewise articulate a personally acceptable means of being dependent upon others. Two survivors are good illustrations of this process.

Dependent and Contented

Mrs. Perry was 87 at the outset of the research. She was living with her husband, a retired pharmacist, while an unmarried son lived in a cottage in their back yard.

> Mr. Perry's health was declining, and he had difficulty controlling his diabetes. Mrs. Perry was in good health and only complained of occasional aches and pains. Her main activities centered on household chores and taking long walks. A year later, his health had declined further, and he had

become agitated and confused. Mrs. Perry and her son secured help in the mornings, while they managed the rest of the caregiving. Because of his increasing health problems, however, she experienced stress from the caregiving chores. By the next year, her husband's condition had worsened to the point they needed 24-hour care. She hired a woman who referred to herself as "Big Mama," an affable but controlling woman who not only took care of Mr. Perry, but also directed her attention to Mrs. Perry's diet and her daily regimen. Mrs. Perry welcomed her company and the extra attention she was receiving, and her previous symptoms of stress disappeared.

The next year, Mrs. Perry was recuperating from a fall and surgery, so both she and her husband received the care and attention of "Big Mama." Her husband had become demented, while Mrs. Perry showed some mental decline as well. She was well dressed, and the house was immaculate amid diapers, catheters, and all the paraphernalia of home care. Mrs. Perry no longer went upstairs, and each day "Big Mama" bathed and dressed her. Although on weekends, Mrs. Perry could handle this personal care, she appreciated the extra assistance. Most of her day was spent on the living room couch, where she contentedly watched TV. "I'm much more cheerful than I used to be. Big Mama takes such good care of me." At the last contact, almost six years after the first, Mr. Perry had died, but his attentive helper stayed on to concentrate her efforts on the care of Mrs. Perry.

At the last contact, "Big Mama" encouraged the interviewer to come over, reassuring her that, "Little Mama is as sharp as a tack." When the interviewer arrived, Mrs. Perry was sitting on the couch watching TV, again clean and well groomed. Her responses were vague and abbreviated, but accompanied by a contented laugh. She also turned to "Big Mama" and her son for help in responding to questions. She described her health as "pretty good," and only complained of a few aches and pains. Her world was confined to the couch surrounded by a commode, television, and a table filled with medications. Each day, she took a walk around the living room, assisted by her helper and a walker. She always stopped at her husband's picture saying, "Hello, Honey, I love you." Her favorite time of the day was bedtime, when she had a glass of brandy. Her son laughingly remarked that she only drank the most expensive brand.

A Full Circle

A shift from autonomy to dependence also occurred in the life of a wealthy upper-class man.

Mr. Reynolds dramatically changed over the course of the study. At age 87, he was still going to work each day at a major law firm where he had been a prominent lawyer for years. He had some health problems that restricted his diet, but he was able to eat a special lunch at his downtown club. He then returned home to "take care of his wife," along with several nurses and servants. She had Alzheimer's Disease that progressively worsened over six years. He was emotionally distant from his children, and most of his friends were dead. "I don't have bad days—I just have boring days. That's what my age means to me—I feel lonely, because there is no one left I have roots to." A year later, it was impossible to complete the interview because of his hearing problems and his anxiety as he awaited word of a possible diagnosis of cancer. Two teams of round-the-clock help came daily to take care of him as well as his wife. He no longer went to work or even left the house.

Another year later, his health was better, and he seemed more contented with his life, possibly because he no longer attempted to be autonomous. He did not have cancer, so his hearing was his main problem. Two helpers took him and his wife out to lunch weekly, and in anticipation of a long-term caregiving arrangement they were renovating their home. Mr. Reynolds was somewhat withdrawn but interested in the current financial news. After six years, at 93 years of age, his situation was much the same. He was dressed in a white shirt, woolen slacks, and sweater. He ate lunch and dinner alone in the formal dining room. His hearing problems had increased his isolation, but he compensated by reading most of his waking hours. By his chair in his study, he had the local newspaper, a stack of Agatha Christie mysteries, and a biography of Margaret Thatcher. He was sleeping more, actually spending as much as twelve hours in bed. He had developed a fear of falling, so he never walked unassisted. He also had numerous health complaints that were carefully tended to by his nurses. He concluded that his life now resembled his childhood when his nanny and his governess were always there to take care of him.

From Activity to Disengagement

Not only do most very old people come to terms with the inevitable physical changes in late life and arrive at the realization that they can no longer be completely independent, but they also usually simplify their social world and limit their social involvements. Early in the research, we recognized a process of disengagement as one element of effective adaptation. In singling out the disengagers among survivors, however, we found examples of both voluntary and involuntary processes. For example, one woman previously described was unable to adjust to her disappearing friendship network and was never quite able to compensate by enjoying her attentive family. Disengagement is forced upon others because of worsening incontinence. Nevertheless, most coped with involuntary changes by some means that kept depression at bay.

Personal Control but Spiritual Retreat

Miss Grieg, the retired banker, was described in Chapter 7 as one who had a methodical and compulsive routine. She is a relevant example here, for her regimen included disengagment from others and a retreat into a spiritual world.

> She was the fifth of eight children in an Irish Catholic family. As the only unmarried child, she recounted her life.

> *I gave up my life for my mother, who lived until 98. From my mid-30s to my mid-60s, I took care of her. I lived a lovely peaceful life with her. I got up each day at five, fed her, bathed her and dressed her, and prepared her lunch. Then I went to work. That was my routine for 30 years. After she died, I took care of her brother until his death.*

> *I did what I could to alleviate pain and suffering, but I loved too much. That was an awful pain for me to bear. I realized at that point in my life that if I wrapped myself up too much in another person, then I would always be in pain. I'd always worry about them. With a family life, you live their life, not your own. It's not your life any more. That's why I never married. I have less to worry about, because I have few attachments. I don't want to use up any energy that dilutes the power of my mind and my prayers.*

> Living out her life in an attractive one-bedroom apartment with noisy cable cars going by frequently, she divided her days between practical efforts to manage her daily tasks and spiritual efforts to give meaning to her life. She recounted how she turned to her religious and spiritual beliefs after having had three nervous breakdowns, crises she traced to her continual worries about others. "When you are young, you have so many goals, you always are disappointed. I learned early to detach myself from people to avoid these disappointments." Most discussions were dominated by her spiritual beliefs and even her tastefully decorated apartment had a framed, handwritten statement, "I am whole, perfect, strong, powerful, loving, harmonious, and happy," an affirmation she said she framed so as to be reminded of many inspiring messages.

> *Old age is just old age. Life is a school. Every problem has an answer if our minds guide us. I am withdrawing from the world and will leave it in God's hands. "Thy will be done." I used to be a worry wart. I am so glad to have reached old age, so I can turn my worries over to others. I am also comforted when my mother comes to me. I see her sitting right there where you are,*

and I talk to her. I have never mentioned her visits to others, for they would think me a senile old woman.

She has devised numerous compensations for her self-determined isolation. "I love sitting under a tree and seeing a spider weave a web." She also described her love of music from the 1920s.

When I hear a song on the radio, I get up and do the two-step. I enjoy my own company. I love corny music, like on the Lawrence Welk show. At my age, I can let my hair down and laugh at my mistakes. I think this is the best time in life, because I don't take things seriously any more.

At the next interview, however, she reversed these views.

I think old age is a terrible thing. I should have been dead years ago. I've had my troubles, and I've had to figure things out for myself. That's when I turned to my religion as a guidepost. Now I know I can turn everything over to a higher power. If I can't sleep, I pray. If I get upset, I say, "Father, take this feeling from my heart and enlighten me." With this help, I can talk myself into an attitude that every day is a good day, if I can see it that way.

On the Outside Looking In

When Mrs. Litsky joined the study, she was an active advocate of Gray Panthers. In fact, we contacted her after reading her letter to a local newsletter for older people about her experience of being verbally abused by her grandson.

This incident, we learned, was a fleeting complaint, for she had a friendly but distant relationship with her grandchildren. Instead her worries focused upon her own health. She had fallen, and her mobility was sharply curtailed. As a further insult to her well-planned life, her male companion had recently died. After a 10-year relationship, his loss was traumatic. Consequently, by our second contact, she spent most of her days in her small apartment, getting around with difficulty with her walker. She seemed lonely and depressed. Her two children lived nearby and dropped in frequently for brief visits, but they provided little companionship.

As her mobility deteriorated, she had to trade her walker for a wheelchair. She also became incontinent. She complained,

I'm getting forgetful and losing my hearing—the only thing I still have is my brain. I think I'm living too long. When you're young, you still have optimism. One door closes but another opens. When you're at the end like I am no more doors open. It's not easy to be a survivor. What hurts the most is the death of my friends. I've lost them all. Here people move in and out all the time. I don't consider myself important anymore, because I have no affirmation from anyone.

> *I always knew if I lived long enough, I'd have to go from being an extro-*
> *vert to an introvert. The good thing is I can be introspective—I can be on*
> *the outside looking in. Now I spend much more time alone, I watch more TV.*
> *I also keep my feelings to myself more. Until now, I always had someone to*
> *talk to. But the funny thing is, I don't mind it, and I'm not lonely. But I am*
> *losing interest in a lot of things, because I'm too tired to get involved. I do*
> *a lot of sleeping during the day.*

Adaptation in the Eyes of the Beholder

In reviewing the data on the survivors, we were impressed by the varied circumstances of each one's life, but we concluded that any judgements about the relative worth of one tack or another is futile. Respondents have either molded their own life-style to suit their competencies and preferences, or they have adapted, sometimes with resignation, to circumstances that are beyond their capacity to control. What was successful to one individual might be the bane of existence of another. In each case, one can observe how these varied evaluations are also in part determined by personality factors as well as the social resources that they can bring to bear.

Coming to Terms with Isolation

Mrs. Palmer and her late husband had moved to the Bay Area from Idaho early in their marriage. Each left their large rural families and only saw a few relatives once or twice in the ensuing 65 years.

"We were separated from our family for so many years, we eventually lost contact." He was a carpenter in the shipyards, and they lived modestly but comfortably, raising two boys and living a life mostly isolated from friends and community involvements. Widowed nine years by the first contact, she lived alone in a second story apartment in a neighborhood that was rapidly changing from a white working-class population to an Asian one. She was suffering from a painful rheumatic disease that limited her mobility. Nevertheless, the major event of her day was walking up and down the stairs, "to keep in shape." Visits to the doctor and a bi-monthly trip to her hairdresser were her only outings. Her beautiful white well-coiffed hair was in sharp contrast to her dark and starkly bare apartment.

In keeping with her rural, Protestant background, Mrs. Palmer was stoical about her isolation, her remoteness from her children and grandchildren, and her continual pain and sleep problems. She was vague about why her son and his family who lived nearby only check on her monthly.

I don't hear from either son very much, but I get along fine. I don't call them, because they have to work, and they aren't home much. I know they are there if I need them. My grandchildren are all good children, but they have their own lives. My son here stops by for an hour each month to pay my bills. That's the only time I see him. The son in Colorado hasn't been here for two years, and I barely know his children—I never see them. I don't even know how many great grandchildren I have there. If anything was wrong, my son wouldn't tell me—he'd know I'd get upset. I'm pretty much by myself, but I don't feel sorry for myself. When the children were small, I was never a gadabout, so it's natural for me to stay at home now. But I'd be lost without my television. I'm content. My only worry is that something will happen to me, and I would lay here alone for days.

At each contact, she reiterated her contentment with being alone despite her increased pain and disabilities. She also reiterated her rationalizations for her children's neglect, "They are busy with their work." By the third interview, her comments were much the same.

I've gotten used to being alone. It would be different if I had gone out a lot earlier. Even as a young girl, I stayed home and helped my mother. As long as I have my TV, I'm okay. I put it on when I first get up, and it stays on most of the day and night. I sleep right here on this sofa. I haven't slept in the bed since my husband died. I keep the TV on at night—it gets my mind off things. After the neighbors complained, I keep the sound off at night and just watch the picture. It keeps me company.

By the last interview, her appearance had become disheveled, indicating that her son was not even monitoring the performance of her weekly home-care worker. Her once beautiful hair was now dirty and uncombed, her nails were uncut, she never dressed, and her messy apartment had a musty odor. Although she expressed some regrets about her life, she remained docile and resigned to her situation.

I'm getting kinda old—not sick, just tired and worn out. I've always been a homebody so being alone here doesn't bother me. I don't feel like I'm 92, and I stay content thinking of all the good things that have happened to me. Old age has even taken some of the pain away. I don't hear from my son in Colorado at all any more, and I don't talk to my son here much. They all have such busy lives. I don't get lonely. I've got my TV and I feel good most of the time.

The Professional Ager

In contrast to the resignation of Mrs. Palmer, Professor Howard tackled the problems of aging professionally, as a university professor with a life-long scholarly career in the study of the biology of aging.

After he retired from the university, he devoted his enormous energies and expertise to the affairs of older people. He taught an adult education course on successful aging and assisted service organizations in designing programs for the elderly. He was also active in community organizations, sitting on boards of local agencies and chairing fund drives. Always a person in control of every aspect of his life, his authority and expertise about aging dominated the interviews to the point that he obscured more personal information. He copy edited any written materials we gave him and suggested many changes in our interview format.

He had been widowed for some years but had remained in the large family home with its office-like den from which he managed his affairs. He was frequently in contact with a divorced daughter who lived nearby. Initially he showed us his pocket date book that indicated numerous civic appointments each day.

> *I have a lot of reasons to be content. I look forward to more involvements with local affairs. I keep up an extensive correspondence. It's not enough to just fill one's days with meaningless retirement activities. I only spend my time on those things that lead to personal growth. It's not a time for continual gratification, it's time to help others. I develop my own contentment by tackling social problems. I feel one must have the will to be contented. I do it by keeping everything in order and keeping in touch with everyone.*

After four years, he was having increased difficulty with his eyesight, although his physical status was good. Despite his aging "by the book," he drew upon his expertise in aging affairs and decided to relocate to a retirement home he selected by the objective criteria of a gerontologist, not one based upon his social characteristics. Leaving his spacious home unoccupied, he moved to a senior residence that, by his opinion was, "the best in the area." He soon found that the social status of most of the residents differed greatly from his upper class Protestant background. Not surprisingly, he commented, "I feel most at home when I am out in the community."

Despite this dislocation in his life, he remained involved in the community, and his appointment book was still filled with activities. He said he was all booked up for the next six months. Even as his living environment changed dramatically from a spacious comfortable home to a one-bedroom apartment, there was little change in his daily routine. He dressed each day in a suit and tie and continued his busy schedule. In fact, his network had actually expanded rather than contracted. He applied his organizational skills and expertise on aging and soon became a leader in the facility. He did not care for the scheduled routines and reported, "When I am in danger of getting bored, I go out and start walking. It has an uplifting effect." Rather than taking long hikes as he had previously, he mapped out a two-mile route through his old neighborhood where he assiduously strode each morning. He was well-recognized by the neighbors on his "daily constitutional." At night before retiring, he reviewed his day and checked off his accomplishments.

Control over Emotions

While Professor Howard controlled the emotional effects of his own aging by judging his status through a professional lens, Mrs. O'Neill followed a life-long pattern of suppressing negative emotions.

The daughter of Irish immigrants, she had lived most of her life in a 12-block radius of the city. After high school graduation, she became a clerk in a bank, where she met her husband. They settled a block from her old high school and began a family. Her husband died at an early age, so she returned to her job at the bank. She raised five children alone and was able to keep the family home. Her children live nearby, and all are in frequent contact.

There is much continuity in her life: a home occupied for 60 years, friendships from childhood, and community involvements for almost as long. She continues her volunteer work at a Catholic meal program in San Francisco's Tenderloin district each week. She even has retained her fashionably slender figure and reports she is still able to fit into her wedding dress. Even her excellent health remained the same, except for failing eyesight. This status she attributes to her sensible diet and having two highballs before dinner. She is proud of her financial acumen and the estate she has built up over the years. "I am a careful person. I've always liked bookkeeping, and I handle everything."

As to her close family relationships, she feels the absence of conflict stems from long-term techniques. "We talk things over and then dismiss is. That's it—I get it off my chest. I have a good feeling about how I raised my five kids. They have turned out perfectly except for my oldest daughter who got a divorce." As to her mood,

> I've never been down in the dumps. I can't see how any human being can be any happier than I am. I'm as happy cleaning out my cupboards as I am going to a party. If someone bothers me on the street, I pretend I don't know English. I strongly believe that sad and happy situations are all part of life. Enjoy the happy ones, and do something about the sad ones—see a priest or find the right person to talk to. Enjoy every day, for you never know what the future holds. I know I have a short future."

When asked about her emotions, she replied,

I'm not very sensitive to other people and how they act to me. That's a waste of time. If people get depressed, they should do what I do, volunteer at church and help with the mailings. There we enjoy chatting and making new friends. That's better than sitting at home and complaining. My worst break was losing my husband. I'm not exactly a humble person. I give myself credit for what I've done alone. I didn't panic. Now my past is past. I don't dwell on it. Nothing upsets me. That's a waste of time. I've been the same every day of my life.

These continuities continued over her six years in the study, as she remained a vital, alert, sociable matriarch in her nineties. In her sparse responses each time to the Affect Balance Scale and the Hopkins Depression Scale, it was evident that dwelling upon her emotional life was an alien experience quite remote from her effective techniques in reducing any negative effects of the aging experience.

The Worst-Case Scenario

Mrs. Elliott was 87 when she joined the research, and she was already very impaired.

The interviewer reported that upon ringing the bell of Mrs. Elliott's well-maintained house, she heard a walker being dragged along a wooden floor, three locks being slowly opened, and then a weak voice asking her to push open the door. Standing there was a tiny woman with a pretty, alert face and a body misshapen by a severe arthritic condition. Tied to her walker was a cloth sack holding her glasses and handkerchief. She was dressed in a pale green two-piece suit and matching costume jewelry. She was waiting for her daily help who would cook her meals, straighten up her house, and shop for her.

Born in England, Mrs. Elliott came to San Francisco with her mother when she was 18, where she secured a job at the telephone company. "I was the best telephone operator in California." She married an engineer she met at work who fell in love first with her voice. Having had the "best possible 47-year marriage," she still mourned the loss of her husband 16 years in the past. They had one daughter who had many problems as she was growing up. At 16, she eloped with an alcoholic, and she eventually picked up the addiction. After having three children, she died at age 44 of alcoholism. Mrs. Elliott's three grandchildren stop by sporadically but offer no sociability or consolation.

With each interview, Mrs. Elliott became even more impaired and at the mercies of her daily helper. To simplify her care, her helper kept her in her bedroom, even though Mrs. Elliott could manage with her walker to get to her living room. She also kept her in her nightgown and robe, which was demeaning to a woman who took great pride in her closet full of clothes, her jewelry, and her life-long emphasis on good grooming. Although her helper was effective in keeping Mrs. Elliott and her house clean, shopping and doing laundry, she offered her no emotional support. When she finished her domestic chores, she spent most of her time in the kitchen talking to her friends on the telephone. Mrs. Elliott did not complain and, in fact, was not despondent, accepting things as they were. She said, "I am waiting to die." She finds Saturday her worst day. Nothing she likes is on television, no one comes, and she can't even bring up the newspaper that is lying four steps down from her front door.

You can't imagine what it is like being so helpless, when I once was so energetic. I began to get sick all the time, first a heart attack, then little strokes, and now this awful arthritis. For two years in a row, I was in the hospital seven times. I've been near death so many times, it is a miracle I'm still here. If I died tomorrow, it would be all right with me. I lived a beautiful life until I got sick. Now there is not much to live for—I have trouble eating, sleeping, and hearing, even though my mind is good. The only time I go out is when I have to be hospitalized. I sit here and look at the four walls.

I don't allow myself to get upset. A few years ago, I went to a series at the Y about getting old. That helped. I saw so many people worse off. Even so, I deserve better. I always lived properly, I worked hard, I did for others, and I kept my house nice. I don't think it is fair. It's been years since someone remembered my birthday. Days go by, and I see no one but the help. Everybody I knew either died, or they got tired of visiting someone who was so sick. I wish I had someone close. As it is, I have no one to love and no one to love me.

All I have lived for is gone. I miss my husband. I don't know what I did to my daughter that led to her terrible life. I wanted to do everything to make her life beautiful, but I must have done wrong things bringing her up. It's very sad, but I realize I have to sit down and talk myself out of bad feelings and be thankful for what I have. I'm not afraid of dying. I'm so tired, I could go to sleep forever. I've had it. Maybe I'll see my husband again. I'll accept what ever comes. I don't believe in Hell, so I have nothing to worry about.

Conclusion

Despite seemingly dramatic differences among individuals, these varied life situations have a thread of commonality. From the very competent Mrs. Albert and Mrs. Carter, who were covering all bases to the lonely and disabled Mrs. Elliott, these survivors had some measure of effectiveness in adapting to seemingly impossible challenges. Most importantly they drew upon quite varied resources and competencies that interpreted satisfactorily the meaning of their long-term survivorship. First, the most effective were the two women who retained their social involvements despite worsening health and functioning and, in doing so, they were able to sustain their mood and motivations. Both were effective, we conclude, at least in part because of their economic and social resources.

The surrender of autonomy and acceptance of dependency were also effective for Mrs. Perry who had increasing difficulty dealing not only with her own health, but the decline and death of her husband. Likewise, Mr. Reynolds, who had been one of the most respected leaders in the city, also welcomed his dependency because it lessened his fears about his health. Both seemed to have come full circle as they reverted to a child-like status with no qualms about their dependency. Mrs. Perry enjoyed her nightly brandy contentedly curled up on her couch after having been fed and diapered by an impressive mother figure, just as Mr. Reynolds equated his helpers in his last years to the attentive governess and nursemaid of his childhood. Their commonality lies in their acceptance of dependency when their status demanded it.

Others dealt with the challenges of late life by disengaging from life. Miss Grieg, a very practical organizer of her days, carried these skills over to organizing her retreat into a spiritual world. She rationalized her rejection of social involvements to avoid anxieties she had previously experienced and, in turn, she organized her days around prayer. Likewise, Mrs. Litsky accepted her change in status after the loss of a significant other and the onset of incontinence, and spent long hours sleeping and watching television.

If adaptation is measured by the outcome of well-being, there are many routes to that end with each being successful by a personal criterion. Mrs. Palmer was a stoical and effective adapter to her isolation by her continual and repetitive rationalizations for her children's neglect. Her television became her best friend both day and night. Professor Howard had his own view of effective adaptation. As a stern taskmaster, he held steadfastly to his professional criteria to evaluate his life, even to the point of using those standards to evaluate each night his accomplishments that day. Also effective was Mrs. O'Neill, who continued her life-long habit of repressing negative experiences and instead concentrating with pride on her list of accomplishments.

It is difficult to find positive aspects of Mrs. Elliott's life, for she has been abandoned by her family and at the mercies of cold and aloof helpers. Nevertheless, she is most exceptional in finding the means to lessen the emotional consequences of her vulnerable situation. By her reports, we find, that she sits down and talks herself out of bad feelings, she looks forward to seeing her husband in the next life, and, in not believing in hell, she has no worries.

Chapter 11

Preparing for Death

Individuals surviving into their late 80s and 90s have even lived beyond the period when their death is a timely event, so some consider themselves "off time" in dying. Consequently, the period shortly before death is of some interest. Researchers interested in this topic, however, have few studies to draw upon unless they venture into more narrowly focused areas of research remote from the subjective aspects of dying. The impetus for much research on the last year of life is motivated by economics and the health care costs of dying patients (Lawton, Moss, & Glicksman, 1990; Lubitz & Prihoda, 1984). Other research literature that concentrates on the quality of life before death is inconclusive. Lawton and his associates (Lawton et al., 1990) found a lowered quality of life at the end of life, but they concluded that is was not necessarily a negative picture for the majority. Likewise, a secondary analysis of a national survey found few, only 14 percent, were fully functional during the last year of life, but even fewer, only 10 percent, were fully restricted (Lentzner et al., 1992). Finally, another report found that decedents were no more disabled than survivors (Guralnik, 1991).

The prolific literature on death and the process of dying usually uses retrospective accounts from family members or the staff of institutions. From a medical point of view, for example, findings are mixed about the extent that terminal patients have more pain and mental distress than other patients. Proxy reports in one study indicate that the majority of older people experienced pain in their last year of life, but the oldest old had less pain than younger old people (Moss, Lawton & Glicksman, 1991). Observations in hospitals (Exton-Smith, 1961) found that the large majority showed no evidence of pain, while another study of mental status of dying patients in hospitals and institutions found that the dying were more depressed and anxious (Hinton, 1963).

Among social and behavioral scientists, much research in the structural-functional tradition focuses upon the impact death has on the structure and functioning of society (Parsons, 1960). Cumming and Henry's disengagement theory (1961) was in that tradition and posited a mutual process of disengagement between the individual and society. Following the popular Kubler-Ross work (1969), other social and behavioral scientists tend to refashion stage theories to apply to the process of dying (Bengtson, Cuellar, & Ragan, 1977; Kalish, 1985; Keith, 1979; Marshall, 1980). One encounters such phrases such as "dying trajectories" (Glaser & Strauss, 1965) or "dying as a social career" (Marshall, 1980). On the whole, this literature agrees on one point, that older people differ from younger people in their attitudes about death. Since they have lived out their allotted time, some suggest, they have less to lose than younger people and can approach their death with more equanimity (Bengtson et al., 1977; Kalish, 1985). Death for them is also predictable and, hence, less disrupting to their loved ones (Moss & Moss, 1989). In a content analysis of essays on death and the dying process, deVries and his colleagues (1993) found that discussions of death in itself were more complex than those about dying, and people usually referred to others' deaths rather than to their own. Marshall's (1980) conceptualization of an "awareness of finitude," may be relevant here. At some point, an individual thinks, not of the time lived, but the time left to live. He suggests that this realization stimulates a changed conception of self.

Such attempts to theorize about death are only partly useful in interpreting the last months of life among the very old. Kastenbaum (1985) most appropriately suggests that such studies need to find new concepts that apply to death and dying among older people. He poses several questions that are relevant to our study. Do adults as they age reshape their thinking to take death increasingly into account? Is there a new process of self-reflection that entails an altered relationship with mortality and new attitudes and values? Also from a practical point of view, do older people avoid seriously ill people? Do they turn to the obituary page or skip it? This chapter will explore attitudes about death and the practical steps the oldest old take in anticipation of their death. Then taking those who died a year or less after being interviewed, we will examine the last year of life, the trajectories to death, and the meanings it has for the oldest old.

An awareness of finitude develops, according to our respondents sometimes after a brush with death or after the death of one's last contemporary. Others mention that point when no one has survived who knew them as children or young adults, or no one knew his or her parents. Many people studied here, as we have noted, develop new attitudes about their imminent death (Kastenbaum, 1985). Their responses tend to take two directions. On one hand, as we have described here, they take practical steps in stripping down their lives by simplifying their physical environment, tying up loose ends, and distancing themselves from the typical hassles of daily life. They also simplify their social world by disengaging from bothersome people and situations and by rejecting those normative constraints that are incongruent with their functional capacities. On the other hand, among these very old survivors, the idea of death is taken increasingly into account as a heightened sense of finitude evolves. Changes in mood and consciousness were also observed in the last months of life.

Practical Preparations for Death

Simplifying One's Life

Most individuals near the end of their lives narrowed and simplified their physical environment and withdrew from problematic social relationships (Johnson & Barer, 1992; 1993). Empirically, some residences appeared bare of all extraneous belongings, as if they had been discarded to make housecleaning easier. Most no longer shopped for new clothes or other belongings except those appliances such as a cane or walker that made their lives easier. One woman began to sell her furniture, so that by our last contact, an easy chair, a card table and two chairs were all that was left in what once was a large living room of furniture. Two respondents never bothered to repair the cracked foundations of their houses after the 1989 earthquake, feeling it was not worth the bother and expense. Others stopped sending Christmas cards or writing to friends. Some no longer voted or followed current events.

For some, this stripping-down process was unintentional, as it came after they had spent most of their money. It is evident in what remained in a safety deposit box of a 95-year-old woman who died after four years in a nursing home, a point when almost all of her money was gone. Although she had had a sizeable estate, most of her assets were used to pay for care during her lengthy decline. To demonstrate the virtual disappearance of her assets, her son showed us an inventory of her assets in her safety deposit box after her death.

CONTENTS OF BOX #2909
5-12-93

1. Notice of balance, Puritan Fund, period ending 1-31-69, $1.00.
2. Unsigned copy of brother's will, 3-13-48.
3. Last Will and Testament of decedent, dated 8-31-71
4. Straight $1000 Life policy, face value, $247, 7-28-43.
5. Driver's License Renewal Examination, 3-31-72.
6. One strand of cultured pearls.
7. Premium Record Policy No. 663 receipt for payment $7.47.
8. Broken cameo (hunter scene) in soft zippered bag.
9. Three plastic passbook covers.
10. Two index cards containing various notes.
11. Fifty-cent piece dated 1964.

Planning for the End

At the first interview, all respondents were asked if they thought about their death and if they had made preparations for it. Over one-half thought about their deaths and most had made practical preparations, such as making a will, leaving instructions, and arranging for the costs for the disposal of their body. These comments convey the impression that once one handled practical matters such as making a will or paying for burial arrangements, they would be ready to die. One woman worried about dying in her sleep because no one would be there to care for her two dogs and one cat. To alleviate her anxiety, she made generous and binding provisions for them. She left her house to the public animal shelter and $30,000 to specific caregivers of each pet.

Not only do most oldest old think of their death without remorse, some talk of their funeral and the disposal of their remains objectively, and some show us pictures of where their body or their ashes will be buried.

"My husbands ashes were fed to the fish, but I want mine to be fed to the birds."

"I've put a bench by the crypt, so people can sit down and be comfortable."

"I just dropped off my pretty pink dress at the undertaker."

"One night I counted everybody who would be at my funeral." An 89-year-old man died 11 months after describing his feelings.

> I'm feeling kinda useless. I don't enjoy anything any more. My wife does everything for me. Now she is the boss, not me. I've turned over my savings box to her. What the heck am I still living for? I'm ready to go anytime— straight to hell. I'd take lots of sleeping pills if I could get them.

Only rarely did these very old individuals avoid making arrangements for their remains. Mrs. Jenkins was one of these exceptions. At 95, she was caring for her husband who was bedfast. Since he wanted to be buried and she wanted to be cremated, no decision had been made. She rationalized this delay by saying, "I know I shouldn't put it off any longer, but I can't leave him alone to go look at cemetery lots." Although she buried her husband a few months later according to his wishes, she remained undecided as to whether she wanted to be buried with him or be cremated.

Personal Meanings about Death

The Finite Self

In addition to general questions about the meaning of life, specific questions were asked that tapped their thoughts about death.

These questions included what it was like to live so long, why they thought they had lived so long, and if they thought about their death. Their responses suggest a sense of a finite self, one who will die soon. One very disabled respondent described the feeling, "Everything is worse. I can't hear my favorite television programs. I feel out of it. I don't understand much of what I read in the paper. It's more than just being tired, it's like I'm slowly disappearing. Not all at once—it's a gradual process."

Another woman reported that she felt that part of her self was already dead. "I dreamed that I was climbing a mountain. When I reached the top, I saw the other side. My grave was down below." Others express a sense of limbo status that comes with the realization that by the time they die, no one will be left who remembers them.

An awareness and acceptance of their finitude often comes with the realization that death becomes a timely event, that one has lived beyond the expected life span.

"I feel left behind. Death is no penalty."

"If I die tomorrow, it would be all right. I've had a beautiful life, but I'm ready to go. My husband is gone, my children are gone, and my friends are gone."

"That's what is so wonderful about living to be so old. You know death is near, and you don't even care."

Even serious illnesses are viewed with equanimity. "I've just been diagnosed with cancer, but it's no big deal. At my age, I have to die of something."

Consistent with other research findings on attitudes about death (Bengtson et al., 1977; Kalish, 1985), the majority thought about their impending death without remorse or anxiety. A common refrain was, "It doesn't bother me," or "I don't care when it happens." One man elaborated about his death, "There is no fear, but no hurry. It really doesn't make any difference." Another man commented, "I should be dead already, considering how much I used to drink. It's just taking me longer to die." Some give practical responses. "I'm ready to go. My funeral and cremation are paid for." Others look beyond death, "I hope my room in heaven will be ready for me."

The major fear is not about their death but about the dying process. Most fear the possibility that they might die in a nursing home after a long illness. The ideal way to die for some is in their sleep, while others want to die on their feet. Only three people expressed sadness or anxiety about their impending deaths. One widow who lived alone was anxious about her death because of severe pulmonary congestion. "I think about my death a lot, particularly when I have shortness of breath. I get panicky when I think I might die alone. It's a terrible thing to think about." At the end of an interview with one 89 year-old woman, she said, "You didn't ask me if I am afraid to die. I am—I don't want to leave this life. I want to hang on. That's selfish maybe, so I don't talk to my family about it."

When death is viewed as a natural and benign event, discussion about it can range from the philosophical to the comic. "I can't die until I get my cupboards cleaned." Others mentioned family reasons for the ideal timing of their death. Some wanted to die in order to avoid outliving their children, and one man wanted to die soon to preserve his father's status as the most long-lived family member. For some, their typical days are regulated around the possibility of death, "I get up each day and say, 'well here's another day. Will I make it to bedtime?' When I go to bed, I say to myself, 'I made it. Thank God for that, but will I make it to morning?'"

The sense of a finite self, that one's life is limited, is sometimes expressed philosophically. Mrs. Faulkner was interviewed once at age 90, approximately three months before her death. As a well-known educator and Jungian scholar, she viewed both her life and impending death philosophically. She reported that many people come to her with questions about the meaning of life and how they can overcome their traumas. She advised them to make connections with the infinite. In discussing her own views, she said,

> Death is not annihilation, for our spirit is immortal. With aging, I'm deepening my spiritual life. I feel good much of the time, and things don't bother me any more. Life is easier at the end, because no one expects much of me. I have become more philosophical about my life—I have more of a connection to the universe.

Trajectories in the Last Months of Life

Chapter 2 compares the survivors with those lost to the research because of death or incapacity. Those who would die were more impaired on their activities of daily living and were less involved with friends. Over time most differences diminish, so that after six years, the survivors and the nonsurvivors are similar in their physical, social and psychological status. This section is a prospective study of the quality of life in the last year of life by singling out those who would die within a year after being interviewed. In the following, we will describe the process of dying, comparing those who died suddenly with those who died of long-term terminal declines. Then we will go on to identify four processes we observed that suggested these respondents, who were near death, were taking death increasingly into account. First, there was a heightened awareness of finitude, that they felt themselves prepared to die. Second, a few respondents took control over the dying process and took indirect steps to hasten their death. Third, emotional states became intensified, where respondents seemed more angry or depressed than previously. Fourth, altered cognitive states were also noted, and these included increased reference to fantasies and dreams.

Sudden Death versus Terminal Declines

Progressive Terminal Declines. Three quarters of the 57 decedents died after a progressive and often insidious decline. During the year before their death, they were quite frail and had nonspecific complaints about fatigue, a chronic cough, and aches and pains. These individuals tended to have a declining interest in current events or in their social relationships. Their fatigue and detachment led many to go to bed for the night sometimes as early as 3:00 in the afternoon. As noted above, as a preparation for death, they commonly simplified their life and shed their belongings, as if they had put their affairs in order and were ready to die. After their death, family members attributed it to a natural event, "She died of old age." Sometimes vague medical conditions were mentioned, such as "fluid on the lungs" or "trouble breathing."

Mrs. Klein illustrates such progressive and prolonged declines that included a few years in an institution before she died. She was age 93 when she joined the project, a German Jewish refugee who joined her sister in San Francisco after World War II. Her only surviving family member was her sister's son who permitted her to remain in the same apartment at a reduced rent. Except for household help several hours a week and delivery of a noon meal, she cared for herself. Even at the first contact, her linkages to her world were weakening. With severe hearing problems, she had difficulty carrying on conversations. "I just sit here alone every day. Nobody has time for me." Her Meals-on-Wheels came at noon. After eating that, she watched TV for a few hours and retired at 5:00 p.m. Despite her restricted life, she remained cheery and said she had always had a special nature—that she never worried.

By Time 2, she had entered a nursing home after a fall and a six-week hospitalization. She was sitting alone in her wheelchair dozing when we arrived. Her cheeriness had disappeared, and she seemed profoundly depressed and cognitively confused. She said she wanted to die—that she was losing her interest in everything. "The nurses are rough with me. My heart is weak. I want God to take me. I pray for that every morning and evening. Here I was a happy lady most of my life and look at me now."

At Time 3, she was curled up in her bed, but greeted us with a big smile. Unlike the previous contact, she was coherent. "It is important to remember the good things in my life. I have to go soon. It is time for God to take me, but my memories make me happy." We stopped in to see her a month before her death. Although a nurse at the desk said she was "doing fine," we found her lying in bed, her breathing labored. She complained of pain and talked of being tired. But she added, "My recipe for life is, be satisfied."

Mrs. Dreifer was interviewed at home in her wheelchair. Nevertheless, she was taking care of her 74-year-old nephew even cooking his meals from her wheelchair. Her body was misshapen by painful arthritis but she remained cheerful. She described her health as good although she was unable to walk. By our second and last contact, she was recuperating from bronchitis and felt that her health was deteriorating. Asked if her health had changed, she replied, "Since I last saw you, I got a year more helpless. I don't think I'll improve. My days are so long and my nights are so long. I can't even listen to music any more—the sound is too distorted. I'm a hopeless case." Asked when her favorite time of the day was, she said, "At twilight. Nature rests and everything is so soft and still. You can hear God speak. He gives me courage." Later on, nonetheless, she said, "Living this long is pure hell. The hardest thing I face is having to go on living. It would be much easier to give up and die, but then who would take care of my nephew?" She died 10 months later, because, according to her nephew, "Her heart just stopped."

Sudden Death. One quarter of the decedents died soon after an accident or an acute episode of a disease such as a cardiovascular episode. Several deaths were reported to be sudden—a heart attack while shopping or diagnosis of cancer with death one month later. Others had pulmonary disease or pneumonia. It is interesting to note that four respondents, or 7 percent, died less than a year after complications from a fall or another accident.

For example, Mrs. Watts was worried about her husband and anxious about living alone while he was in the hospital. She said she was getting confused about her medications without him there to help her sort them out. Shortly after that, she fell down the stairs and was unattended for 12 hours. She died in a coma 10 days later. Another woman forgot her keys and was forced to spend a cold night outdoors locked between her front door and a security gate. She blamed her subsequent deteriorating health upon this incident. Some respondents were able to maintain most activities and were without life-threatening diseases at our last interview with them. In other words, at our last interview, they expressed no premonition of the nearness of death and in comparison to most others in the sample, their physical status showed no indication of decline.

Heightened Awareness of Finitude

This concept refers to the process when individuals take death increasingly into account, a process that triggers self-reflection about their past and their limited future (Marshall, 1980). Our respondents spoke frequently about death, but often in general terms. Among those soon to die, however, discussions of death had a more personal referent.

Mr. Gregory also continually confronted death while sustaining his positive view of life. He lived with his second wife and their teen-age daughter. He reported that his health was good, although he needed transfusions to combat fatigue. While he kept his mind active by studying French, his favorite activity was sleeping. By our second contact, he still drove, and his activities were unchanged, although he said he was going downhill. "My memory is lousy. I can't remember what year and day it is. And I know I must have leukemia. I am so tired all the time. I get to feeling the only one left older than me is God. I know I have to die sometime, and now I feel it is not far off."

A year later, he was relieved upon learning he did not have leukemia. He had developed minor arthritis and had his glasses adjusted to his worsening eyesight. He was still studying French, and spoke of how much he loved his wife. As to his reports on his situation, he said, "I'm here, there, and maybe nowhere. I'm getting toward the end, I know." Eleven months later, his wife called to say he died suddenly of a heart attack. She had to cancel a golf game he had scheduled for the next day.

Very old people like *Mr. Ewing* have continual reminders of their impending death because they have witnessed the deaths of so many contemporaries. Sometimes these reminders come at a time when the isolating effects of poor health intensify thoughts about death. At age 87 initially, Mr. Ewing exhibited few changes over a four-year period except for evidence of declining personal hygiene. He had been widowed 10 years, and over that time had never seemed to form new social ties. At each interview, he commented that the worst thing to happen to him was the death of his wife, and he complained each time of the deaths of friends. His two children lived within a two-hour drive, and he saw them or his grandchildren every two or three weeks. Except for those visits, his social contacts were confined to clerks in stores and a cleaning woman twice a month. He had given up driving but was able to walk to a nearby shopping center. He was continuing a life-long habit, smoking a pack of cigarettes a day. When describing his day, he commented, "I spend most of my time just sitting right here in this chair." When he arose from that chair, the interviewer noted a wet spot that was consistent with an odor of urine in his apartment.

By the second contact, he commented,

It's gotten to the point I have to stop and get my breath, but I still can do everything. I am never sick though—no colds or headaches. I just think I'm getting toward the end. All my friends are dead—nine friends and acquaintances in the last year. I'm not overly happy about my life.

By the third contact, he was unshaven and had stains on his clothes. The smell of urine was stronger only adding to the aroma of cigarette smoke. He again commented, "My friends are dropping like flies." Six weeks after this contact, he died sitting in the chair where he had spent most of his waking hours. He was waiting for his grandson to pick him up and take him to his son's for the holidays.

Control over the Dying Process

Mrs. Bromley, one of the most strong-willed participants in the study, deemed herself ready to die, so she stopped taking her medications for hypertension and congestive heart failure. At 89, she was a cantankerous retired teacher who lived in subsidized housing. Her only child was ill with cancer. She typified a person who obsessively took control over her life and even her dying. Her one-room apartment was crowded with physical evidence of her many hobbies—stuffed animals she made, two sewing machines, a harmonica and an accordion. And there were four canes lying about. She described her health as fair. "It's up and down. I can't breathe lying down, but nothing bothers me." Yet she had a string of complaints, many about being lonely. She said she was angry most of the time, an emotion she said that kept her alive.

She admitted she had spent all of her money by age 75, and now lived on Supplemental Security Income and various entitlement programs. She did not want to make friends with the many minority elderly living in her subsidized senior housing, and she would not attend any organization that referred to older people as "seniors." As to her physical status, she had prescriptions for hypertension medications and Lasax. She talked extensively about death at our first contact. "Last year I thought I would die, but then I realized, I am a Mormon, and Mormons are blessed. I was told as a child, 'You are a blessing in your father's house. You will live to a ripe old age.' I realized last year that I could die when I pleased. I wasn't ready then. I had so many things to do. It was my blessing, you see."

At the next contact, she remained grumpy and complaining, even though her social life had improved considerably. A downtown bar reserved a back room for talent shows one night a week, and she went there by taxi every week to play her harmonica. As to her mood, she said, "I get angry a lot, but I'm terribly happy. I have a good life—I feel like flying to the moon. It gets better every day, even though I'm mad a lot." As to her health, she reported it was excellent. "I have pain, but it has nothing to do with old age. I did have two bad spells—difficulty breathing when trying to sleep." She was particularly angry at her doctor and had not seen him in eight months. "My feet swell and I have trouble breathing, but I'd rather die than enter a hospital. I've thrown out all my medications, so I'm on my own now." According to the manager of her building she died three months after that interview.

Mrs. Parker, at 93 years of age, offers a good example of preparing for death, because she said, "I want to face the unknown with grace and style." She had lived in a retirement home for almost 20 years. At our first contact, she appeared as an attractive and elegantly dressed woman in excellent health and active socially. Her one concession to life in her 90s was giving up visits to her daughter who lived 100 miles away, claiming the trip made her too tired. Her major complaint was her cognitive problems, "I don't handle my bank account very well any more. There is a little cog in my brain that prevents me from adding and subtracting." Six months after the first interview, she wrote in a Christmas card to us, "I am proud to be three-fourths through my 94th year and I am still counting. But I have not kept faith with the spirit of Christmas. I didn't get through my Christmas card list."

Fourteen months later, she said she had blackouts and a "little stroke." Increasingly fatigued, she spent most of her day in bed, admitting that she was withdrawing from a lot of activities and spending more time alone. She had lost her ability to dial telephone numbers, so she talked less to others. She still took walks, but just short ones around the block. When asked about any stress in her life, she said, "I have no diseases, but I realize I have to give in to the medics. Here I've never had to rely on anyone before. Now being in this place, it is easy to just fade into the unknown in style." About 10 months later, she died, and according to her daughter, she died at the time she had predicted.

Altered Emotional States

Anger, anxiety, and depression were noted among some of those who would soon die. *Mrs. Clemens* became depressed with worsening vision and hearing. Although continually comforted by her attentive family, she was always remorseful, saying she was going through hell on Earth. During her waking hours, she was rarely alone. Her grandson ran his carpentry business out of her basement, while a granddaughter ran a mail-order business from her dining room table. Her mood improved somewhat when her grandson left his parrot with her, for she loved the company. Her eyesight was too poor to see the bird droppings all over her clothes. Despite the welcome distractions, she still complained. "Losing my eyesight is like hell on Earth. There is nothing to do. I go to bed at 5:00." She still felt lonely even though her daughter visited four times a week and at least one grandchild was there daily. When asked about being depressed, she replied, "It's my natural style. I am scared of being alone. The hardest thing is to cope with the length of the days."

At our third contact, her grandson was working in her yard, and her granddaughter was working on sewing projects at her dining room table. She had a new bird that was noisy, adding to the squeaking of her hearing aid. She was now using a walker. A visitor could observe what a warm relationship she had with her grandchildren, but she was nevertheless demoralized. "I get so discouraged and bored. My eyes are progressively worse. Each day I awake and say, 'Oh God, why am I still here? Why haven't you taken me?'" When asked about her health, she replied, "My health is good, but my legs don't work so well. And I can't sleep. I wake up at 3:00 a.m. and just lie there and think and think. When I get up, I don't know whether or not I am rested. Then I go to bed at 5:00, because I have nothing else to do. The hardest thing is the loneliness and boredom."

At the next and last contact, she had a daily companion who sat in on the interview. She still enjoyed the company of her bird, but her major fear was that it would fly outside and she would not see it. She was also afraid she would step on the bird. She reported that her hearing was getting even worse. With nothing to do, she went to bed at 3:00 after her second meal of the day and when her companion left. Again she complained about still surviving, "I am angry at the creator. I don't deserve this life. I've been a good person—I haven't lied or stolen. I just wish I'd go." Then in the next comment, she spoke of her happiness when her great-grandchildren visit. Three months later, her granddaughter called to say Mrs. Clemens had died in the hospital where she was admitted with breathing difficulties. She commented, "She wanted to die more than anything."

Anger was common for some like *Mrs. Fordham*, who at the first contact still worked in a part-time clerical position and retained active membership in a religious organization. She described her health as excellent, after having survived 10 surgeries for colon cancer. At the three subsequent contacts, we observed progressive physical and cognitive declines. With considerable weight loss, she had become so frail that she had been blown over by the wind when taking her daily walk, an event she felt contributed to her decline. She also described her increasing helplessness, "My daughter is doing everything but breathing for me." At each contact, she became even more dependent upon her daughter but angry at her for taking over her life. Her memory declined to the extent her daughter left a list of what she should discuss during the interview. When her mood became so unpleasant that she could not get help, she entered a nursing home where she died within a few months. Unlike others in similar situations, she never came to terms with and accepted her disabilities, her dependency, and her imminent death.

Mrs. Livingston, at age 90, died one month after the fourth interview, a time when she reported she had changed. Although she still retained her activities in many clubs, she reported at the last interview, "I've been falling quite a bit—the last one nearly finished me off. It has affected my whole system and my way of thinking." She also admitted, "I'm more bitchy and not pleasant to be around." Soon afterwards, her husband called us to notify us of her death.

> She always said that when she had to go, she wanted to go quickly. It was morning and I was working at my tool bench in the basement, and she was getting ready to go somewhere. She had taken a shower and put her undergarments on. The phone rang, and when she went to answer it, she fell. I found her lying on a heap on the floor. Her heart beat for three days, but they could get no response from her nervous system.

Others who appeared anxious and depressed most of the time were without family members or reliable caregivers. For example, *Mrs. Massey*, at 90, was not sleeping, instead playing solitaire most of the night. Except for our interviewer, she had had no visitors in a year. She, like others in her situation, expressed fears about who would look after her, or who would find her when she died.

Altered Consciousness before Death

We have some information about mental status changes shortly before death. Such changes were noted among 26 percent of the decedents with approximately one half exhibiting forgetfulness and confusion. Of these, one half showed prominent cognitive decline with one having died of Alzheimer's Disease. Others slipped in and out of consciousness near the end of their lives. *Mrs. Bloom*, the centenarian described in Chapter 1, was very impaired but she initially was able to visit with friends, read fiction, and even write poetry, yet she reported, "I have periods of aloneness when I feel unrelated to what is going on." She continued living in her home with the assistance of a daughter who arranged for live-in help. By the second contact, however, it was difficult to schedule an interview, for she had been hospitalized for overmedication. Afterwards, her condition varied from being lucid to being comatose. At our last contact, she began the interview telling us about her early life. She had Jane Austen's *Pride and Prejudice* open on her lap. After 30 minutes, she ceased speaking and appeared to be asleep. This fluctuating status continued until she died two months later.

Increased confusion and wandering appeared to shorten *Mrs. Schultz'* life. At the beginning, she walked home from the senior center daily, a 40-block distance. While she remained lively and energetic, she did become increasingly forgetful. After three years, and at the instigation of her family she moved to a senior residence near her daughter. Undaunted, she made new friends at the facility, but her mental confusion increased. She also began wandering. One night she was found two miles away where she had fallen and broken several bones. After a hospitalization, she entered a nursing home where she became totally helpless, confused, and was eating less and less. Her daughter was alarmed about her decline and moved her to her home where she died two weeks later.

Mr. Harley, age 92, a widower with one surviving son, was interviewed only once, two months before he died. He was still running a small insurance agency and had a rewarding relationship with a woman, who came each afternoon to cook his dinner and spend the evening with him. They also went frequently to her family parties and had season tickets to San Francisco Giants baseball-games. While his life seemed to be going well, he was anxious and distraught, because he made a bad investment for his companion and lost some of her money. While she appeared to take this loss in her stride, he was so obsessed that he wanted to die. "I feel like I'm 100 years old, I am so troubled by my errors. I hope the good Lord will take me before I abolish all good things." Despite his seemingly good health, he died suddenly of a heart attack two months later.

Two other childless women adapted to their aloneness through creating a fantasy world. *Miss Lowden* was a retired, never-married teacher, who moved from her own apartment to a board-and-care home and then to a nursing home during the course of the study. Her only surviving family members were in the Midwest, and most of her friends were dead or institutionalized. When interviewed the last time at the nursing home, she answered our questions as if she were back in her former life—how she shopped, cooked, visited friends, and attended church. At the same time, she was worried about what would happen to her when her money ran out. "I pray but it doesn't work." She concluded the interview with a fantasy. "My friend's son came to see me. He said, 'Mary, it's foolish to end your life this way. I love you. I've never loved anyone but you. I will make a living, and take care of you.'" Another childless woman, still struggling to manage in a downtown hotel, was similarly anxious about the future and how she would survive. At our final contact, she invented two children who had called her from the East Coast to say they were coming to get her.

Others refer to dreams or extrasensory experiences that are consistent with their feeling of being a detached self. Dreams can also depict an experience where one returns from death. One woman described her hospitalization for pneumonia.

> I had a dream I was shipwrecked at sea and had to swim to shore. I realized I didn't care if I drowned. Then I awoke choking as if I were drowning. I told myself, the best thing is to be passive—to breathe slowly. Once I got my breath, I started to fight for my life.

"Out-of-body" experiences were reported that they referred to as "the other side of life," or they were already dead but had come back to life. Still others dreamed about long-deceased family members. One never-married man, who maintained he had never dreamed, became baffled by frequent dreams about his parents and siblings during his childhood. Another man, who gave otherwise lucid responses throughout the last interview before his death described his recent dreams or fantasies.

> *My only problem is that I don't know who is sleeping with me at night. It isn't my son. He died. I think my aunt is sleeping with me. I'm never certain though, because she gets up early. When I wake up in the morning, my wife is in bed with me. Then I go into the kitchen and there is my aunt fixing my breakfast. It's a mystery. Someday I'll figure it out.*

Conclusion

This chapter has reviewed the respondents attitudes about death and their practical preparations for that event. To examine the last year of life, we present a prospective account from the interviews with decedents a year or less before their death. Our findings agree with those in the literature; namely, those who have lived beyond the anticipated life span, have few worries or anxiety about their impending death. In fact, if they are in pain, they may welcome death. By their 80s and 90s, the survivors have witnessed so many deaths of others close to them that their own death is expected in the offing. Consequently, some of the processes we have observed in the last year of life may be specific to advanced old age. Death is faced without fear, as the very old make practical preparations for that event and mentally work through its meanings.

Through observations and content analyses of respondents' discussions, we have identified both practical actions and mental processes among those soon to die. Practically the simplification of daily life is quite common as is specific planning for one's remains. Parallel to that are ruminations on the meanings of life and death and the development of a new awareness that one is finite. As a finite self, death is usually seen as a natural part of life at their age.

In looking at specific cases, each end-of-life situation is unique to that person, but there appears to be some commonalities among those who would die soon. First, they developed a heightened awareness of finitude and increasingly talked about their own death. They began to identify with their deceased friends, bemoaning constantly, "My friends were dying like flies." Others described changes in their emotional life because of increased depression, anger, or anxiety. A few felt that they could take control of their life and decide when they would die. One woman determined that she was ready to die, so she took charge of her dying by refusing to take her medications or go to her doctor. Others experienced altered states of consciousness, whether it was anxiety, listlessness, or confusion. Dreams and fantasies also were reported that may be related to the nearness to death. In other cases, much of the day and night was spent sleeping.

Despite evidence of some cognitive and emotional changes, however, most of the very old accepted the inevitability of their imminent death, some with resignation, some with positive anticipation, and some, like Mrs. Parker, who wanted to "go out into the unknown with grace and style."

Chapter 12

Conclusions

Since little was known about the oldest old at the time we began this research project, we posed relatively general research questions. Namely, what competencies do the oldest old need to adapt and survive outside institutions? How do very old people manage their physical environment and the activities of daily living? Are they able to maintain sufficient social integration so that needs for sociability and support are met? How do they sustain their motivations and a sense of well-being? Given the scope of these questions, we have cast a broad sweep through several research disciplines. Anthropology has provided the methodological focus in how we addressed these research questions and established guidelines for the interview process. Always central to our inquiry was the collection of emic material, the phenomenological aspects of each respondent's experiences. We let the respondents speak for themselves and made every attempt to repress any of our own preconceptions.

Intriguing findings appeared with each wave of interviewing; namely even though the oldest old had experienced many social and physical losses, most were contented with their lives. Therefore, our objectives in later waves of interviews concerned, why do they do so well? Even more of an enigma was the finding that over six years, their level of disability increased significantly, yet their subjective well-being actually improved. These counterintuitive findings, that morale seems unaffected by rising disabilities and many social losses, has become one of our central interpretations. Moreover, in attempting to find associations between subjective well-being and disability over time, it became apparent that social, physical, and environmental factors in themselves brought incomplete explanations. Thus, we came to view the individual as an active agent in managing their daily lives or, if incapacitated, in mobilizing help from others. These participants also reacted to their situation existentially, as they drew upon cognitive and emotional processes that provided meanings to their experiences. As we have demonstrated, these psychological processes have beneficial effects.

In contradiction to common taken-for-granted views among gerontologists, some processes observed in the course of the study may be unique to late life. As to the social needs of the oldest old, the optimistic views about family resources is not borne out by our findings. In fact, living so long imposed the risk of out-living one's family, as happened to at least 24 percent of the respondents. Also from a developmental perspective, conceptions about continuity in the self as a positive feature in the aging process is contradicted here. To adapt, the oldest old must reconstitute a self-concept that is consistent with the realities of late life. Consequently, discontinuities rather than continuities in self may be necessary or even desirable. Moreover, instead of the efficacy of being in control and engaged in life, it is sometimes more adaptive to surrender control, accept some measure of dependency upon others, and disengage from troublesome and overdemanding social ties.

To briefly summarize the findings presented here, demographically the 150 participants in the research in most respects resemble the oldest old described in national statistics of whites living outside institutions. They are predominantly women, who are widowed and who live alone. Almost one third have no children, and almost as many have witnessed the death of at least one child. A large proportion have difficulty functioning on their activities of daily living, yet they continue to live more or less independently and to view their health as good.

Understandably, there was a high attrition rate, so that after six years, only 33 percent remained in the study. Most of those lost either died or became too mentally or physically incapacitated to continue. After almost three years, in comparison to survivors, those lost were more disabled at the outset, and they were less involved with family, friends, and in community associations. They also exhibited more cognitive losses. However, most of these differences between survivors and those lost because of morbidity and mortality diminished after six years. Over time the survivors became more incapacitated and thus similar to those lost to the study.

The Context of Survivorship

Our working proposition evolving during the earlier contacts concerned the effects of chronological age. Namely, we proposed that these long-term survivors were different than younger old people. To address this proposition, it was necessary to widen the age range and draw a second sample of those 70 to 84. With an age range of 70 to 103, we found age differences in the types of problems individuals faced. Not surprisingly, the younger old were more physically active, had a better mood, and were more likely to be married. Nevertheless, they reported dealing with problems more typical of middle age—financial shortages and emotional demands from family members. Other than their physical problems, the oldest old in comparisons to the younger respondents had detached themselves from financial and family worries, and they complained less of emotional problems. They also felt less need to exert mastery or control over their lives. Consequently, they faced fewer stressors and hassles from outside forces than did the younger respondents. Instead, by delimiting their physical and social environments, the oldest old eliminated some sources of stress. Since others placed few demands on them, they were free to cope with their limitations without distractions.

Chronological age also is an important indicator of how one adapts to late-life transitions. The transitions from marriage to widowhood and from living with others to living alone are more likely to occur in the 70s, some years before the onset of disability and the risk of dependency, transitions likely to occur in one's 80s. Consequently, by the time the very old need help, most have no one in their household to turn to. It is here that gender differences are important. Men undergo the transition to widowhood later than women. If they are widowed in their 70s, most remarry. In contrast, those men widowed in their 80s have great difficulty in adapting. At that age, remarriage is not usually considered an option. Their long dependence upon their wife in managing their household and social affairs has left some men quite helpless and distressed when they are left alone.

Throughout the study, physical disabilities dominated most respondents' concerns about their situation, so we tracked their physical status carefully over the six years. In order to link physical status changes to later outcomes, the 63 participants at Time 4 were categorized into three trajectories on the basis of their functioning: the functionally fit, the chronically disabled, and increasingly disabled. Then by analyzing outcomes fifteen months later, it was possible to identify the precursors to morbidity and mortality. Interactions between health and social and psychological factors were particularly prominent among those whose functioning declined rapidly because of an acute illness or an accident. These individuals were more likely to be hospitalized, to experience mental status changes, and to be institutionalized. Most of those who became too incapacitated to participate were in this trajectory of rapid decline. Thus, functioning on the activities of daily living is a good predictor of later status.

The role of the family in sustaining community-living is critical, for the actions of children are key determinants in forestalling institutionalization. The problem for members of this cohort, however, is the high rate of childlessness. While two thirds had at least three generation families, as many as one third had no descendants. In fact, the proportion of childless oldest old is so large that among those in their 80s, they outnumber those parents who have four-generation families. Consequently, the much-heralded verticalizaton of the family as older people bask in the affections of four generations is not as prevalent as previously assumed. Most childless are able to construct some family-like relationships or strengthen their bonds with nieces and nephews. Nevertheless, 24 percent of the oldest old, most of whom are childless, no longer have ongoing family relationships except for intermittent letters or phone calls. For the parents, nonetheless, their children are important supporters who make it possible for them to remain in the community.

Beyond the family, most participants had as many social relationships as they wanted. While respondents continually complain about the deaths of friends, the majority still can identify a close friend, and almost as many continue to form new friendships. To maintain friendships, however, the criteria used to define friendships usually need to be redefined to include many who formerly would have been identified as acquaintances. Thus, there is an array of relationships ranging from close friends to casual relationships met at community associations. Neighbors can be important for the oldest old, because with their proximity, some provide important supports if the family is not available. Otherwise, resourceful individuals can form friendships with their helpers, thus assuring that social needs are met.

The Processes of Adaptation

Adaptation is a multilayered process that empirically takes several forms. First and most importantly, to adapt, individuals are actors and reactors. As actors, they concentrate on behavioral attempts to manage their physical and social environment, often by narrowing and simplifying their physical environment and carefully scheduling their activities. In doing so, they are adapting within their given physical and social resources. They also are reactors who draw upon cognitive and emotional processes that make their long-term survivorship more meaningful. As reactors, they reappraise their life and reconstitute their self concept to account for revised aspirations and expectations as to who they are and who they want to be.

The process of adaptation is also a relative concept, because it is lodged in a given cultural context. With culturally lodged norms and values, any notion of successful or unsuccessful aging is relative to that cultural context. Thus, our conception of adaptation is a process that is defined, negotiated, and evaluated within this cultural context. Viewing adaptation as relative to a given cultural and personal context, we suggest, makes the pursuit of criteria of successful aging a moot point. For example, numerous factors are used to define success (Baltes & Baltes, 1990): the length of life, physical health, mental health, cognitive efficacy, social competence, and personal control. When success is evaluated by health and functioning (Rowe & Kahn, 1987), social competence (Maddox & Wiley, 1976), or environmental resources (Lawton, 1982), the outcome is based in large part on factors beyond the personal control of most very old individuals. If successful aging hinges upon health and functioning, most are unsuccessful, but by criteria resting upon cognitive and emotional factors, many are effective adaptators. Consequently, we continually emphasize how the meanings respondents apply to their life are manipulated and brought into congruence either with reality or some ideal view they hold of a desired social world.

The objective indicators are those behaviors readily observable in managing their daily lives, coping with problematic situations, and mobilizing effective social resources. Less observable indicators are the subjective factors, those intrapsychic processes that may potentially sustain well-being and avoid depression.

In order to familiarize ourselves with how the oldest old carried out their daily activities despite their disabilities, we questioned them extensively on how they spent their time on typical days. These discussions reflect how enterprising many oldest old are as actors who devise a daily regimen that permits them to accomplish needed tasks. They also simplify their environment to make it more manageable. Many ritualize the most mundane activities, carefully regulating their time so as to make their lives more predictable and, in the process, convey more significance to what they do.

There is some evidence among the oldest old of a greater acceptance of dependency and a surrender of control over selected areas of their lives, changes that do not usually undermine their sense of well-being. Some respondents actually welcome such alterations in their relationships and are relieved to turn to others for help. In other words, staying active and in control may be unrealistic for many toward the end of their life. As a matter of fact, their success in adaptation may hinge upon having the initiative to cease attempts to exercise control and to resist futile efforts to continue a vestigial life-style more appropriate to an earlier stage of life.

To come to terms with their situation late in their lives, some individuals also become increasingly introspective, exhibiting interiority, a personality characteristics pointed out by Neugarten (1977) some time ago. As many intentionally narrow the boundaries around their social world, this increased introspection can lead to a process of disengagement among the more disabled of the very old. In fact, sociable individuals who do not alter their preferences for social activities over solitary pursuits tend to have more difficulty dealing with their physical impediments, as well as with the inevitable deaths of friends and age peers in their family.

To control the emotional consequences of change, discourses are used as an adaptive strategy that helps individuals develop personal meanings about significant areas of their lives. While their bodies may be disabled, their minds continue to actively examine and interpret their predicament in a process that can perhaps alleviate distress and forestall demoralization. The subjective life, consequently, can serve not only to sustain mood and motivations, but also to give the very old some control over the emotional consequences of their losses.

Theories of self are useful in organizing these discourses, as for example, when they reconstitute themselves as very old yet fairly healthy. They also tend to view themselves as semi-detached from problematic roles and relationships. In their temporal orientation, most live in the present, "one day at a time," and contrary to common ideas, few reminisce about their past. If they should think of the past, they are consciously careful to be selective and to remember the best parts of their life, "to whitewash their past." A present temporal orientation, some told us, is an effective maneuver to cope with their increasing propensity to confuse or forget the temporal sequence of their lives.

In an exploration of their emotional life, we find that few are clinically depressed, and in fact, their subjective well-being is high and actually improves over time. In discussing their mood, resignation to the realities of late life is common and is most likely a positive force, or at best a neutral one. As respondents answered our questions about mood, they demonstrated how effectively most cope with those forces that ordinarily would undermine their well-being. The mood of most participants lies somewhere in a neutral zone. One response illustrates this status, "I'm not exactly happy, but I'm not sad either." Moreover, when the respondents described negative emotions, they usually added a counterpoint to negative feelings by describing their strategies for dealing with those emotions. "I get sad, but then I talk myself out of it."

The lives of the 48 survivors illustrate the multiple levels of adaptation, as they initiate task-oriented behavior as well as cognitive processes that explain, justify, and rationalize many aspects of their lives. In adapting, some effective individuals cover all bases and retain control of the physical, social and psychological forces impinging upon them. Others are forced to be more selective in coming to terms with life in late life. For example, some retreat into a dependent status with relief at the welcome security others provide for them. Others disengage into a spiritual world or into a body-centered existence relatively remote from others.

Adaptation is also a relative process, in the eyes of the beholder. What seems a dreary or desolate situation to an outside observer is not necessarily interpreted as such by those living out that particular life. Given this relativity, we found very few who were without some competencies in adapting. Moreover, as they prepared for their death, the oldest old in this study simplified their lives, stripping down extraneous features and preparing themselves practically and emotionally for the end. Just as in other areas of adaptation, thus, they are effective in preparing for death.

Implications of This Research

In reviewing the varied lives of the participants in this study of the oldest old, we are always impressed by the great diversity in this sample of white urban Americans. Certainly we need to know more about even greater diversity in how the oldest members of ethnic groups or those in rural and small-town America are faring. Such studies of cultural subgroups may single out the universals in the aging process as distinguished from specific cultural patterns. Another variation that needs to be more carefully studied is the age differences after age 65. While more information is becoming available, most researchers on the elderly still neglect age distinctions in old age or they use chronological age in regressions that control its effects.

This longitudinal study of the oldest old permits us to make several generalizations which have practical implications. First, the oldest old are especially vulnerable to seemingly unimportant events. A fall may lead to a hospitalization where pneumonia may occur. Problems with medications may lead to symptoms of dementia and a diagnosis of irreversibility. Eviction from a long-term residence may lead to social isolation and perhaps an unnecessary institutionalization. We have seen that most of the problems of the oldest old are the difficulties of getting through each day. Few need round-the-clock care. These problems can be solved by resources outside the health care system.

This situation stands in marked contrast to the emphasis in the literature, where much of the national surveys and policy decisions have become strongly medicalized in their emphasis. They focus upon how poor health and disability can lead to high risks, vulnerability, and the need for long-term care. Not that such important factors can be ignored, we merely want to point out that much what the oldest old need can be addressed by small interventions. For example, provision of a bi-weekly helper, meals-on-wheels, and reliable transportation.

The problem for many is the lack of familiarity with the social service system. Most middle-class elderly tend to view the social worker as a helper of the poor, so they do not know the services for which they might qualify. Knowing where to turn and taking the first step in finding formal assistance is a difficult and unfamiliar endeavor and one that often fails to secure needed help. Large numbers of low income homeowners are particularly vulnerable. While they are not eligible for subsidized services, they lack sufficient funds to afford services that can keep them in their homes. Such problems of access to health care are rarely encountered. Most of the oldest old are regular users of health care and have Medicare and often other insurance to cover costs.

Some participants in our study are incredibly impaired on their activities of daily living, and some have suffered from cognitive loss. Yet most of these have sufficient competence to get through their days without full-time help. The affordability of social services, even such minimal help as described here, is particularly important for the oldest old. Having never expected to live so long, some had spent most of their money. Now they live on that financial borderline that makes them ineligible for the services they need.

Hopefully this book has illustrated that in addition to large-scale surveys that are so common today, small-scale, naturalistic studies such as ours are a very necessary adjunct. As social involvements diminish, much that happens in the lives of the oldest old is found in the emotional and cognitive domain. These interior processes are best tapped by an open-ended interview process rather than a few forced-choice items on surveys. With systematic qualitative research techniques, that world can be tapped.

Over the course of the study we were frequently asked: "How can you do such depressing research?" Such a query seemed alien to our experiences, for the study of the oldest old was rarely depressing and often uplifting. In other words, despite the variations in levels of adaptation, a common theme underlying most interviews was, "It's tough to be this age, but I can handle it." Even some felt that their current stage in life was more satisfying than earlier stages. Thus, we have much to learn from the oldest old, and hopefully this book is a start in understanding more about both the objective and subjective facets of life in late late life.

Afterword

It has been my privilege to be associated with Colleen Johnson and Barbara Barer in the Oldest-Old Project from its early stages. Participating in planning, interpreting, and some analyses, was an experience that has influenced both my professional and personal thinking. One of the associated activities that has affected me most on a personal level is interviewing a few of the respondents. Meeting these very old people, who are, in fact, less than a generation older than I, has primarily raised my awareness of what I expect in my own future. I suppose all the interviewers shared my awe at the unanticipated competence of so many men and women in their late 80s and 90s, but the fact that I am older than the others may have made the impact even more powerful for me.

More than a decade ago, Mildred Seltzer and I (Seltzer & Troll, 1986) wrote a paper on what we called "expected life history." Earlier, Victor Marshall (1975) had suggested that we tend to base our anticipations for length of life on the ages at which our parents died. It seemed to Millie and me that we base more than our anticipated time of death on the lives of our parents, that we also base our expectations for what our remaining years will be like on what theirs were like after they were our age. My mother lived to be 93, and while her last years were relatively competent ones—she could still read and take care of her personal needs up to the last heart attack—they showed a clear diminution of functional capacity over her final seven years, after she moved in with me. Because she was living with me, I could see the details of these gradually increasing problems and the growing depression that accompanied them, and I felt sure that I was looking at my own future. I expected that I would follow her path in behavior, in physical condition, and in feelings. When she retired at 80, she moved to an apartment on the coast of California, and read and walked and looked out her window at the ocean. Then she came to live with me in the East and felt isolated and restricted. I had a compulsory retirement at 71, but have continued to write and engage in research until now, at 80. However, the parallel with my mother is evident in my moving to California after my retirement and buying a condo on the coast, although in my case it is the bay, not the ocean. Like my mother, I read and walk and look out the window at the water. Would I now, at 80, stop my other activities and also just read and walk and look at the water?

During my repeated interviews with my few assigned oldest-old respondents over the eight years of the study, I could not help compare their appearance and behavior with that of my mother at their age. It is true that several respondents fell along the way. One man was relocated by his son to be near him and died soon after. The husband of one woman was dying and she was too absorbed in this process to have the energy to be interviewed. Another woman's growing cognitive deterioration made her responding taxing. And one woman became gradually more and more incapable of communicating. The two respondents who did survive over the eight years, however, were not only as "good" as my mother—whom we had all considered remarkable—they were even "better." (It is easy to forget about those who did not continue because they fit my expectations for their advanced age.) It was the vitality of these two remarkable, antistereotypical survivors that has dominated my thinking. They both maintained their own large homes until the end of the study. They were both interesting, fun people to talk with. Mrs. Karl particularly impressed me because she managed her own finances, in contrast to my mother—and to me. I must scuttle each year to an accountant for help with my income tax report. Mrs. Karl not only knows how to do all the organizing, bookkeeping, and calculations required, but continues to make money year after year by astute care of her estate and investments. (Of course, she had been a financial officer for a large corporation during her working years.)

My first impression of Mrs. Karl was indicative. When she appeared at her door to let me in, she seemed to me tall and powerful. She radiated health and vitality. Yet she was 90 years old! In our conversation, it is true, she mentioned some health problems, chiefly of a digestive nature. She rarely went to a doctor and had never been to a dentist. (During our last, sixth, interview, she mentioned that she had needed a cavity filled that year and felt that she must be growing old. At that point she was 97 years old.) Her walls were covered with her own paintings, and her comments about city and national affairs were intelligent and spirited. It is true that she was reserved in manner and did not have many intimate friends, but that had also been true of my mother. Mrs. Karl had been married and was now widowed but had no children. She had a close though ambivalent relationship with her next-door neighbor of 35 years, a recent widow several years older than she. Also, as the oldest of 12 children, her family relationships were numerous. Brothers and sisters, brothers-in-law and sisters-in-law, nephews, and nieces seemed to be around frequently, although none lived in San Francisco.

Over the following five interviews, she seemed to lose some of the stature that had so impressed me at our first meeting. During her 90s, that is, she gradually began to look "older." She continued to have digestive attacks that took her to the hospital periodically, although she scorned her neighbor for calling for this emergency help. These hospital visits were unnecessary, she believed, because she knew how to take care of herself. She eventually began to talk of not always having the desire to paint and mentioned that the droughts made it impossible for her to work on her garden—her other passion. She complained of becoming more passive.

When I did not get an answer to my telephone attempt to set up the sixth interview, I feared the worst. It is true that she had talked from time to time of moving to Fresno to be near many of her siblings, but she had promised to let me know if she did. I would have given up and assumed that she was dead or in a nursing home, but Colleen decided to call Information in Fresno, and was given a number for her. She had moved. When I phoned her, she gave me clear and concise directions to her house. I expected to find her in a smaller dwelling that would be easier to maintain, so I was astonished when I drove up to the address she had given me to find myself in front of a house that was even larger than her previous one in San Francisco. She greeted me warmly, told me the details of the sale of her San Francisco house, and explained that she had to buy this larger one in Fresno because of investment and taxes. She was still living alone, with a woman who came to clean a half day every other week, and said that the cleaner had so little to do that Mrs. Karl had asked her to drive her shopping on those days. A brother-in-law had helped her start a garden, and her art studio was set up in her huge two-car garage, which, since she no longer drove, she did not need.

Mrs. Karl and my other oldest-old respondents raised questions in my mind about my own "expected life history." Where before I had been pleased to model it on my mother—93 being "nothing to sneeze at"—I now wished to increase my aspirations to match these even more successful survivors. But in a way, seeing the survivorship exhibited by these two women also made me anxious. After all, if something is not possible, one is not likely to waste effort wishing for it. And there is also the law of averages. How could I know whether I would live even to my mother's 93—especially in good health? My father had died at 78. Asking for 97 or 98 or 100 would be hubris.

Interest in the very old is not limited to the staff of this research project. Old-age survivors have become heroes and heroines of our time. They have beat the odds. One definition of a hero is a person of extraordinary achievement. Many of the respondents in this study seemed to feel they had achieved extraordinary status by virtue of outliving most of their friends. The celebration of their 90th birthday was often a large family event, just as the celebration of 100th birthdays is marked nationally by presidential telegrams and radio announcements. One has only to read the vignettes from the interviews included in this book—or the interview protocols from which they came—to sense the feeling of satisfaction, in a way of accomplishment, that comes with surviving.

The contents of this book cover a wide range of topics related to old-age survival. They discuss, among other topics, self and time, the quality of life at the end of life, health and physical status, and family and other social relationships. Three issues might be mentioned as relevant to these data. One question we might ask is whether the current trend toward longer lives and longer life expectancy will continue, or whether this cohort will be a unique peak in human existence and our life expectancies will decline from here? I have heard journalists and others assume that the present trend will continue, some say indefinitely, to Biblical proportions.

Even I have played with the fantasy of a time when centenarians will be as ubiquitous as 50-year olds are today (Troll, 1995). That depends, of course, on future medical and social policy, and on the health of the environment, among other things.

Another relevant issue is that raised by Erik Erikson (1950) over 40 years ago, when he delineated eight stages of human development, from infancy to old age. At that time, he felt that the last stage of life had to do with ego integrity. People either had to feel that their life had consistency, that it made sense, or they would despair and feel depressed and unhappy. A reading of this volume shows that both these resolutions appear among the study respondents. Some of them felt despair. The majority, however, managed to feel consistency and integrity. Their morale stayed impressively consistent over the years, even though their physical condition and consequently their quality of life deteriorated tragically.

A final issue, related to this, has to do with continuity and change. In the eyes of the beholders, the subjects of this story appear vastly changed. They look very different from the way they must have when young. I always found it hard to take when they showed me photographs taken many years earlier. Their health and vigor is drastically altered and thus, their way of life and capacity for experience. And yet, so many of them, to themselves, feel familiar. They assert that they are the same person they have always been.

As I noted earlier, I am less than a generation younger than these oldest-old. I could call myself "young-old." And they seem truly "old" to me. But I wonder whether I, too, will feel integrity and consistency as the same inevitable changes occur to me and I move into the world of the "oldest-old."

LILLIAN E. TROLL

References

Erikson, E. (1950). Childhood and society. New York: Norton.

Marshall, V. (1975). Age and awareness of finitude in developmental gerontology, *Omega 6*, 2: 113–129.

Seltzer, M. M., & Troll, L. E. (1986). Expected life history: A model in non-linear time. *American Behavioral Scientist, 29*, 6 (July/August), 746–764.

Troll, L. (1995). Some psychological implications of an explosion of centenarians. In M. M. Seltzer (Ed.), *The impact of increased life expectancy: Beyond the gray horizon.* New York: Springer, 71–86.

Appendix A

Physical Status

1) *Perceived Health Status* (1 = excellent to 4 = poor). Also included were questions on vision, hearing, appetite, activity restrictions, sleep, and presence of pain (1 = positive to 3 = negative).
2) *Activities of Daily Living, ADL* (Katz et al., 1963). (six items, with 1 = no impairment and 3 = impaired).
3) *Instrumental Activities of Daily Living, IADL* (Duke University Center for the Study of Aging and Human Development, 1978), (eight items, with 1 = no impairment and 3 = impaired).
4) *Disease Checklist*

Social Resources

1) *Instrumental Supports* (sum of the number of relatives and/or friends who provide practical and material supports. These services include help in household tasks, money management, and transportation.)
2) *Expressive Supports* (sum of the number of relatives and/or friends who provide less tangible kinds of supports, such as positive sociability, shared activities, and emotional rewards.)
3) *Confidante* refers to the presence of a person to whom they could turn when troubled or feeling "down."
4) *ADL/IADL Help* is a need-based variable measuring the total assistance from family and friends on those activities of daily living which respondents cannot perform alone.
5) A *Family Caregiver* (yes/no), the identification of someone who provides help on a regular basis with any impaired functioning in daily activities. If unimpaired, the respondents are asked who would potentially perform that role.

6) *Social Contacts*, a sum of the total number of relatives and/or friends seen at least weekly.

7) *Social Integration*, coded measures of integration into family system, friendship networks, and community associations (1 = integrated, 5 = not integrated).

8) *Formal Supports*, the total number of services received from visiting nurses, choreworkers, and so on.

Psychological Competencies

1) Mood: a. *Affect Balance Scale* (eight items, with 1 = positive and 4 = negative) (Bradburn, 1969).

   b. *Hopkins Symptom Checklist* (eleven items, with 1 = not depressed and 4 = depressed) (Derogatis et al., 1974).

2) Competence:

   a. *Mastery Scale*, eight items (8 = little mastery and 32 = mastery exercised) (Pearlin & Schooler, 1978).

   b. *Measures of Adaptation*, include coded 5-point measures (1 = positive and 5 = negative) on a sense of control and effectiveness in managing the physical and social environment and in sustaining morale and motivations.

3) Mental status. a. Initial evaluation by telephone contact in setting up the interview when we reviewed the day's date, their date of birth, address, and telephone number and later in person by the interviewer's assessment.

   b. Interviewer assessment of reality orientation and cognition (1 = no impairment to 6 = very impaired).

Appendix B

Examples of Trajectories among 22 Survivors with Increased Disability over 46 Months

Events Leading to Institutions: ($n = 9$)

Female, never married, childless, lived alone. Fell → Confused → Flu → Institution.

Female, new to the area, lived alone, one son, no social supports. Anxiety, depression → Limited mobility → Institution.

Female, lived with elderly sister. Multiple events beyond sister's caregiving capacity. Heart condition → Hernia surgery → Multiple falls, broken wrist → Increased confusion → Hospital → Institution.

Female, never married, childless, lived alone. Stroke → Institution → Further cognitive decline.

Male, widowed, lived alone. Multiple events, but cognitive decline beyond daughter's caregiving ability. → Stroke → Hospital → Cognitive decline → Incontinence → Institution.

Male, married, lived with spouse. Multiple events and wife's illness. Cataracts, colon problems → Hospital, angioplasty, bowel resection, hip fracture → Institution, wheelchair bound. Wife also institutionalized.

Female, childless, lived alone. Limited mobility, bladder problems → Hospitalized for diverticulitis → Home with 24-hour care → Kidney dialysis → Institution.

Female, childless, lived with elderly sister who died. Crushed ver-
tebrae, pain → Caregiver died → Institution.
Female, childless, lived alone. Fainting spells, agitated → Slipped
disc → Mastectomy → Home care → Institution.

Events Leading to Formal Supports at Home (n = 8)

Female, childless, lives alone in own home. Arthritis, GI problems
→ 3 hospitalizations → viral infections → Bedfast. Hired live-
in help.
Female, lives alone, sons not in proximity. GI problems, incontinence → Energy decline → Hospitalized, heart problems →
Hired home health care.
Male, married, wife impaired, own home. Surgery for prostate
cancer → Hired 24 hour nursing care at home for self & spouse.
Female, married, spouse terminal, own home, supportive son
nearby. Good health, tired → chronic back pain → Fall, hospital → Hired home care help → Fall, hospital → Hired 24-hour
home care.
Female, childless, lives alone in own home. Fall, fractured verte-
brae → Cognitive decline → Flu, weight loss. Hired home
health care.
Female, childless, lives alone in own home. Arthritis, hypertension
→ Fall, hospital, seizure, institutionalized 1 month → Home
with formal supports.
Female, childless, lives alone. Arthritis, good health, memory problems → Increased confusion, VNA, physiotherapy and home
care instituted.
Female, lives alone, 1 daughter nearby. Spastic colon, polyps,
arthritis → Depleted energy → Hospital for bleeding ulcer →
Wheelchair. Hired home care help.

Events Leading to Family Care (n = 5)

Male, widowed, lives in own home with son, other son next door.
Hypertension, shortness of breath → Health improved →
General decline, no complaints.

Female, lives alone, supportive daughter nearby. Arthritis → Hospitalized, fluid on lungs → Informal supports at home with formal supports implemented twice a week.

Male, married, lives at home with wife. Hospitalized, back tumor, radiation → T3, Too sick for interview → T4 Health improved. Wife, caregiver.

Female, lives with daughter. Confused, fearful → Hospitalized, GI distress → Daughter caregiver.

Female, 7 children, lives in basement apartment in daughter's home. Limited mobility, pain → Fall, home health care → Falls, weight loss. Multiple family supports.

Bibliography

Abler, R. M., & Fretz, B. R. (1988). Self-efficacy and competence in independent living among oldest old persons. *Journal of Gerontology, 43(4)*, S138–S143.

Adams, R. G., & Blieszner, R. (Eds.) (1989). *Older adult friendships.* Newbury Park, CA: Sage.

Aldous, J. (1990). Family development and the life course: Two perspectives. *Journal of Marriage and the Family, 52(3)*, 571–583.

Allan, G. A. (1989). *Friendship: Developing a sociological perspective.* Newbury Park, CA: Sage.

Allan, G. A., & Adams, R. G. (1989). Aging and the structure of friendships. In R. G. Adams & R. Blieszner (Eds.), *Older adult friendships* (pp. 59–72). Newbury Park, CA: Sage.

Antonucci, A., & Akima, H. (1987). Social networks in adult life and preliminary examination of the Convoy Model. *Journal of Gerontology, 42*, 519–527.

Arling, G. (1976). The elderly widow and her family, neighbors, and friends. *Journal of Marriage and Family, 38*, 757–768.

Atchley, R. C. (1994). *Social forces and aging: An introduction to social gerontology.* Belmont, CA: Wadsworth.

Baldwin, W. H., & Nord, C. W. (1984). Delayed childbearing in the U.S.: Facts and fictions. *Population Bulletin, 39*, 1–42.

Baltes, P., & Baltes, M. M. (1990). Psychological perspectives on successful aging: The model of selective optimization with compensation. In P. Baltes & M. M. Baltes (Eds.), *Successful aging: Perspectives from the behavioral sciences* (pp. 1–34). New York: Cambridge University Press.

Baltes, P. B. (1993). The aging mind: Potentials and limits. *Gerontologist, 33(5)*, 580–594.

Barer, B. M. (1992). The relationship between homebound older people and their home care worker. *Journal of Gerontological Social Work, 19*, 129–147.

Barer, B. M. (1994). Men and women aging differently. *International Journal of Aging and Human Development, 38*, 29–40.

Barer, B. M., & Johnson, C. L. (1990). A critique of the caregiving literature. *Gerontologist, 30(1)*, 26–29.

Bass, D. M., & Bowman, K. (1990). The transition from caregiving to bereavement: The relationship of care-related strain and adjustment to death. *Gerontologist, 30(1)*, 35–42.

Becker, E. (1971). *The birth and death of meaning*. New York: Free Press.

Bengtson, V., Cutler, N. E., Mangen, D. J., & Marshall, V. W. (1985). Generations, cohorts and relations between age groups. In R. Binstock & L. George (Eds.), *Handbook of aging and the social sciences* (pp. 304–335). New York: Van Nostrand Reinhold.

Bengtson, V. L., Cuellar, J. B., & Ragan, P. K. (1977). Stratum contrasts and similarities in attitudes toward death. *Journal of Gerontology, 32(1)*, 76–88.

Bengtson, V. L., Rosenthal, C., & Burton, L. (1990). Families and aging: Diversity and heterogeneity. In R. Binstock & L. George (Eds.), *Handbook of aging and the social sciences*. New York: Academic Press.

Bennett, K. M., & Morgan, K. (1992). Health, social functioning and marital status: Stability and change among elderly recently widowed women. *International Journal of Geriatric Psychiatry, 7*, 813–817.

Berkman, L. F., & Syme, L. S. (1979). Social networks, host resistance and mortality: A nine year follow-up study of Alameda County Residents. *American Journal of Epidemiology, 109*, 186–204.

Blau, Z. (1973). *Old age in a changing society*. New York: Viewpoints.

Blazer, D., Hughes, D. C., & George, L. K. (1987). The epidemiology of depression in an elderly community population. *Gerontologist, 27*, 281–287.

Blieszner, R., & Adams, R. G. (1992). *Adult friendships*. Newbury Park, CA: Sage.

Bowling, A., & Browne, P. (1991). Social networks, health, and emotional well-being among the oldest old in London. *Journal of Gerontology, Social Sciences, 46*, S20–S32.

Bradburn, N. M. (1969). *The structure of psychological well-being*. Chicago: University of Chicago Press.

Brock, A. M., & O'Sullivan, P. (1985). From wife to widow: Role transition in the elderly. *Journal of Psychosocial Nursing, 23(12)*, 6–12.

Brody, J. A., & Miles, T. P. (1990). Mortality postponed and the unmasking of age-dependent non-fatal conditions. *Aging (Milano), 2,* 283–289.

Burton, L. M., & Sorensen, S. (1993). Temporal context and the caregiver role: Perspectives from ethnographic studies of multigeneration African American families. In S. H. Zarit, L. I. Pearlin, & K. W. Schaie (Eds.), *Caregiving systems: Formal and informal helpers* (pp. 47–66). Hillsdale, NJ: Lawrence Erlbaum Associates.

Bury, M., & Holme, A. (1990). Quality of life and social support in the very old. *Journal of Aging Studies, 4,* 345–357.

Carstensen, L. L., & Turk-Charles, S. (1994). The salience of emotion across the adult life-span. *Psychology and Aging, 9(2),* 259–264.

Chown, S. M. (1981). Friendship in old age. In S. Duck & R. Gilmour (Eds.), *Developing Personal Relationships, 2* (pp. 231–276). London: Academic Press.

Cicirelli, V. (1981). *Helping elderly parents: The role of children.* Boston: Auburn House.

Clipp, E. C., & George, L. K. (1993). Dementia and cancer: A comparison of spouse caregivers. *Gerontologist, 33(41),* 534–541.

Cornoni-Huntley, J., Brock, D. B., Ostfield, A. M., Taylor, J. O., Wallace, R. B., & Lafferty, M. E. (1986). *Established populations for epidemiological studies of the elderly, vol. I: Resource data book.* National Institutes of Health Publication No. 86-2443. Bethesda, MD.: National Institute on Aging.

Crohan, S., & Antonucci, T. (1989). Friends as a source of support in old age. In R. G. Adams & R. Bleiszner (Eds.), *Older adult friendships* (pp. 129–146). Newbury Park, CA: Sage.

Cumming, E., & Henry, W. (1961). *Growing old.* New York: Basic Books.

de Vries, B., Bluck, S., & Birren, J. F. (1993). The understanding of death and dying in a life-span perspective. *Gerontologist, 33(3),* 366–372.

Derogatis, L. R., Lipman, R. A., Rickers, K., Uhlenhuth, E. H., & Covi, L. (1974). The Hopkins Symptom Checklist (HSCL): A measure of primary symptom dimensions. *Pharmacopsychiatry, 7,* 79–110.

Dowd, J. (1986). The older person as stranger. In V. Marshall (Ed.), *Later life: The social psychology of aging* (pp. 147–190). Beverly Hills, CA: Sage.

DuBois, C. (1974). The gratuitous act: An introduction to the comparative study of friendship patterns. In E. Leyton (Ed.), *The compact: Selected dimensions of friendship.* St. John's, Newfoundland: Memorial University of Newfoundland.

Duke University Center for the Study of Aging and Human Development. (1978). *Multidimensional Functional Assessment: The OARS Methodology*. Durham, NC: Duke University Press.

Ekman, P., Serenson, E. R., & Friesen, W. V. (1969). Pan-cultural elements in facial displays of emotion. *Science, 164*, 86–88.

Evans, D. A., Scherr, P. A., Cook, N. R., Albert, M. S., Funkenstein, H. H., Beckett, L. A., Hebert, L. E., Wetle, T. T., Branch, L. G., Chown, M. J., Hennekens, C. H., & Taylor, J. O. (1992). The impact of Alzheimer's disease in the United States population. In R. M. Suzman, K. G. Manton, & D. P. Willis (Eds.), *The Oldest Old* (pp. 283–299). New York: Oxford University Press.

Ewing, K. (1990). The illusion of wholeness: Culture, self, and the experience of inconsistencies. *Ethos, 18*, 251–278.

Exton-Smith, A. N. (1961). Terminal illness in the aged. *Lancet* (August 5), 305–308.

Fitting, M., Rabins, P., Lucas, M. J., & Eastham, J. (1986). Caregivers for dementia patients: A comparison of husbands and wives. *Gerontologist, 26*, 248–252.

Fry, C. (1985). Culture, behavior, and aging in the comparative perspective. In J. Birren & K. W. Schaie (Eds.), *Handbook of the psychology of aging* (pp. 216–244). New York: Van Nostrand Reinhold.

Gallagher, D. E., Thompson, L. W., & Peterson, J. A. (1981). Psychosocial factors affecting adaptation to bereavement in the elderly. *International Journal of Aging and Human Development, 14(2)*, 79–95.

Gallo, J. J., Anthony, J. C., & Muthen, B. O. (1994). Age differences in the symptoms of depression: A latent trait analysis. *Journal of Gerontology, 49(6)*, P251–P264.

Geertz, C. (1973). Person, time and conduct in Bali. In C. Geertz (Ed.), *The interpretation of cultures* (pp. 360–411). New York: Basic Books.

George, L. K., & Gold, D. T. (1991). Life course perspectives on intergenerational and generational connections. In S. P. Pfeifer & M. Sussman (Eds.), *Families: Intergenerational and generational connections* (pp. 67–88). New York: Haworth.

Gergen, K. J. (1977). Summary, change and chance in understanding human development. In N. Datan & H. Reese (Eds.), *Life-span developmental psychology: Dialectic perspectives on experimental research*. New York: Academic Press.

Glaser, B. G., & Strauss, S. I. (1965). *Awareness of death*. Chicago: Aldine.

Golander, H. (1995). Rituals of temporality: The social construction of time in a nursing ward. *Journal of Aging Studies, 9(2)*, 119–135.

Gouldner, A. (1960). The norm of reciprocity: A preliminary statement. *American Sociological Review, 25,* 161–178.

Guralnik, J. (1991). Prospects for the compression of morbidity: The challenge posed by the increasing disability in the years prior to death. *Journal of Aging and Health, 3,* 138–154.

Gussow, M. (1995, September 18). Music, his music, lures Bowles back. *New York Times,* p. C13.

Hagestad, G. O. (1990). Social perspectives on the life course. In R. Binstock & L. George (Eds.), *Handbook of Aging and the social sciences* (pp. 151–168). New York: Academic Press.

Hagestad, G. O. (1992). Family networks in an ageing society: Some reflection and explorations. In W. J. A. van den Heuvel, R. Illsley, A. Jamieson, & C. P. M. Knipscheer (Eds.), *Opportunities and challenges in an aging society* (pp. 44–52). Amsterdam: North Holland.

Hall, E. (1983). *The dance of life.* Garden City, NY: Anchor/Doubleday.

Hazan, H. (1980). *The Limbo People: A study of the constitution of the time universe among the aged.* London: Routledge and Kegan Paul.

Health Care Financing Administration (1981). *Long term care: Background and future directions.* HCFA Publication no. 81-20047. Washington, DC: US Department of Health and Human Services.

Heidrich, S. M., & Ryff, C. D. (1993). Physical and mental health in later life: The self-system mediator. *Psychology and Aging, 8(3),* 327–338.

Hendricks, C., & Hendricks, J. (1976). Concepts of time and temporal constructions among the aged with implications for research. In J. Gubrium (Ed.), *Time, roles, and self in old age.* New York: Human Sciences Press.

Herth, K. (1990). Relationship of hope, coping styles, concurrent losses, and setting to grief resolution in the elderly widow(er). *Research in Nursing and Health, 13,* 109–117.

Hess, B., & Waring, J. (1978). Parent and child in late life: Rethinking the relationships. In G. Spanier (Ed.), *Child influences in marital and family interaction.* New York: Academic Press.

Hing, E. (1987). *Use of nursing homes by the elderly: Preliminary data from the 1985 National Nursing Home Survey.* Advance data no. 135. Bethesda, MD: National Center for Health Statistics.

Hinton, J. M. (1963). The physical and mental distress of the dying. *Quarterly Journal of Medicine, New Series XXXII* (No. 125, January), 1–21.

Homans, G. (1958). Social behavior as exchange. *American Journal of Sociology, 63,* 597–606.

Izard, C. (1977). *Human emotions*. New York: Plenum.

Johansson, B., Zarit, S. H., & Berg, S. (1992). Changes in cognitive functioning of the oldest old. *Journal of Gerontology, 47*(P75–P80).

Johnson, C. L. (1983a). Dyadic family relations and social supports. *Gerontologist, 23,* 377–383.

Johnson, C. L. (1983b). Fairweather friends and rainy day kin: An anthropological analysis of old age friendships. *Urban Anthropology, 12,* 103–123.

Johnson, C. L. (1985). The impact of illness on late life marriage. *Journal of Marriage and the Family, 46,* 165–172.

Johnson, C. L. (1988a). *Ex-familia: Grandparents, parents and children adjust to divorce.* New Brunswick, NJ: Rutgers University Press.

Johnson, C. L. (1988b). Relationships among family members and friends in later life. In R. M. Milardo (Ed.), *Families and social networks.* Newbury Park, CA: Sage.

Johnson, C. L. (1993). The prolongation of life and the extension of family relationships: The families of the oldest old. In P. A. Cowan, D. Field, D. A. Hansen, A. Skolnick, & G. E. Swanson (Eds.), *Family, self, and society* (pp. 317–330). Hillsdale, NJ: Lawrence Erlbaum.

Johnson, C. L. (1994). Differential expectations and realities: Race socioeconomic status and health of the oldest old. *International Journal of Aging and Human Development. Special Issue: Social and Cultural Diversity of the Oldest Old, 38,* 41–50.

Johnson, C. L. (1996). Determinants of adaptation of oldest old Black Americans. *Journal of Aging Studies, 9(3),* 231–244.

Johnson, C. L., & Barer, B. M. (1992). Patterns of engagement and disengagement among the oldest old. *Journal of Aging Studies, 6(4),* 351–364.

Johnson, C. L., & Barer, B. M. (1993). Coping and a sense of control among the oldest-old. *Journal of Aging Studies, 7,* 67–80.

Johnson, C. L., & Barer, B. M. (1995). Childlessness and kinship organization: Comparisons of very old whites and blacks. *Journal of Cross-Cultural Gerontology, 10,* 289–306.

Johnson, C. L., & Catalano, D. J. (1981). The childless elderly and their family supports. *Gerontologist, 21* (December, no. 6), 610–618.

Johnson, C. L., & Catalano, D. J. (1983). A longitudinal study of family supports to impaired elderly. *Gerontologist, 23,* 612–618.

Johnson, C. L., & Johnson, F. A. (1983). A microanalysis of senility: Responses of the family and the health care professional. *Culture, Medicine, and Psychiatry, 7,* 77–96.

Johnson, C. L., & Troll, L. (1992). Family functioning in late late life. *Journal of Gerontology, Social Sciences, 47(2),* 566–572.

Johnson, C. L., & Troll, L. (1994). Constraints and facilitators to friendships in late late life. *Gerontologist, 34(1),* 79–87.

Johnson, C. L., & Troll, L. (1996). Family transitions from 70 to 103 years of age. *Journal of Marriage and the Family, 58(1),* 178–187.

Kalish, R. A. (1985). The social context of death and dying. In R. H. Binstock, & E. Shanas (Eds.), *Handbook of Aging and the Social Sciences* (pp. 149–170). New York: Van Nostrand Rinehold.

Kastenbaum, R. (1985). Dying and death: A life-span approach. In J. E. Birren & K. W. Schaie (Eds.), *Handbook of the psychology of aging* (pp. 619–643). New York: Van Nostrand Reinhold.

Katz, S., Ford, A. B., Moskowitz, R. W., Jackson, B. A., & Jaffe, M. W. (1963). Studies of illness in the aged: The index of ADL. *Journal of the American Medical Association, 185,* 914–919.

Keith, P. M. (1979). Life changes and perceptions of life and death among older men and women. *Journal of Gerontology, 6,* 870–878.

Knipscheer, C. P. M. (1988). Temporal embeddedness and aging within the intergenerational family: The care of grandparenting. In J. E. Birren & V. L. Bengston (Eds.), *Emergent Theories of Aging* (pp. 426–446). New York: Springer.

Kolata, G. (1992, November 16). New views on life spans alter forecasts on elderly. *New York Times,* p. A1.

Kovar, M. (1986). *Aging in the eighties (advanced data).* Vital and Health Statistics, No. 115 (May 1). Washington, DC: USDHHS.

Kovar, M. G., & Stone, R. (1992). The social environment of the oldest old. In R. M. Suzman, D. P. Willis, & K. G. Manton (Eds.), *The oldest old* (pp. 303–320). New York: Oxford University Press.

Kubler-Ross, E. (1969). *On death and dying.* New York: Macmillan.

Larsen, R. (1978). Thirty years of research on subjective well-being of older Americans. *Journal of Gerontology, 33,* 109–125.

Lasch, C. (1979). *Haven in a heartless world: The family besieged.* New York: Norton Press.

Lawton, M. P. (1982). Competence, environmental press, and the adaptation of older people. In M. P. Lawton, P. G. Windley, & T. O. Byerts (Eds.), *Aging and the environment: Theoretical approaches.* New York: Springer.

Lawton, M. P., Greenbaum, M., & Liebowitz, B. (1980). The lifespan of housing environments for the aged. *Gerontologist, 20,* 56–64.

Lawton, M. P., Kleban, M. H., Rajagopal, D., & Dean, J. (1992). Dimensions of affective experience in three age groups. *Psychology and Aging, 7*, 171–184.

Lawton, M. P., Moss, M., & Glicksman, A. (1990). The quality of the last year of life of older persons. *Milbank Quarterly, 68*, 1–28.

Lazarus, R., & Folkman, S. (1984). *Stress: Appraisal and coping.* New York: Springer.

Leach, E. (1961). *Rethinking anthropology.* London: Athlone.

Lentzner, H. R., Pamuk, E. R., Rhodenhiser, E. P., Rothenberg, R., & Powell-Griner, E. (1992). The quality of life in the year before death. *American Journal of Public Health, 82(8)*, 1093–1098.

Levenson, R. W., Carstensen, L. L., Friesen, W. V., & Ekman, P. (1991). Emotion, Physiology, and Expression in Old Age. *Psychology and Aging, 6(1)*, 28–35.

Lieberman, M. A., & Tobin, S. S. (1983). *The experience of old age: Stress, coping and survival.* New York: Basic Books.

Lipowski, Z. J. (1983). Transient cognitive disorders and delirium, acute confusional states in the elderly. *American Journal of Psychiatry, 140(11)*, 1426–1436.

Litwak, E. (1985). *Helping the elderly: The complimentary roles of informal networks and formal systems.* New York: Guilford Press.

Longino, C. (1988). Who are the oldest Americans? *Gerontologist, 28*, 515–523.

Longino, C. F., Jackson, D. J., Zimmerman, R. S., & Bradshaw, J. E. (1991). The second move: Health and geographic mobility. *Journal of Gerontology, 46(4)*, S218–S224.

Lopata, H. Z. (1973). *Widowhood in an American city.* Cambridge, MA: Schenckman Publishing Co.

Lopata, H. Z. (1979). *Women as widows: Support systems.* New York: Elsevier.

Lowenthal, M., & Haven, C. (1968). Interaction and adaptation: Intimacy as a critical variable. *American Sociological Review, 33*, 20–30.

Lowenthal, M. F., & Robinson, B. (1976). Social networks and isolation. In R. H. Binstock & E. Shanas (Eds.), *Handbook of aging and the social sciences* (pp. 432–456). New York: Van Nostrand Reinhold.

Lubitz, J., & Prihoda, R. (1984). The use and cost of medicare services in the last two years of life. *Health Care Financing Review, 5*, 117–131.

Maddox, G. L. (1965). Fact and artifact: Evidence bearing on disengagement theory from the Duke geriatrics project. *Human Development, 8,* 117–130.

Maddox, G. L., & Wiley, J. (1976). Scope, concepts, and methods in the study of aging. In R. Binstock & E. Shanas (Eds.), *Handbook of Aging and the Social Sciences.* New York: Van Nostrand Reinhold.

Manton, K. G. (1992). Mortality and Life Expectancy Changes Among the Oldest Old, In R. M. Suzman, D. P. Willis, & K. G. Manton (Eds.), *The Oldest Old* (pp. 157–182). New York: Oxford University Press.

Manton, K. G., & Soldo, B. J. (1992). Disability and Mortality among the Oldest Old: Implications for Current and Future Health and Long-Term-Care Service Needs, In R. M. Suzman, D. P. Willis, & K. G. Manton (Eds.), *The Oldest Old* (pp. 190–250). New York: Oxford University Press.

Manton, K., & Suzman, R. (1992). Forecasting health and functioning in aging societies: Implications for health care and staffing needs. In M. Ory, R. Abeles, & P. Lipman (Eds.), *Aging, Health and Behavior* (pp. 327–357). Newbury Park, CA: Sage.

Markus, H., & Nurius, P. (1986). Possible selves. *American Psychologist, 41(9),* 954–960.

Marshall, V. W. (1980). *Last chapters: A sociology of aging and death.* Monterey, CA: Brooks-Cole.

Maslow, A. H. (1954). *Motivation and personality.* New York: Harper.

Matthews, S. (1986). *Friendships through the life course.* Newbury Park, CA: Sage.

Mayer-Oakes, S. A., Oye, R. K., & Leake, B. (1991). Predictors of mortality in older patients following medical intensive care: The importance of functional status. *Journal of the American Gerontological Society, 39,* 862–868.

Merton, R. K., Fiske, M., & Kendall, P. L. (1956). *The focused interview: A manual of problems and procedures.* Glencoe, IL: Free Press.

Mitteness, L. S. (1995). Catastrophe and chronic illness: The self in the context of Rheumatoid Arthritis. Paper presented at the Southwestern Anthropological Association Annual Meetings, San Francisco, April, 1995.

Moen, P., Dempster-McClain, D., & Williams, R. (1992). Successful aging: A life-course perspective on women's multiple roles and health. *American Journal of Sociology, 97(6),* 1612–1638.

Moore, S. F., & Myerhoff, B. (1977) Introduction: Forms and meanings. In S. F. Moore & B. G. Myerhoff (Eds.), *Secular rituals.* Amsterdam: Van Gorcum.

Moss, M., Lawton, M. P., & Glicksman, A. (1991). The role of pain in the last year of life of older persons. *Journal of Gerontology: Psychological Sciences, 46(2)*, P51–P57.

Moss, M. S., & Moss, S. Z. (1989). The death of a parent. In R. A. Kalish (Ed.), *Mid-life loss: Coping strategies* (pp. 89–114). Newbury Park, CA: Sage.

Myerhoff, B. (1984). Rites and signs of ripening: The intertwining of ritual, time and growing old. In D. Kertzer & J. Keith (Eds.), *Age and anthropological theory*. Ithaca, NY: Cornell University Press.

Neugarten, B., Moore, J. W., & Lowe, J. C. (1968). Age norms, age constraints, and adult socialization. In B. Neugarten (Ed.), *Middle age and aging* (pp. 22–27). Chicago: University of Chicago Press.

Neugarten, B. L. (1977). Personality and aging. In J. E. Birren & K. W. Schaie (Eds.), *Handbook of the psychology of aging* (pp. 626–649). New York: Van Nostrand Reinhold.

Neugarten, B. L., & Hagestad, G. O. (1976). Age and the life course. In R. Binstock & E. Shanas (Eds.), *Handbook of aging and the social sciences* (pp. 35–55). New York: Van Nostrand Reinhold.

Newmann, J. P. (1989). Aging and depression. *Psychology and Aging, 4*, 150–165.

O'Bryant, S. L., & Straw, L. B. (1991). Relationship of previous divorce and previous widowhood to older womens's adjustment to recent widowhood. *Journal of Divorce and Remarriage, 15(3/4)*, 49–67.

Ostor, A. (1984). Chronology, category, and ritual. In D. Kertzer & J. Keith (Eds.), *Age and anthropological theory*. Ithaca, NY: Cornell University Press.

Paine, R. (1974). Anthropological approaches to friendship. In E. Leyton (Ed.), *The compact: Selected dimensions of friendship*. St. John's, Newfoundland: Memorial University of Newfoundland.

Palmore, E. (1979). Predictors of successful aging. *Gerontologist, 19*, 427–431.

Palmore, E. B., Nowlin, J., & Wang, H. S. (1985). Predictors of function among the oldest old: A ten year follow-up. *Journal of Gerontology, 40*, 244–250.

Parsons, T. (1960). Toward a healthy maturity. *Journal of Health and Human Behavior, 1(Fall)*, 163–173.

Pearlin, L. I., & Schooler, C. (1978). The structure of coping. *Journal of Health and Social Behavior, 19*, 2–21.

Perls, T. T. (1995). The oldest old. *Scientific American*, (January), 70–75.

Pihlblad, C. T., & Adams, D. L. (1972). Widowhood, social participation and life satisfaction. *Aging and Human Development, 3,* 323–330.

Preston, S. H. (1992). Cohort succession and the future of the oldest old. In R. M. Suzman, D. P. Willis, & K. G. Manton (Eds.), *The oldest old* (pp. 50–57). New York: Oxford University Press.

Pruchno, R. A., & Resch, N. L. (1989). Husbands and wives as caregivers: Antecedents of depression and burden. *Gerontologist, 29(2),* 159–165.

Quinn, A. (1995, May 7). "A little rebellion is a good thing:" The letters of Jefferson and Madison provide a record almost as amazing as their friendship. *New York Times Book Review,* p. 11.

Rathbone-McCuan, E., Hooyman, N., & Fortune, A. (1985). Social support for the frail elderly. In W. J. Sauer & R. T. Coward (Eds.), *Social support networks and care of the elderly.* New York: Springer.

Regier, D. A., Boyd, J. H., Burke, J. D., Rae, D. S., Myers, J. K., Kraemer, M., Robins, L. N., George, L. K., Karno, M., & Locke, B. Z. (1988). One-month prevalence of mental disorders in the United States. *Archives of General Psychiatry, 45,* 977–986.

Reid, D. W. (1984). Participatory control and the chronic illness adjustment process. In H. LaCound (Ed.), *Research with the locus of control concept.* New York: Academic Press.

Riegel, K. (1975). Adult life crises: Toward a dialectical theory of human development. In N. Datan & L. Ginsberg (Eds.), *Life-span developmental psychology: Normative life crises* (pp. 99–128). New York: Academic Press.

Riley, M. (1983). The family in an aging society: A matrix of latent relationships. *Journal of Family Issues, 4,* 439–454.

Roberto, K. A. (1989). Exchange and equity in friendships. In R. G. Adams & R. Bleiszner (Eds.), *Older adult friendship: Structure and Process* (pp. 147–165). Newbury Park, CA: Sage.

Rodin, J., Timko, C., & Harris, S. (1985). The construct of control: Biological and psychological correlates. In C. Eisdorfer (Ed.), *Annual Review of Gerontology and Geriatrics* (pp. 3–55). New York: Springer.

Rodin, J. (1986). Aging and health: Effects of a sense of control. *Science, 233,* 1271–1276.

Rosaldo, M. Z. (1984). Toward an anthropology of self and feeling. In R. Schweder & R. L. Vine (Eds.), *Culture theory: Essays on mind, self and emotion* (pp. 137–157). London: Cambridge University Press.

Rossi, A. S., & Rossi, P. H. (1990). *Of human bonding: Parent-child relations across the life course.* New York: Aldine de Gruyter.

Rowe, J. W., & Kahn, R. L. (1987). Human aging: Usual and successful. *Science, 237*, 143–149.

Rubinstein, R. L. (1990). Personal identity and environmental meaning in later life. *Journal of Aging Studies, 4(2)*, 131–147.

Rubinstein, R. L., Alexander, B. B., Goodman, M., & Luborsky, M. (1991). Key relationships of never married, childless older women: A cultural analysis. *Journal of Gerontology: Social Sciences, 46*, 270–277.

Ryff, C. D. (1989). Happiness is Everything, or Is It? Explorations on the Meaning of Psychological Well-Being. *Journal of Personality and Social Psychology, 57(6)*, 1069–1081.

Ryff, C. D. (1993). The self in later life. *Gerontology News, (March)*, 2, 11.

Ryff, C. D., & Essex, M. J. (1991). Psychological Well-Being in Adulthood and Old Age: Descriptive Markers and Explanatory Processes. *Annual Review of Gerontology and Geriatrics, 11*, 144–171.

Sankar, A., & Gubrium, J. F. (1994). *Qualitative methods in aging research.* Thousand Oaks, CA: Sage.

Scherer, K. R., & Ekman, P. (Eds.) (1984). *Approaches to emotion.* Hillsdale, NJ: Erlbaum.

Schliefer, S. (1989). Bereavement, depression and immunity: The role of age. In L. L. Carstensen & J. M. Neale (Eds.), *Mechanisms of psychological influence on physical health, with special attention to the elderly* (pp. 61–80). New York: Plenum Press.

Schulz, R. (1985). Emotion and affect. In J. E. Birren & K. W. Schaie (Eds.), *Handbook of the psychology of aging* (pp. 531–543). New York: Van Nostrand Reinhold.

Schulz, R., & Brenner, B. (1977). Relocation of the aged: A review and theoretical analysis. *Journal of Gerontology, 32(3)*, 323–333.

Seltzer, M., & Troll, L. (1986). Expected life history: A model in nonlinear time. *American Behavioral Scientist, 29*, 746–764.

Shanas, E. (1979a). The family as a social support system in old age. *Gerontologist, 19*, 169–174.

Shanas, E. (1979b). Social myth as hypothesis: The case of family relationships of old people. *Gerontologist, 19*, 3–9.

Siegel, J. S. (1994). Plotting the course: Individual aging and population aging in the West. *Gerontologist, 34(3)*, 420–426.

Soldo, B., & Manton, K. (1985). Changes in health status and service needs of the oldest old: Current patterns and future trends. *Milbank Memorial Fund Quarterly/Health and Society, 63*, 286–323.

Sprey, J. (1991). Studying adult children and parents. *Families: Intergenerational and generational connections, Pt. 2. Marriage and Family Review, 16*(3–4).

Stone, R., Cafferata, G. L., & Sangl, J. (1987). Caregivers of the frail elderly: A national profile. *Gerontologist, 27,* 616–626.

Suttles, G. (1970). Friendship as a social institution. In G. McCall (Ed.), *Social relationships.* Chicago: Aldine.

Suzman, R. M., Manton, K. G., & Willis, D. P. (1992). *The oldest old.* New York: Oxford University Press.

Svanborg, A. (1988). Aspects of aging and health in the age interval 70–85. In J. J. P. Schroots, J. E. Birren, & A. Svanborg (Eds.), *Health and aging.* New York: Springer.

Taeuber, C. M., & Rosenwaike, I. (1992). A demographic portrait of America's oldest old. In R. M. Suzman, D. P. Willis, & K. G. Manton (Eds.), *The oldest old* (pp. 17–49). New York: Oxford University Press.

Thomae, H. (1980). Personality and adjustment to old age. In J. Birren & R. Sloane (Eds.), *Handbook of mental health and aging* (pp. 285–309). Englewood Cliffs, NJ: Prentice-Hall.

Tobin, S. (1991). *Personhood in advanced old age: Implications for practice.* New York: Springer.

Tobin, S. S., & Lieberman, M. A. (1976). *Last home for the aged.* San Francisco: Jossey-Bass.

Todd, H., & Ruffini, J. (1983). *Law, disputes and the urban elderly* (Final Report IROI MH/AG28823). Medical Anthropology Program, University of California at San Francisco.

Treas, J., & Bengtson, V. L. (1987). Family in later years. In M. Sussman & S. Steinmetz (Eds.), *Handbook on marriage and the family* (pp. 625–648). New York: Plenum.

Troll, L. (1986). *Family issues in current gerontology.* New York: Springer.

Troll, L. (1994). Family-embedded vs. family-deprived oldest old: A study of contrasts. *International Journal of Aging and Human Development, 38,* 51–64.

Troll, L., & Bengtson, V. (1992). The oldest old in families: An intergenerational perspective. Symbolic and intergenerational links. *Generations, 17*(3), 39–44.

U.S. Bureau of the Census. (1990). *Marital status and living arrangements.* March 1989. Current Population Reports, Series P. 20, No. 445. Washington DC.

Uhlenberg, P. (1993). Demographic change and kin relationships in later life. In G. L. Maddox & M. Powell (Eds.), *Annual Review of Gerontol-*

ogy and Geriatrics, Vol. 13, Focus on kinship, aging and social change (pp. 219–238). New York: Springer.

Uhlenberg, P. (1995). A note viewing functional change in later life as migration. *Gerontologist, 35(4)*, 549–552.

Verbrugge, L. (1984). Longer life but worsening health: Trends in health and mortality of middle aged and older persons. *Milbank Memorial Fund Quarterly, 62(2)*, 475–519.

Walster, E., Walster, G., & Traupmann, G. (1978). *Equity: Theory and research*. Boston: Allyn & Bacon.

Watkins, S., Menken, J., & Bongaarts, J. (1987). Demographic foundations of family change. *American Sociological Review, 52*, 346–358.

Wood, V., & Robertson, J. (1978). Friendship and kinship interaction: Differential effects on the morale of the elderly. *Journal of Marriage and the Family, 40*, 367–375.

Wright, R. H. (1989). Gender differences in adults' same- and cross-sex friendships. In R. G. Adams & R. Bleiszner (Eds.), *Older adult friendships*. Newbury Park, CA: Sage.

Wu, A. W., Rubin, H. R., & Rosen, M. J. (1990). Are elderly people less responsive to intensive care? *Journal of the American Gerontological Society, 38*, 621.

Zarit, S. H., Todd, P. A., & Zarit, J. M. (1986). Subjective burdens of husbands and wives as caregivers: A longitudinal study. *Gerontologist, 26*, 260–266.

Author Index

Subject Index

ADULTHOOD AND AGING
Research on Continuities and Discontinuities
Vern L. Bengtson, PhD

In this volume, distinguished scholars explore and apply the theoretical models of continuity and discontinuity to their research in adult development. The chapters address the different ways in which continuity over time is affected by change over the life course, as well as how individuals negotiate and maintain crucial continuities by adaptive change.

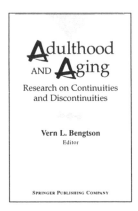

Diverse topics examined include adult life crises, illness, sibling relationships, and gender identity. As a special feature, each chapter is followed by an insightful commentary. Contributors include W. Andrew Achenbaum, Robert H. Binstock, James Birren, Bertram J. Cohler, Margaret Hellie Huyck, Boaz Kahana, Eva Kahana, Sheldon S. Tobin, Lillian E. Troll, and Steven H. Zarit, among others.

Partial Contents:
Psychological Immunity and the Late Onset Disorders • Conceptual and Empirical Advances in Understanding Aging Well Through Proactive Adaptation • A Non-Normative Old Age Contrast: Elderly Parents Caring for Offspring with Mental Retardation • Perspective on Adult Life Crises • Continuities and Discontinuities in Sibling Relationships Across the Life Span • Continuities and Discontinuities in Public Policy on Aging • Public Support for Programs for Older Americans: Continuities Amidst Threats of Discontinuities

1996   360pp   0-8261-9270-X   hard $52.95 (outside US $57.80)

536 Broadway, New York, NY 10012-3955 • (212) 431-4370 • Fax (212) 941-7842